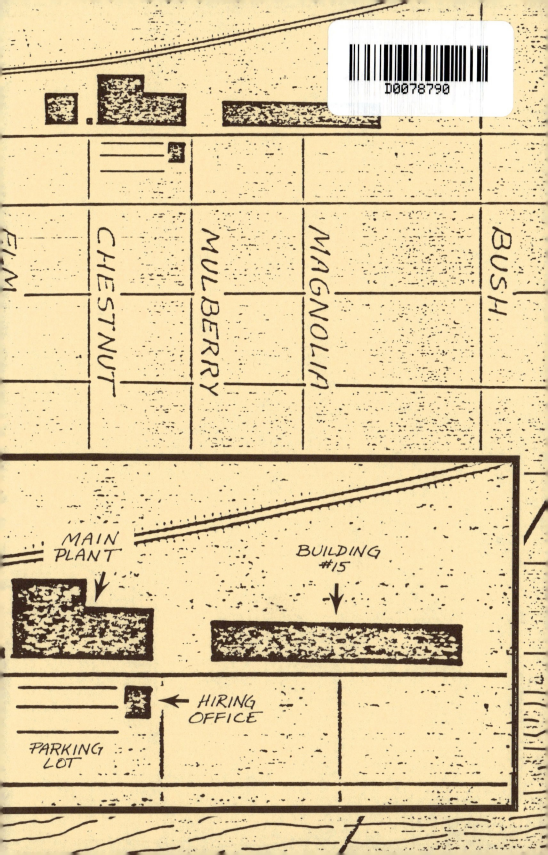

January 26, 1989

To Sara Evans,

You realize you are an inspiration to a generation of people — with your warmth, balanced perspective, creative spark, and wise counsel.

Thank you for your encouragement. Thank you for caring.

With love,
Margaret R. Beegle

I
Remember
Like Today:
The Auto-Lite Strike
of
1934

I
Remember
Like Today:
The Auto-Lite Strike
of
1934

by
Philip A. Korth
and
Margaret R. Beegle

Michigan State University Press
1988

All Michigan State University Press books are produced on paper which
meets the requirements of American National Standard for Information
Sciences—Permanence of paper for printed materials. ANSI 239.48–1984

Michigan State University Press
East Lansing, Michigan 48823-5202

Production: Julie L. Loehr
Editing: Dawn Tawa
Typography: the Copyfitters
Cover: Lynne A. Brown

Library of Congress Cataloging-in-Publication Data

Korth, Philip A., 1936—
    I remember like today.

    Bibliography: p.
    1. Auto-Lite (Firm) Strike, Toledo, Ohio, 1934—History.   2. Automobile Workers
    Federal Union. Local 18384—History.   3. Trade-unions—Automobile industry
    workers—Ohio—Toledo—History—20th century.   4. Strikes and
    lockouts—Automobile industry—Ohio—Toledo—History—20th century.   5.
    Toledo (Ohio)—Economic conditions.   I. Beegle, Margaret, 1952–   II. Title.
    HD5325.A82 1934.T655 1988 331.89'28292'0977113 87-63610
    ISBN 0-87013-255-5

The main assembly plants for Auto-Lite in 1934 stood between the Elm Street Bridge
and Bush Street and the railroad tracks and Champlain Street. The main entrance gate
was on Champlain Street at the foot of Chestnut Street between the office building and
the factory building. A chain link fence with a large gate to allow trucks and automobiles entrance connected these two buildings. Behind the factory buildings ran railroad tracks and beyond them were open fields. The map printed on the endsheets
represents the physical layout in 1934.

Contents

Dedication

*For Nadine,
Dirk, Kim, and Viki*

Acknowledgments

A work of this nature incurs debts to institutions and people that its publication hopes to repay. The primary debt, upon which all subsequent debts accrue, I owe to the Humanities Program of the Rockefeller Foundation, for without its support this project would never have been done. Historian Dr. Peter Wood exercised the essential judgment and carried the program officer's responsibility for providing the financial support that brought this project to life. Since oral histories are so expensive to gather, not only in terms of equipment and transcription but in terms of time and travel, the grant from Rockefeller was crucial.

People we interviewed, whether they appear in this work or not, generously contributed their time and patience; they gave us their memories. I hope they feel that this book justifies their faith and trust.

Institutions that helped guide the search include the Walter Reuther Library at Wayne State University; the Toledo Public Library, particularly the Local History Division; the Michigan State University Libraries; the Toledo *Blade*; the Toledo Police Department; and Toledo's Local 12 of the United Automobile Workers of America.

Special mention is due Marc Van Wormer from Toledo; Martha Jane Soltow, MSU labor librarian; Warner Pflug, archivist at the Reuther Library; Tana Mosier Porter of the Toledo Public Library; and Clem Holowinski, former president of Local 12, UAW in Toledo.

Transcribing oral histories, as any practitioner knows, consumes immense time and energy. I was fortunate to secure the help of Sue Cunningham, who did a marvelous job of transcribing the spoken word to print. Dr. Nancy Pogel and Judy Easterbrook also worked with tape and typewriter to create the rough material from which this book evolved.

The project benefited from the energy of Claude Kazanski and Margaret Beegle, undergraduate students in 1973 in James Madison College of Michigan State University. They helped search the printed sources, plot strategy, and conduct interviews in Toledo. Margaret stayed with the project through its final stages, suggesting cuts, revisions, organization, and language that helped structure and clarify much that this book contains. To Claude and Meg: thanks. I hope the result is adequate reward for your efforts.

A number of people have read all or portions of this manuscript in its various stages, offering suggestions both gracious and useful. Dr. Charles P. Larrowe made particularly useful suggestions in the final stages of its preparation. Dr. James McClintock, Dr. Reed Baird, and Dr. Bruce Curtis always found the sensitive way to show me how badly my manuscripts needed further work. These readers are not responsible for its shortcomings, of course, though they helped create its virtues.

Finally, Dr. Richard Chapin saw the manuscript's virtues with sufficient clarity to decide to publish it. Julie Loehr, Dawn Kawa, and Lynne Brown—the very capable staff at MSU Press—helped in the final editing, organization, and construction that turned a manuscript into a book.

This book is meant to convey a very special thanks to three people: Dr. Hyman Berman, Labor Historian, University of Minnesota; Dr. J. C. Levenson, Edgar Allan Poe Professor of English, University of Virginia; and, most of all, Dr. Mary C. Turpie, Professor Emeritus of American Studies, University of Minnesota.

Philip A. Korth
East Lansing, Michigan
May 1, 1988

Introduction

American unions formed over a century before the Auto-Lite strike of 1934. Workers, usually craftsmen, banded together to protect standards in the trade, to control working conditions, and to set wages and hours for their labor. After the Civil War, workers' local and regional efforts expanded and developed into national organizations such as the National Labor Union and the Knights of Labor.

The most successful workers often had a skill which involved training and apprenticeships. Printers, carpenters, shoemakers, machinists, and cigarmakers tried to maintain high quality in the exercise of their trade. The solidarity they sought rested on their craft nexus; carpenters joined with other carpenters, machinists with other machinists, and cigarmakers with other cigarmakers. This mode of organization followed in the tradition of fraternal and guild organizations whose origins go back into European medieval history.

In the nineteenth century, many of these crafts adapted to emerging industrial realities and preserved craft standards even as they adopted machine techniques. However, workers in some crafts were overwhelmed by industrial developments, because machines began to perform many of the skilled functions in production. For example, cobblers once made an entire shoe, practicing a complex, sophisticated technique requiring great skill. A shoe sewn by hand and soled by hammer and nail might fit better and wear longer than a machine-made shoe, but it took a cobbler a long time to make one. The introduction of the sewing machine and the nailing machine altered the process of shoe production dramatically. Machine production reduced the time and cost of making a shoe, because one worker on a sewing machine could sew uppers at an amazing rate, and one worker operating a nailing machine similarly could attach a sole and heel quickly. The rate of production rose sharply and cost fell. Two workers, trained to tend machines, could easily out-produce the cobbler, even though neither machine tender could make an entire shoe. Moreover, learning to run the machine might take only hours, whereas learning to cobble took years. The introduction of machines thus debased crafts by breaking them into simple repetitive operations.

This difference had enormous consequences for workers. It altered their work itself and lowered their standard of living, their status, and their power. Skilled craftsmen could demand both status and money so long as they controlled the trade, but semi-skilled workers suffered low status and earned little money because they could not control their work. One person could easily replace another; women replaced men and children replaced both. Sometimes children replaced their own parents, for employers could pay children the lowest rates and thereby reduce the cost of production and increase profits.

Workers resisted this emerging nightmare with any weapons and methods available. Mass demonstrations preceded and sometimes reflected organizing, as E. P. Thompson showed in his powerful work, *The Making of the English Working Class.* Demonstration occasionally resulted in organization, but direct resistance and the strike proved powerful and effective. Unions in the United States grew in numbers and significance in the antebellum period when carpenters, printers, and other craftsmen formed local organizations. Some, such as the Knights of St. Crispin (shoemakers) or the Sons of Vulcan (iron puddlers), revealed in their names the fraternal traditions to which they appealed. Early unions that lasted gathered skilled workers and attempted to set standards, wages, and working conditions. After the Civil War, which marks the beginning of America's industrial "take-off," workers' efforts led to national organizations that tried to advance workers' economic demands as well as develop broad programs, sometimes with social and political dimensions.

Thoughtful workers perceived the implications of uncontrolled industrial development for the worker's future and read the European socialists as they analyzed their own experiences. By the 1870s, both socialists and anarchists found voices and followers among American workers. In December 1869, the Noble Order of the Knights of Labor formed a national organization in Philadelphia and appealed to class, loosely defined, when it asserted that "An Injury to One is an Injury to All." For two decades the Knights occupied center stage among national labor organizations, leading both in organization and numbers. Trade unionists also formed national organizations independent of the Knights, some that even transcended single crafts, but preserved the craft nexus. In December 1886, the American Federation of Labor emerged to challenge the Knights' comprehensive goal of organizing all workers, including unskilled industrial workers, and asserted a craft basis for American unions.

The Knights lost influence and virtually disappeared in the mid-1890s, but the AFL and its craft philosophy prevailed. In 1987, it remains the largest organization of American workers. It compromised with industrial unionists in the fifties, accepted their view that unions without a craft nexus could and should be organized, and merged with the Congress of Industrial Organizations. Now the AFL-CIO speaks for virtually all organized American workers.

The last century has been filled with successes and setbacks whose history can easily confuse, for it is filled with contradiction and paradox. It should be remembered that the CIO had not emerged in 1934.

Important for understanding the context of the Electric Auto-Lite Company strike of 1934 is the legal status of the labor union in the twentieth century. On the eve of the strike, it was not certain that labor unions were legal or that they could appeal to the legal system for fair and impartial redress of disputes. Common law precedents in the nineteenth century viewed unions of workers as akin to organizations of manufacturers. In strikes, unions found themselves accused of violating the right of freedom of trade. Unions, courts asserted, were really conspiracies that attempted to restrain trade.

In the late 1880s, corporate abuses of trade practices brought about the Interstate Commerce Act (1887) and the Sherman Anti-Trust Act (1890), which were intended to regulate the conduct of business and to assure that business did not conspire to manipulate or monopolize trade. These acts were not intended to apply to relationships between an employer and employees but to relationships among employers.

However, corporations fighting union organization found ways to use this legislation and the courts against unions. For example, the American Railway Union, which struck the Pullman Company in 1894, was destroyed and its president, Eugene V. Debs, imprisoned through injunctions issued by federal courts and enforced by federal troops. Those injunctions revealed to employers the potential in the

Interstate Commerce and Sherman anti-trust acts once one accepted their applicability to unions.

The most celebrated cases—the Danbury Hatters (1903), the Bucks Stove and Range (1906), and the Hitchman Coal and Coke Company (1910)—put labor on the defensive. In the first instance, the courts found that individual union members were liable for triple damages under Sherman because they had instituted a boycott. In the second, officers of the AFL, including its president, Samuel Gompers, were sentenced to jail terms because they violated a sweeping injunction forbidding the union from "interfering in any manner" with the sale of Bucks Stove products. In the Hitchman Coal case, the United Mine Workers was declared under the Sherman Act as an illegal conspiracy. Clearly, the courts could prove effective weapons against unions.

Progressives in Congress attempted a remedy in 1914 through Sections 6 and 20 of the Clayton Anti-Trust Act, which stated in part: "The labor of a human being is not a commodity or article of commerce. Nothing contained in the anti-trust laws shall be construed to forbid the existence and operation of labor organizations; . . . nor shall any organizations, or the members thereof, be held or construed to be illegal combinations in restraint of trade, under the anti-trust laws." Gompers declared Clayton to be labor's "Magna Carta." However, within a decade, employers and the courts not only found ways around Clayton but found ways to use it against unions. Section 20 had prohibited injunctions against unions except when "necessary to prevent irreparable injury to property, or to a property right, of the party making application, for which injury there is no adequate remedy at law. . . ." Any strike attempts to close down a business, so strikes remained targets of injunctions. A wave of cases in the twenties limited union activity so severely that any attempt to organize might be declared illegal. Thus, labor unions risked indictments as conspiracies in restraint of trade, subject to damages.

The Norris-La Guardia Act of 1932 attempted to set fair labor standards and explicitly limited the use of injunctions in labor disputes. The act declared as a matter of policy that workers had the right to organize, to strike, and to choose their own leaders. But Clayton had appeared to speak with equal clarity.

When Franklin Delano Roosevelt defeated Herbert Hoover for the Presidency in 1932, he put together a coalition that made a place for workers and their unions. He sought to bring the country out of the Great Depression through the National Industrial Recovery Act, which was passed in 1933. This act cancelled, temporarily, anti-combination provisions of both the Sherman and Clayton anti-trust acts, allowing corporations to meet to set prices and production quotas. It contained a provision, Section 7(a), which stated explicitly that workers had the right to form unions and to select their own leaders. William Green, then president of the AFL, declared that this provision gave workers "their charter of industrial freedom." However, the final resolution of this issue occurred after the Auto-Lite strike of 1934. Congress passed the Wagner Act of 1935, which explicitly declared that workers had the right to organize and which asserted a national policy that trusted in collective bargaining to resolve differences between workers and their employers.

One thing was clear to workers in 1934: they could not rely on legislation for protection. Unions that had survived, even in the face of a hostile judicial system, had been well organized and strong. They had depended on their own organizational power and not on the vagaries of political favor. The political and legal climate in 1934 might encourage workers to organize, but those who organized and stuck together had the best chance of success.

It is hard to gauge how much of this history workers knew in detail, but we can make a good estimate of the number of workers who had been touched by unions. In 1933, organized labor's rolls had dropped to less than 2.5 million from a high in the early twenties of about 5 million.* The national work force in 1933 was about 40 million, so about 6 percent were organized. Therefore, few workers had actual experience with unions. Toledo may have benefited from greater union activity than the national average, but we should not be surprised that workers at Auto-Lite knew little about unions.

---

*Joseph G. Rayback, *A History of American Labor*, (New York: The Macmillan Company, 1961), 315.

1

An Overview

The strikes at Auto-Lite in Toledo in the spring of 1934 secured a victory for the fledgling Automobile Workers Federal Union Local 18384 of the AFL and permanently altered the nature of worker-employer relationships in Toledo. This victory assured that working men and women in Toledo would have some power over their working lives and a voice in their community. Workers in Toledo today owe a debt of gratitude to the "unholy thirteen" who huddled over the fires burning in drums in front of Auto-Lite and who dreamed of freedom and dignity. And as today grows out of yesterday, so the workers in 1934 faced a set of conditions and attitudes shaped decades before by the industrial evolution of Toledo, the development of the automobile industry, and the historical struggles of their ancestors.

In the twenties, some workers at Auto-Lite had discussed the possibility of forming a union, but nothing had materialized. The nature of production work in a factory created in many minds—particularly in the minds of craft union advocates—an insuperable obstacle to forming a union. The factory operative enjoyed no inherent power, for he or she could be moved from job to job or speedily replaced because the machine performed the skilled functions while the operative tended it. The parts industry, like the automobile assembly industry itself, experienced the seasonal cycle of production and lay-offs, even in the best of times, so operatives at Auto-Lite faced constant uncertainty. They understood their vulnerability: employers could dismiss a worker at will or refuse to rehire a worker who got out of line. Forming a union in the twenties and thirties proved fully as out of line then as now. Workers at Auto-Lite lived with fear and uncertainty, for with the exception of the model shop and related operations where a few workers made new products and cut dies, the Auto-Lite employed operatives almost exclusively. One need not look far to understand their reluctance to take the risks of forming a union.

In 1933, a few workers from Auto-Lite's Department Two, the punch press room, notably Charles Rigby, Lester Byrd, Chester Dombrowski and John [J. J.] Jankowski, began to act upon their belief that semi-skilled factory workers should and could form unions, and they approached the Toledo Central Labor Union for advice. Although sympathetic, no single craft union found them within its jurisdiction. Factory operatives simply did not fit the craft form of organization. Rigby and his friends were referred to a new Federal Labor Union, which had recently formed in Toledo.

Federal Labor Unions appeared in the AFL well before 1933. Produced by the debates between craft union advocates and industrial union advocates, the Federal Labor Union provided the structure to organize entire industrial plants or complexes. During the initial organizing period, all workers, regardless of skill or work assignment, would be recruited into a single Federal Labor Union chartered for a particular plant or factory system. Once organized, workers would be assigned to new or existing locals of the appropriate craft international. The organizers initially targeted Spicer Manufacturing Company, Bingham Stamping and Tool Company, Logan Gear Company, and City Auto Stamping Company. Through Rigby and his friends, the Auto-Lite, one of the largest employers in Toledo, joined the list. Membership from Auto-Lite, initially small, included strong and imaginative leaders.

Local 18384 had an unusual jurisdiction that included a number of distinct companies. Normally, a separate charter would have been issued for each, but Local 18384 covered five companies, each with its own shop committee to direct plant affairs. The officers reflect the atypical composition of Local 18384. When Lawrence D. Haynes, the first president of Local 18384, found a new job in Detroit in early March of 1934, the members declared the office vacant and elected Floyd L. Bossler to fill it. Bossler did not work at any of the plants in Local 18384's jurisdiction. A city employee in the street department, he had built a reputation in Toledo by speaking on socialist themes and by campaigning actively for the new mayor and former Socialist,

Solon Klotz. However, members of the Auto-Lite shop committee sat on the executive committee of the local—William Siefke, for example—and the local's financial secretary, George Addes, also came from Auto-Lite. Other officers and executive committee members came from the remaining four companies targeted for organizing. Thomas Ramsey, business agent for Local 18384, worked at City Auto Stamping. This reflected the nature of work in the auto parts business. The worker followed the work, sometimes from plant to plant around the city.

From August 1933 to February 1934, Local 18384's activities grew from a series of furtive, secret meetings in workers' basements to open meetings attracting a few hundred workers at the rented Moose Hall. There, in February, the membership decided to strike Spicer, Bingham, and Logan to enforce the union's demands for recognition, wage increases, and a seniority system. Members of the Auto-Lite shop committee insisted that Auto-Lite be included, although the union had little active support there. Charles Rigby, chairman of the Auto-Lite shop committee, argued persuasively that a strike there could be effective since union supporters dominated the punch press room, Department Two, which made the stampings for the entire assembly operation. This obvious tactical advantage convinced Local 18384's executive committee to include Auto-Lite in the strike; and it agreed to continue the strike at Spicer, Bingham, and Logan until Auto-Lite settled.

On February 23, Local 18384 struck Spicer, Bingham, Logan, and Auto-Lite. Production at Spicer, Bingham, and Logan slowed significantly as a result of the strike, but at Auto-Lite production continued unabated. On the morning of February 23, fifteen workers out of Auto-Lite's work force of fifteen hundred clustered with their picket signs and union badges around a fifty-five gallon drum salamander in front of the factory on Champlain Street, watching the mass of workers report for work. Support by strikers at Spicer, Bingham, and Logan, who refused to return to work unless Auto-Lite reinstated its strikers, sustained them.

The handful of strikers huddled around fires in late February surely felt the chill of winter; but just as surely, they felt chilled because they were so few in number. Fear thawed from their faces four days later, however, when they won an agreement and reinstatement. On February 28, the strike ended. The Auto-Lite strikers returned to work under a thirty-day agreement, knowing they had survived where others had not but fully aware of their precarious situation and of the immense organizing task before them. They had achieved an important moral victory, for they demonstrated to their fellow workers and to themselves that Auto-Lite was not invincible.

Assuming that they had won recognition, the Auto-Lite shop committee arranged meetings with management. The meetings quickly demonstrated that Auto-Lite had merely acknowledged the existence of Local 18384 but did not recognize it as the bargaining agent for Auto-Lite workers. The nucleus of workers in the punch press room, building upon their successful reinstatement, signed up workers in anticipation of the inevitable showdown. The company also prepared by adding new workers to the force and, more ominously, by secretly purchasing tear gas and arms from Federal Laboratories, a munitions manufacturer.

The April 1 deadline of the February agreement passed without a contract, but the union continued to try to negotiate. On April 12, six weeks after their modest victory, the membership voted to strike; and on Friday, April 13, approximately four hundred Auto-Lite workers set up picket lines. An equal or greater number of workers crossed the picket lines, entering the factory without serious incident. The strike appeared to divide the work force equally, but many new hires were among those entering. The company responded by increased hiring, replacing those workers who had struck. Minor incidents, such as pushing, shoving, and some fist fights, occurred on the picket lines and at homes around the community when union members tried to persuade those still working to join the strike. From the first day of the strike, the Toledo Police Department assigned officers to patrol the picket lines, but they made no attempt to disperse the pickets.

The picket lines rallied strikers, kept their spirits high, preserved their solidarity, and generated fear and guilt in those who sought to cross them. Workers from other plants around Toledo and from other unions joined Auto-Lite strikers on the picket lines, as did members of the Lucas County Unemployed League, which had been organized in 1933 by members of the American Workers party. Thus, the picket lines became a major target of the Auto-Lite management, which went to court to attack them. On May 3, counsel for Auto-Lite appeared before Judge Roy R. Stuart in the Court of Common Pleas seeking injunctive relief from the pickets.

Bringing the case before the Court of Common Pleas invoked the county's jurisdiction. Judge Stuart granted the injunction and limited pickets to twenty-five. He assigned responsibility for enforcement to Lucas County Sheriff David Krieger, a Republican who had run for office with the support of C. O. Miniger, president of Auto-Lite. Krieger began to hire special deputies to enforce the injunction. He did not require previous police experience for the job. The deputies dressed in street clothes and wore only arm bands and badges to identify themselves. Auto-Lite paid their wages. Fifty Toledo police force members had recently been laid off because of the city's strained financial situation, but none joined Krieger's force of special deputies.

On May 5, leaders of the Lucas County Unemployed League announced in a public letter to Judge Stuart that they intended to violate the injunction against mass picketing. Two days later, as the leaders picketed Auto-Lite, Sheriff Krieger arrested them and charged them with contempt of court. Judge Stuart convicted them but then suspended their sentences and released them. They returned to the picket lines, where they were joined by dozens of union members who had also agreed to break the injunction. Additional arrests ensued; but in large measure the league and the union defeated the injunction, for the city and county, unable to handle mass arrests, had to release the pickets shortly after their arrests. The pickets quickly lost whatever respect they had had for the sheriff and the courts.

Ironically, the injunction proved crucial, for the strike seemed doomed until its issuance. Auto-Lite operated with non-strikers supplemented by the newly hired. Although less efficient, production of generators, meters, and gauges continued. In addition, some strikers filtered back into the plant. However, the hated injunction had aroused the strikers. Their ability to break the injunction in fact, if not in law, encouraged other workers in the community to join them, and the picket lines swelled.

Auto-Lite remained intransigent. It intended to break the picket line. When crowds of up to six thousand rallied in front of Auto-Lite on May 21, 22, and 23 to hear speakers from the American Workers party and the union, Auto-Lite hastily added to its cache of arms. The company encouraged Sheriff Krieger to enforce the injunction more energetically. Adding to his force of special deputies, which now included Auto-Lite workers who remained at work and scabs, Krieger set out on May 23 to disperse the pickets. He stationed deputies well supplied with tear gas on the roof while others were stationed in front of the plant. The subsequent melee began when someone threw a heavy steel bracket from the building and hit a female picket, Alma Hahn, in the ear and neck. Outraged, the pickets surged forward and attempted to storm into the building to attack the person who threw it. The special deputies fired tear gas down on the pickets, who then fell back across the street. News of the fighting quickly spread across Toledo and attracted larger crowds. Attendance at movie houses declined as the Auto-Lite strike became the most exciting show in town.

The Auto-Lite factory also became a symbol, a target for Toledo workers' pent-up exasperation, frustration, and anger. The strikers, determined to halt production at Auto-Lite, surrounded the factory on the afternoon of May 23 and refused to let the strikebreakers out when the shift ended. Strikers, sympathizers, and children from the area showered the factory building with bricks and stones until no window remained unbroken. Managers herded the strikebreakers into the adjoining building behind the main plant where they spent the entire night in darkness and terror. The special deputies soon exhausted Auto-Lite's stockpile of tear gas, so an emergency call went out to Cleveland for additional supplies. The crowd overturned cars and set them afire as they dodged tear gas canisters and projectiles.

Frantic calls for help from inside the factory persuaded the governor to intervene, and, at midnight, units of the Ohio National Guard were mobilized and sent into Toledo. They arrived at 4:30 in the morning, deployed on Michigan Avenue two blocks away, and marched to the plant, dispersing the crowd as they advanced. Within hours, the guardsmen had moved the crowd back and had taken up positions, setting up machine gun emplacements at key intersections near the plant. At 7:30 that morning, the guard released the strikebreakers and escorted a bus carrying some of them away from the building.

The guard ended the siege of the Auto-Lite factory, but it did not end the struggle. The crowd remained, restless and hostile. The young, frightened, and poorly-trained guardsmen failed to intimidate the crowd. Rocks and bricks soon accompanied the taunts and insults passing back and forth across the picket lines. On Thursday afternoon, May 24, a full battle between guardsmen and the crowd erupted in front of the Auto-Lite factory. Guardsmen hurled back rocks thrown from the crowd, also pausing to throw tear gas canisters and to fire tear gas shells. Members of the crowd donned gloves to hurl the tear gas back into the guardsmen's ranks. With fixed bayonets, guardsmen charged into the crowd repeatedly, only to retreat again as the Battle of Chestnut Hill raged back and forth in front of the factory. During one charge, guardsmen fired, wounding more than a dozen and killing Frank Hubay, a young unemployed worker who had once worked for Auto-Lite. But the gunfire did not disperse the crowd. Later that night, guardsmen fired again and wounded two more. The adjutant general of the guard, Frank D. Henderson, ordered the nine hundred guardsmen reinforced, bringing the total on duty at Auto-Lite to 1,350. Friday, May 25, saw no serious encounters; but on Saturday, amid union demands that the plant close completely and the guard withdraw, a crowd of five thousand clashed with the guard. Two hundred were injured and fifty arrested.

The following week the plant remained closed. No further violent confrontations occurred as federal mediators, the company, and the union attempted to work out an agreement. Auto-Lite suggested that the Automobile Labor Board, which President Roosevelt had appointed on March 25, be asked to intervene; but Local 18384, sensing victory, rejected the suggestion. On Friday, May 31, the guard withdrew, and an agreement negotiated directly between the union and Auto-Lite management emerged. On June 4, the union ratified this agreement in which Auto-Lite recognized Local 18384 as the legitimate bargaining agent for its members. On June 5, the Auto-Lite plant reopened.

However, Local 18384 did not win an unqualified victory. The order of rehiring placed strikers second in importance to old employees who had remained at work during the strike, and it secured bargaining rights only for its members. Shortly before the strike, some workers who aligned themselves with Auto-Lite management formed a competing organization called the Auto-Lite Council. Management recognized this company union's bargaining rights and gave them priority in rehiring. The order of rehiring created few difficulties in practice, however, since virtually all old workers were rehired at the same time, striker and non-striker alike. Newly hired strikebreakers found themselves ignored, and many were not rehired until months later when production began to accelerate.

The Auto-Lite Council hung on for two more years; but Local 18384 won the real victory, of course, for its recognition established the basis for collective bargaining. Auto-Lite workers understood this and rushed to join Local 18384. Within months, the Auto-Lite Council was a paper organization. Preferential treatment that Auto-Lite management promised council members never materialized, and its members realized that they could expect no more in their negotiations than the union already had won.

Local 18384's success in establishing a conventional collective bargaining relationship with Auto-Lite management failed to fulfill the hopes of the leaders of the American Workers party, the Communist party, and other radical supporters of the strikers who had seen in the Auto-Lite strike the potential for a more dramatic and revolutionary outcome. Likewise, the plan of the AFL leadership to distribute the membership of Local 18384 among existing craft unions never reached fruition because the CIO formed in 1935. Local 18384 then evolved into Local 12 of the United Automobile Workers, CIO. Members of Local 12 became leaders of the UAW and supported the organization of other strikes such as the Chevrolet transmission plant strike in 1935 and the great Flint sit-down strike of 1936–1937.

Ultimately, Auto-Lite closed because the expanding assembly companies began to produce their own parts and no longer needed Auto-Lite. In the fifties, Ford Motor Company bought the Auto-Lite name and some of its patents. In the early sixties, the Toledo plant and its remaining operations were absorbed by a conglomerate. The Auto-Lite factory on Champlain Street, scene of the tragedy and triumph of 1934, closed its doors in 1962. When the following interviews were conducted in 1973, the building stood virtually abandoned, a storehouse for industrial implements.

When Auto-Lite closed, the workers, many of whom had struggled there in 1934, were given the option of retirement or transfer to other plants far from Toledo. Some, who had lived in Toledo their entire lives, did transfer to protect their small pensions. Others remained, unwilling to disrupt their lives. Some received pensions of thirty to fifty dollars per month after working for Auto-Lite for thirty or more years. Some received no pensions at all. Although Local 12 was able to find jobs for some Auto-Lite workers at other plants it had organized, it could not do so for all. Thus, it confronted the central assumption unions make and also discovered the limits of its power: unions assume that the employer wants to remain in production. When an employer does not wish to remain in production, a union cannot force him to do so. If an employer chooses to discard a factory and cease production, he can do so. Therefore, many Auto-Lite workers found themselves unemployed: too young to retire and too old to hire. Discarded much like old industrial machinery, these workers had to subsist on small pensions and on Social Security.

This brief summary of events tells us what happened when and where but not how and why. The rest of this book will answer those questions, but a review of issues may also aid in an understanding of the strike. The dynamics of organizing help us understand some of these events, because organizing requires a worker's personal commitment, a willingness to stand up and be counted. A committed worker knows in a most personal way who stands up with him and who "sticks." One worker must rely on the word of another for, in truth, even today, the only real power workers have is the power of their solidarity. Therefore, loyalty to one's brothers and sisters in the movement becomes the essential virtue. The importance of this loyalty helps to explain the intensity of commitment and also the rancor that divisiveness created at Auto-Lite.

Loyalty arose on both sides at Auto-Lite. Union organizers appealed to a felt, common plight on the job and to class solidarity. They declared that mutual loyalty among workers would generate the unity necessary to improve working life and to secure their dignity and freedom. If they stuck together, they could win. Conversely, the company identified the organizers as a small group of malcontents not really part of the corporate family and who were even considered "outsiders." Managers appealed to the workers' sense of loyalty to the company as the supplier of jobs, of livelihoods. The company made clear the consequence of joining a union that peers had created. Unions represented disloyalty and thereby removed one from the family's protective embrace. For some workers, that appeal proved persuasive, notably for those who internalized the company's viewpoint and who believed that unions disrupted the harmony of industrial life. Some also carried with them a vague sense that unions were somehow illicit.

Section 7(a) of the National Industrial Recovery Act passed in 1933 appeared to resolve the legal question. It asserted:

> (1) that employees shall have the right to organize and bargain collectively through representatives of their own choosing, and shall be free from interference, restraint, or coercion of employers of labor or their agents, in the designation of such representatives. . .,
> (2) that no employee and no one seeking employment shall be required as a condition of employment to join any company union or to refrain from joining, organizing, or assisting a labor organization of his own choosing. . . .

Although unenforceable and unclear (even allowing the formation of company unions dominated by management), the act suggested that government approved unions. The act, therefore, had a psychological impact far greater than its legal precedent. No organizer in Toledo declared, as organizers did elsewhere, that "President Roosevelt wants you to join a union"; but the act's implications encouraged key organizers to act, and thousands of workers responded. Without doubt, company assertions that unions were not respectable lacked credibility.

The act also discomfited workers who had hidden behind feelings of helplessness that rationalized doing nothing. The act compelled them to confront the reality of their conditions and to recognize that they could legitimately act to assert their dignity and freedom. The federal government certainly did not play an activist role in Toledo on behalf of organizing efforts; but Section 7(a) lowered one barrier to organization and encouraged workers to unite and to seek negotiating meetings with management. The inconclusiveness of such negotiations, however, convinced workers that the law would ultimately be enforced only through their own united efforts.

Additional stimulus for organizing came from leftist political parties, such as the American Communist party, the Socialist party, the Socialist Workers party and the American Workers party. Members of the Conference for Progressive Labor Action and graduates and staff from Brookwood Labor College founded by A. J. Muste also focused their attention on Toledo. Trained at Brookwood as organizers, they used their skills to help raise the consciousness of Auto-Lite workers. They not only counseled strike leaders but actively supported them through innovative organizations such as the Lucas County Unemployed League, which rallied potential strikebreakers in support of the strikers.

The crushing weight of the Great Depression on the industrial worker also created conditions that lead to the strike. Some Americans, assuredly, scarcely felt the depression and others eluded its debilitating effects; but industrial workers felt its full weight. Wholly reliant upon wages and a steady job, they quickly felt the disintegration of business activity. Possessing modest skills and easily replaced, they found themselves in constant competition for survival with other desperate men and women. If unemployed, they were forced to seek others' jobs. If employed, they could feel hungry eyes on themselves.

The resultant uncertainty and anxiety permeate the interviews in this book. If a strike failed, overt union sympathizers would surely lose their jobs and would likely be blacklisted. Relief—charity, in the view of many—was demeaning and clearly a final, desperate measure. Nevertheless, these deep anxieties did not defeat the movement toward unity and organization. Those who overcame their fears, who took the risk, live vividly in the memories of the men and women who will speak to us in this book.

The workplace itself, where these men and women mingled, where they earned their bread and discovered the ties of solidarity, compels our attention as it controlled their lives. The conditions they encountered—the character and posture of their supervisors, the pace of their work, the nature of the machines they operated—all helped create an environment conducive to organizing. As long as resentment troubled only the individual, it could be isolated and rendered harmless. Consequently, the first organizing step required breaking down that isolation and generating awareness of a common plight. What was the common plight of the Auto-Lite workers? How did Auto-Lite deal with its employees? What was the workplace like? What did it feel like to be an employee of Auto-Lite? Workers and managers alike will answer questions such as these in the interviews.

Clearly, loyalty among workers at Auto-Lite proved more powerful than a sense of obligation to company managers. Personal bonds among a few men who worked in the same small department created the initial unity, but trust and faith had to spread broadly throughout the plant for organizing to succeed. A modest success—simple reinstatement after the February strike—provided the encouragement; personal bonds and peer sympathy then brought workers together.

This reconstruction of events and review of issues in the 1934 strike at the Auto-Lite factory provides a context for the personal recollections that follow. (See Appendix A: The Narrators for a descriptive listing of the individuals who contributed oral histories to this book.) The complexity of such an event, coupled with differing individual experiences and points of view, emerges in the oral histories that complete this volume. These oral histories help create an understanding of the human drama of such a strike, of the hundreds of personal decisions and actions which made it live.

Many of the people interviewed for this book have passed away; but much to our good fortune, their stories survive. They are not illiterate; but many have not, generally, expressed in writing their fears and hopes, their attitudes and sentiments. Because our culture relies so heavily on written documents to define historical reality, the experiences of these people are often shared with only a few. Some are not shared at all, and we are the poorer for it. This book aspires to save some of those experiences and to enrich our understanding of the Auto-Lite strike of 1934.

2

Toledo and the
Auto Industry: 1920–1934

Two realities dominated the consciousness surrounding the Auto-Lite strike: the depression and industrialism. Though complex, they fall within our understanding because they fell within our narrators' abilities to cope. Those whom the depression and industrialism destroyed do not speak to us here, although the survivors who speak here bear scars created by their confrontations with these forces. And, however discrete and personal these confrontations felt, they were not unique. The weight and breadth of these realities assured shared experiences. Few could escape them.

In this chapter, our narrators will recount their individual experiences with the depression and with the world of industrialism. We asked two basic questions: "Where were you born?," which led to discussion of family and work traditions, and "What was it like during the depression?"

The depression had mixed effects. For some it was an inconvenience, for others it was devastating, and for most it represented a shock and an assault on their dignity and security. Ironically, our narrators initially interpreted this social and economic disaster as a personal failure; they, like so many other Americans, internalized the depression. Relief, our narrators tell us, represented a confession of failure—a confession that one could not cope, could not provide for one's dependents or even one's self at the most basic level of subsistence: food, clothing, shelter. One avoided situations which would reveal this failure. For example, many refused to attend school because of shabby

19

clothing. Entertainment often consisted of popcorn and cards in private homes, where the absence of money for a date could be overlooked. Even the relatively secure who could think of college determined their credit loads by the amount of tuition they could afford. Those who had savings accounts felt bank closures sharply, but many scarcely knew the purpose of banks. Others who did, who owed on mortgages, might have wished they did not.

Bank closures hurt workers who had savings or property, but the loss of a job incapacitated any worker, for that job provided the basis for respectability and identity. Without work, one had no claim to legitimacy. Layoffs in the auto industry, and specifically at Auto-Lite, had occurred with some frequency during the twenties; but they were often seasonal and were thus predictable. One could temporarily shift into another line of work, or prepare for a layoff and hope for a job afterward. The depression was different. Layoffs for indefinite periods spread over the entire economy and hopes for jobs constantly dashed upon reality. Without a job and without money, the worker could not pay his way. American traditions that insisted the individual was master of his or her destiny increased the worker's suffering by aggravating that sense of guilt and inferiority.

Traditions can create security, and some of our narrators found security in family; but the family tradition could create individual problems as well. Family roles reversed: children supported parents. Often, any working family member brought home wages and shared them in an attempt to assure survival of the family. A wage that might have sustained one person was transformed by large families into a scratching existence for many and security for none.

The depression disrupted patterns of work that had created some security when wages were high enough to support life and when jobs, though not continuous, were regular. The few jobs available in 1934 were often of short duration and only part time. Wages earned on these jobs could not adequately sustain a worker and his or her family. In seasonal industries like auto production, many workers had found odd jobs during the off-season. But in 1934, odd jobs became primary jobs. In Toledo, Auto-Lite—the hope of many workers because of its size and its employment of the semi-skilled and unskilled—had difficulty remaining in production even with a reduced work force.

Women constituted a major proportion of Auto-Lite's work force in jobs that must have been better than their alternatives. Domestic service for paternalistic employers at oppressively low wages could easily convince young working class women to try factory work. Their class origins opened no doors to college and career; commonly, before completing high school, they entered the work force in a job defined as "women's work." There were many such jobs at Auto-Lite.

Perhaps the greatest poignancy is found in the sense of loss accompanying the rural to urban migration. Rural life had its own struggles: the farm was not always the island of harmony and self-sufficiency portrayed in sentimental literature. However, rural life could have a sense of community, an integration with others and with nature. Therefore, the migration to the city represented a loss which heightened one's awareness of the isolation and emptiness of the new life of concrete, electricity, and assembly line. Of course, this alienation of worker from worker and of worker from meaningful work obstructed any movement for a union and was also symptomatic of the sickness the union might cure. The sense of loss is clear in the recollections from her youth of Elizabeth Nyitrai, who began working at Auto-Lite as a teenager.

ELIZABETH NYITRAI
Production worker at Auto-Lite; crossed picket lines and worked during the strikes.

I was raised on a farm, and I was the only girl among six brothers for the longest time. So, I was a tomboy. Of course, I wasn't very strong, but I went everywhere the boys went, climbed trees—the highest tree—whatever they did, went hunting with them, and things like that. Frog hunting, and roasted over a fire. I was a regular tomboy, but I wasn't strong enough to be a tomboy. So you know I had spunk, and I had feelings for my parents, too, you know. I had to give up high school. See, I started my freshman year down there before we sold the farm and then, of course, when we came to Toledo, I had to give it up because I didn't have the nice clothes to go to a city school, where down there, you know, I loved it. Then, of course, you couldn't raise your vegetables. Mother, down there, had a big garden, and we raised a few hogs for meat in the winter and maybe had a calf now and then.

Well, I'll tell you, I had the blues for about five years after we moved. I missed all my friends, and I missed going through the woods looking for birds' nests and walking through the fields. Like my mother would send me out in the fields to pick the dried beans out in the cornfield. I'd sit there listening to the birds and watching them; and at that time, I could tell by their singing what type of bird it was: a redbird or—I could tell, because I'd seen them and everything. And I loved nature, picking the first spring flowers in the woods; and over here, nothing but concrete. It was awful. I hated it.

Before the farm, we lived in this small coal mining town, and we were like one big family. The closest hospital was in Columbus, so if anybody had a baby, they had midwives. In them days you didn't get up right away and work, like now they send you home in three days. So, you know what the women in the neighborhood would do? They'd cook their choicest foods, fried chicken, their best cakes and pies, and they'd pack it in a basket that big, and they'd cover it with their fanciest cloth—they did a lot of fancy work, embroidery and all that—real fancy cloth.

One day, one mother would bring a basket of goodies. The next day, another mother would bring a basket of goodies. And, of course, your turn came if one of them got sick or like down with the flu and wasn't able to cook, why then they all pitched in and we paid each other back. But they don't do that here.

I know we moved here and rented a house. Well, one of my little brothers, two years old, was leaning against the picket fence and my dad heard the neighbor lady yell at him, "Get away from that fence; you'll break it!" So then my dad says, "This will never do," because down home—we did live in town before we bought the farm—everybody looked after each other's children. And if they did bawl them out, we never got angry because we knew they'd do it for their own good and we'd do the same. They looked after each other, helped each other. So, my dad didn't like her being so nasty. So he says, "We have to look for a house." So, he found a house about three blocks farther up. It was a junky old house, but my mother fixed it up. She raised thirteen children there.

At first, I worked as a domestic, as a maid for one year. Three dollars a week. Come home Thursday afternoon and Sunday afternoon. Three dollars a week. Do all the laundry and ironing and cleaning a big home and take care of the baby. Three dollars a week. But they were wonderful to me. But that wasn't much, and I know my mother was still washing clothes on our washboard. It took my mother three days to do the laundry for such a big family. I remember I felt so sorry for her. So, one week I went back to work and I told the lady I worked for, I says, instead of paying me by the week, pay me once a month. When she got rid of her laundress, she raised me little by little because I threatened to quit. I think I was getting maybe eight dollars a week.

Anyhow, fifteen dollars a month was the payment I had to make on a washing machine. I went down and bought my mother a double tub Dexter.

Of course, my mother was fussy with her washing. She'd wash it out of one water, wring it into the next tub, wash it out again. It would get special clean. Because down at home we had them big copper wash boilers, and after we'd rub the clothes out, why then she'd put it in this tub with some lye in it and put it on top of the coal stove and boil it. All our white clothes were boiled. And then in the winter you'd have to hang them outside, and they'd get real stiff while that freezing bleach did some more. With all them kids, she kept a very spotless home.

As we all grew up and got jobs, we all pitched in and helped. Like when I come home from the Auto-Lite, I never saw my check. I'd sign my name on it and hand it to my mother. And if I wanted a dollar sometimes, if she was hard up, I didn't get that dollar. I had to go down and borrow from one of my friends. But then a lot of times when Easter come, and I would tell her, gee, I'd like to have a new Easter outfit. I know one time she gave me twenty-five dollars to go down and buy myself an Easter outfit. But she was good at saving her money. We never went hungry. I never remember a time when we ever went hungry.

ELIZABETH DOMBROWSKI

Elizabeth joined her husband, Chester, a punch press operator in Department Two at Auto-Lite and union organizer.

We lived on Hamilton years ago. I remember I was about eight or nine years old. When my father was out of work, we sat under a big tree in the backyard and you know what we had for supper? Graham crackers and lemonade. My mother didn't have no money. She was really a thrifty person, but my father only made twelve dollars a week and when they got out of work, or there were no orders, he stayed home.

I worked at Champion Spark Plug when I was eighteen years old. I was young and I thought, well, I can work and I don't have to. So, I got kinda sassy. The foreman says, "What kind of work do you want to do?" There was no union there, you know. I said, well, my mother said I couldn't work on a punch press 'cause she didn't want my fingers cut off. I was scared to death. Then they put me on the biggest press that was in the shop. He said, "Watch that so they don't cake up on you, you know, plug up on you." I had those little brass rings that were punched on. In a few minutes, I had about two bushels of that stuff around me. I couldn't see the top, I was just covered. I got scared and I said, stop this. Something is wrong. Here comes the foreman. Boy, was he mad. [He said,] "What did you do?" I said, I don't know. Something broke. He said, "Something broke! You broke this whole damn thing." Excuse my English, but that's just what he said. He said, "If you weren't a new—" I was only there, I guess, second or third day then— "a new girl, I'd fire you." So, he went to a higher foreman, the ones with the little lids on their chest, you know, and them long yellow coats. He come and said, "God sakes, she really did it." It took the fellow the whole afternoon with wheelbarrows with chunks of that press to take out to get repaired. I didn't see that thing for weeks.

VIRGIL BARNHART
Owned small candy business near the Auto-Lite factory; wiped out by the depression and hired into Auto-Lite in 1935.

I operated the Barnhart Candy Company until sometime in 1932, I believe it was, and, of course, business was getting tighter and tighter. Unemployment was steadily getting worse and our candy business— well, as I said, people didn't have the money to buy bread, let alone buy candy. There was only one recourse: we owed the wholesalers, we owed our suppliers, we owed even our help, and we finally had to file bankruptcy. There was no recourse but to close the business; we couldn't make ends meet.

I think that we was paying twenty dollars a month rent for a three-room apartment, and I distinctly remember the bedroom had been attached to the building, and it had a flat roof and come to rainy weather, we had to take a piece of canvas and mount up over the bed to keep dry. All it needed was a coat of tar, and I didn't even have enough money to buy a bucket of tar to put on it. And I couldn't get the landlord to do anything with it.

Well, after we went bankrupt, there was no recourse but to go on public welfare. There was a food distribution place on, I believe, Galena Street—about ten blocks from where we lived—and if you wanted the food, you had to go there and pick it up and carry it home.

The food consisted of bread, and dried beans, and cornmeal, flour; it was all dried food distribution. I don't recall whether there was any federal distribution at that time; I think it was all city and county welfare, if I remember right. We managed to get a few dollars, enough to pay the rent, by my wife working part time at Titke's down on Cherry Street. 'Course she'd have to walk back and forth, and that continued until the WPA [Works Progress Administration] program. And it wasn't any comfort, but everybody else was more or less in the same circumstances. You'd see people that'd been in business, that'd been independent all their life. You'd meet 'em in the food line; that was their only recourse. They maybe had some property, but they couldn't get any money from the bank because the banks were all closed.

I'll tell you, for the first week or so, I went down the alley; didn't walk down the street. That's how ashamed I felt about taking welfare, but after I got over the first shock of having to be in that circumstance, and finding that there were hundreds of other people in the same circumstances, it became a way of life. That's about the only way I can describe it. Of course, the legislators were attempting, and did eventually get, money available to attempt to utilize the manpower to really start some worthwhile work in and about the city, to make the person feel that he was a part of society and pulling his own weight. That was set up under the WPA program.

RUTH LYONS UNFERDROS_____

Daughter of the president of the Auto-Lite Council; observed the strikes.

INTERVIEWER: *Did you have to work during the depression?*

Try and find a job! I worked at the telephone company in 1931, 1932. My mother was working part time, and this day my mother came home from work and there sat my father and I. We were both laid off the same day. And it was terrible. My father said one of the biggest mistakes he made in life was that he didn't go on relief, but he felt just above going on relief, so consequently, after the depression was over, we had a great big grocery bill to pay; we had a great big coal bill to pay. Like I said, Mother and Father just scraped enough for the taxes together and fifteen dollars a month interest payments on the house. Father said afterwards if it ever happened again, he'd be the first one down in the relief line, but pride kept him out of it. It was terrible, and I think that's one reason why I don't like pancakes. I ate an awful lot of pancakes. And my husband, he won't eat soup, and I think the reason he won't eat soup is because that's practically what they lived on.

LYNN G. WATERS
Toledo policeman; on patrol at Auto-Lite during the strikes.

I worked in the Willys-Overland Company, automobile manufacturer, a while and then I went and worked for the Canadian Tracks Company. The Overland were having it tough over there—they worked at that time twenty-three hundred men—and they went broke. I had to get a job but quick to support my family. Then I went from there on to the police department in 1928.

INTERVIEWER: *You were originally attracted to Toledo by the Overland Company?*

Well, yes. Because anyone could get a job there then. They employed four or five hundred men a day, that many would quit. They used to bring them in here on buses from Tennessee and Kentucky. Every morning the old Blue Goose Line would bring a couple of bus loads of workers to the Overland.

INTERVIEWER: *Then you went on the police force. What attracted you to the police force?*

It was a job and it was steady, and I originally thought, well, I'll take that job as a stop gap. Then when things commenced to get good, by then I had fifteen or twenty years in there. See, Toledo, I think, was hardest hit financially, of any city in the state and possibly in the nation. All of our banks closed but one.

INTERVIEWER: *When was that?*

1932, I believe it was. All the banks closed except the Toledo Trust.

INTERVIEWER: *So, a policeman's job was a pretty good job then?*

That's right. It was steady.

ELIZABETH SZIROTNYAK
Production worker at Auto-Lite; crossed picket lines and worked during the strikes.

I had been working already from 1928. In 1928, I was hired at the

Auto-Lite, and then worked until 1933. Then I was off that whole year of the depression. So then when I got back, I was out of everything—clothes and money—I didn't go nowhere all that while. We couldn't afford even a fifteen-cent show. And what I did in the meantime for three dollars a week, you wouldn't believe. I worked in a hamburg joint for four dollars a week and on your feet all that time. We were open twenty-four hours. And then six people come in; they want six different things. You don't know which way to go. That's why I went back to the Auto-Lite. I said, I'll go back and work for three dollars a day there, rather than do what I used to do: housework and take care of two dogs. I had to clean up after those dogs. The dogs were more important than even me. She cooked special—noon—for the dogs. Of course, we ate out of the same thing, because it was that good. Oh, yeah! Chicken broth, chicken and dumplings, she'd make the dogs. We ate the same things. (Laughter.)

THOMAS PROSSER⎯⎯⎯⎯⎯⎯⎯⎯⎯⎯⎯⎯

Toledo policeman; on patrol at Auto-Lite during the strikes.

INTERVIEWER: *What attracted you to police work?*

Well, mostly things were kind of tough at the time I went on, and there was a pension involved. And, of course, it was a little bit of adventure, you know, and excitement.

When I went on the department the only training you got was you went out with a policeman three nights, and from then on you was a policeman and was on your own. And you had no scout cars, no radios, anything like that. All you used was a call box. If you got in trouble, you either got out of it or that was it. You had to fight your way out. No help or anything.

I worked a district when I first went on from Michigan Street on Adams out to Twenty-first Street, and it was the toughest district in Toledo at that time—the bootleggers, pimps, everything. In 1933, Mayor Solon T. Klotz cut our wages. We were up to two hundred dollars a month, which was pretty good money in those days. Then they cut us back to a hundred and fifty; finally, it was a hundred and thirty-five. Then they paid us in scrip for almost a year, and we had a terrible time. Scrip was issued by the city. Eventually, they redeemed it, but at the time you couldn't spend it; nobody would take it. The only way you could get rid of it was—I had a friend in the plate glass company down there and he used a lot of water for grinding glass, and they could take the scrip and pay their water bills. So, he'd take the scrip and give me cash for what he thought he'd use for the water bill, and that's the only way I'd get any money. It was pretty rough for a while. It just happened that I had a landlord that would take the scrip and hold it.

JOHN SZYMANSKI_____
Auto mechanic, self-employed during the strikes; later, Auto-Lite machinist and union supporter.

I lost my father when I was eleven years old in 1921. I wanted to go to school, you know. In fact, I wanted to go to the seminary to be a priest, to be frank with you. That fell through, naturally, because I lost my father and we were a family of ten children. I was about the fifth or sixth in line. So, while I was still in grade school, I enrolled in Northwest Ohio Motor School. That's where I picked up mechanics and had my training. I was nuts about this stuff. So naturally when this depression happened, people were up against it. They'd bring me cars to fix. Maybe they'd give me chickens or eggs or produce or something or do something for us. We had our own garden, too, you know, chickens and ducks and stuff.

INTERVIEWER: *What year was that?*

This was back in 1930, 1931, 1933, in through there, see, and I'll tell you frankly, brother, there were guys on CWA [Civilian Works Administration] at that time—then they went to WPA. Them poor devils. It was the most unusual thing. The government would take these people from Toledo and send them to Bowling Green. Then from Bowling Green, they'd send them to Toledo. They were digging ditches, planting trees, working in the zoo and—oh, you name it, they did it. They were doctors, lawyers, professional people—highly educated—professors who teach in school and so forth. Well, how could you go to school without money? Those who were extremely rich, I suppose, were the only ones who could go to school.

Oh, yes, at that time, too, there was prohibition, you know. I was never involved in anything illegal as far as prohibition was concerned, but some of these guys had some pretty good boats. They had planes, boats, automobiles; you name it, they had it. And naturally, they'd ask you to do work for them. Well, you work for everybody. And they paid you well. I'd sometimes go out there in a day and ride around for an hour or so on a speed boat, run around that bay, up and down the river. These guys would cut across that lake, pick up a load, and then they'd come in, you know. Well, I didn't ask them their profession, because I found out that the less you asked questions, the better off you were. And I figured that these guys could afford it.

And naturally I always felt sorry for the underdog. When a guy came to my shop, the poor devil had a flat tire or—he was trying to get to his job and the old tire was flat—let's say I put a tire on it. The fellow would say, "Well, I ain't got any money now." [I'd say,] Well, don't forget. Stop by when you get around to it. Well, I was a trusting soul. I still am. I lost more money in my day than some people accumulate all their life. You trust too many people. Naturally, you felt sorry for them because some were in very dire need; there's no question about it. And there's a tendency for people to take advantage of people. So, that's part of the business stuff.

SEYMOUR ROTHMAN
Newspaperman just entering the trade in 1934; reported some events during the Auto-Lite strikes.

I'm Seymour Rothman, a reporter at the *Blade* for many years. At the time of the Auto-Lite, I was going to the University of Toledo and carrying copy on the morning newspaper here, the Toledo *Times*. These were, of course, depression times and everyone was understaffed, and so in the case of something like the strike that required so many people, I was permitted to go out with reporters and make myself useful out there instead of staying in the office doing copyboy's work.

We had been living in a depression, everybody was in it, and at least as far as I or my friends were concerned, it was just a way of life. We weren't depressed mentally. Of course, you'd think about getting a job. Any job you could get was a good one, whatever it paid. And your dates were by streetcar, and you spent a lot of time in other people's houses. The idea of spending a lot of money just didn't seem to be important.

Tuition at the university, I think, was twelve dollars a semester for as many hours as you could carry. Now, that didn't cover books; that was tuition. But there were some other small charges. In those days, you kind of worried about getting the twelve dollars.

JOHN [J. J.] JANKOWSKI_____

Punch press operator in Department Two at Auto-Lite; union organizer.

In 1928, I got married in Toledo, but I lived in Detroit. My wife was a graduate nurse, and she worked in St. Vincent's Hospital in Toledo. Before, when I was keeping her steady company, I was working in the Hudson Motor Car Company. When I told the boss I'm going to be married Saturday, he says, "Well, be back here Monday." And I says to myself, okay, I'll come back Monday. The wedding lasted—them Polish weddings them days I didn't know because in Detroit, in my neighborhood, we forgot that old tradition like they had over here. That wedding lasted clean up to goddamn Wednesday. When I reported to work Thursday, the boss said, "Get gone, you're done." So then, I went over to Detroit, shoveled coal, worked on garbage disposal, canning season—when they had extra garbage in Detroit. Carted extra trucks, or drive one of them trucks. Done all kinds of jobs around there.

In about the beginning of the year, just about when they change models at the Hudson Motor Company, they give us some work pretty good there for a while. Then, just about February, it started slacking way down. And there was no unions at Hudson Motor. They'd say, "Come in one day a week." We'd work one day. "Don't come in 'til next Monday," 'cause there mostly everybody was working one, maybe two days a week. That's in 1928. One day, two days. In 1929, it was the same thing. It was in 1928 when I lost my job at the Hudson.

Then one weekend I come over to my mother-in-law on a Friday night. She says, "How things going over there? In Detroit?" Oh, I told her, working one day a week, sometimes two, sometimes none at all. She says, "Why don't you try another company?" Well, with one kid and wife to support, I'm stuck. And she says, "Well, why don't you try over here at the Auto-Lite? They're hiring people; they're working ten hours a day." Well, I says, I don't know. [She says,] "Try and stay over 'til Monday and go there. Try it."

It's the last week in February when I done that and went over there Monday morning, went in there every morning trying to get a job, kept a-going there every day. There was a bunch of men, boy, it was packed full. So finally, on a Friday about 9:30 in the morning, the personnel manager he come out there and he says, "I need four punch press operators. I got any volunteers?" Well, there's a lot of people that's ascared of punch press. I run 'em in Detroit at Hudson. I said, I accept it. So, he hired four of us.

He led us across the street to the department we worked. That's in Two, Department Two. The foreman's desk was right in the middle of the floor. It was not private, caged-in, it was right in the middle of the floor, all the presses all around. Walked us up there and he says, "Here's your men." It was March 1, 1929.

ROBERT A. CAMPBELL
Auto-Lite machinist and member of Mechanics Educational Society of America (MESA); continued to work during the strikes.

In 1929, during the depression, while I was working with Auto-Lite, I heard rumors to the effect that officials were drawing their money out of the Security Bank, which is a large bank in Toledo, and so I went home and told my father. My father called the branch manager of our bank in East Toledo, and he said there was no reason to worry about his, that they weren't having any problems. A week went along, and then things looked like they were getting worse as far as people drawing their money out of the bank. So, my father went down to draw his out, and they said, "Well, you can't draw. We can't give it to you for thirty days. We have a thirty-day notice on withdrawals on any deposits." So, after thirty days they closed their doors. And every bank in Toledo was closed. So, they issued bank claims. You had a claim for the amount of money you had in the bank. What a lot of business places were doing if people actually needed money to live on, why, they were buying these claims for sometimes as much as a 20 percent discount.

I knew fellows at the Auto-Lite that were affected. Some of the older men lost their homes, and they bought a cheaper home and started over again and saved their money.

TED SUSKA
Auto-Lite production worker and early union supporter.

I was married in 1923. We bought this home and we moved in here in 1925, and so we had a mortgage and stuff like that, you know. I had been working at the Auto-Lite, and then the depression came. I was working two and three days a week, you know, and just about existing to meet the mortgage of thirty-five dollars a month for the house here.

It was bad here in Toledo. I was too proud to go over and beg from anybody, to go on relief or anything, so my wife went over and borrowed money from her mother. Not like today, you know. The first you know, you're on relief. It was a tough situation, and the wages weren't very much. You made maybe twenty, twenty-five dollars a week then, you know. You had a home to pay for, children, married. It was a tough life.

INTERVIEWER: *How would you get to work every day?*

Me, I tell you, when I first was there I'd start out of here at 6:00 in the morning and walk to the Auto-Lite. I walked about five years, and then when I got a little bit on my feet, then I started riding the buses. And then I got a bonus from the Army from the first World War, and I bought myself a car and from then on we kind of enjoyed it a little more. But back in 1934, I couldn't ride the car because I didn't have any money to buy gas, so we had to walk. I had a car but no money to buy gas.

CHESTER DOMBROWSKI_____
Punch press operator in Department Two at Auto-Lite; union organizer. [His wife, Elizabeth, joined the interview.]

During the depression, I had a little money in the bank. Her and I had just gotten married. I think we were just in our twenties—early twenties. I had three hundred dollars in the bank, and I went into the bank during the depression and I says to the guy, look (just for the heck of it), I need a dime for a loaf of bread. I says, I put my money in here, could I have a dime to buy a loaf of bread? He says, "I'm sorry, but I can't give it to you. I haven't got it. All our money is tied up in homes or in loans and stuff like that." I says, I'm sorry, but I didn't invest in a home or a loan. I said, I brought it in here for an interest. I could use a dime for a loaf of bread. He says, "I'm sorry, I can't give it to you." It was the Opieka Bank. Today, it's the Lucas County. They changed their name. Just like the Auto-Lite changed their name to Eltra, from Electric Auto-Lite, when they moved out of Toledo. Then the bank moved down someplace I discovered. They didn't even let me know. They didn't notify us or nothing. I discovered that they moved on Superior Street, and I went there and I asked them for money.

ELIZABETH: We got a little bit, didn't we?

Yeah, I got twenty dollars. They sent me a paper—it was something about the size of a check, almost—and it says that I could expect twenty dollars from all the money that I had in there and no more.

ELIZABETH: From three hundred dollars.

And some old woman was in there, some old lady. I remember she was ahead of me. Whatever he told her, she was crying. She probably had her savings in there, and he told her that she wouldn't get anything. I remember she was crying, and I didn't know what to say. I just stood there and I looked and I talked to this guy and the guy says, "Well, you'll hear from us." And I remember getting a piece of paper and it said, you will receive, within the next ten years or something, twenty dollars, and that I shouldn't expect any more. That was it.

DOROTHY MATHENY
Teacher; organizer and member of Toledo Federation of Teachers; witnessed Auto-Lite strike events.

I'm Dorothy Matheny, ex-teacher of English. I retired in 1965. I taught for thirty-eight years.

INTERVIEWER: *Were you teaching in Toledo in 1933 when the Toledo Federation of Teachers began?*

Yes. I was over at Woodward High School. The person who was organizing at that time in the school was head of the English Department, Mr. Raymond Lowery, who became president of the National Federation of Teachers. But we had around 95 percent of the teachers organized in the federation at that time. Partly because, in 1929, you see, the banks closed and teachers were not getting any money and the public didn't have any money—or thought they didn't have any money—to give us raises anyway. Teachers were desperate, so the federation looked pretty good to them.

We had all kinds of difficulties. Everybody was horrified. In the first place, the unions, at that time, were not acceptable at any level, from any group. The whole attitude was anti-union and nobody who belonged to the right class of people joined unions. So, the fact the teachers were organizing was way off. They just thought the teachers were supposedly better than union people. Union people were all thugs and people who went around beating other people on the head, were uneducated and crude, and this kind of thing, and they felt that teachers were not that class of people.

I remember one time coming on to Thanksgiving that the youngsters in this homeroom class wanted to take part in donating something to somebody, so they collected food and several of us went over, and the youngsters went over into this house. They had no furniture; they were using orange crates and whatever else they could bring home. There wasn't really chairs; they'd burnt the furniture. They had no food in the house. I don't even know if they had a refrigerator. They weren't the only family; there were hundreds and hundreds like that because they had been out of work.

STEVE ZOLTAN

Set-up man at Auto-Lite; stayed out with the strikers but did not picket; later became a plant superintendent.

But back then, in one of my first jobs before Auto-Lite way back in— what was it, 1920?—I joined the AFL and we started organizing. In those days, of course, we got fired. I ain't back yet you know. They fired the eight of us. I had a little fun with them. I asked our business agent, I said, look, I'm out of work now about seven or eight months. I said, what are you going to do about it? He gave me an unemployment stamp in my book so I don't have to pay dues. "Well," he said, "if you organize 100 percent, they can't fire you all." That's the answer I got. That was a position for me to hate, you know. I didn't have the nerve to organize 100 percent—I wasn't built that way. I never tried to force anybody into anything. I was talked into this. I was one of the eight that joined. I joined the leader. I said, well, maybe we should organize. I lost my job and I ain't back yet. That's a long time.

Of course, when the depression set in, the banks closed, no money to be had. Everybody was mean, hungry, vicious, and, as a result of the Auto-Lite strike, other plants begin to organize. No one was satisfied. Couldn't get your money out of the bank. Banks closed. I can tell you one thing, too, that we had banks in those days like we have today; but those banks weren't for my type of people, the men who worked in the shop. Banks were for people who wanted to build—borrow money. Tell you the truth, 'til 1930, I didn't know what the banks were for.

Prior to the union, you really had to have the ability in order to get a two- or three-cent raise. But what I do recall as no good is the amount of increase that the company used to give the employees prior to the union. You worked there six months you got a one- or two-cent raise. Then another six months you got another two. You never heard of a nickel or dime, never. When I served my apprenticeship in the Millburn Wagon Works, oh, my God, about 1912–1913, I had to work one whole year as an apprentice to get a two-cent raise. I was getting seven cents an hour, I finally went to nine cents. I worked another year—the second year—I got one-cent raise, I got a dime an hour. They paid twice a month, and it was in coin. Like if it was ten dollars, you'd get a ten-dollar gold piece, five dollars, a five-dollar gold piece— not silver dollars. For one pay, I'd get eleven dollars and the other pay twelve dollars, for thirty-one days. That was my wages for the month— twenty-one to twenty-two dollars. People don't believe that. That's the truth. I went to the Libby Glass House—six dollars a week. Now you wonder why they organized? That's why they organized. Yet, the profits those days were just as great as they are now. Did you ever hear of anybody making a billion dollars profit? General Motors does; Ford makes it; Chrysler makes it.

I met my present wife, and in order to marry I had to get a job. So, I got a job in the Auto-Lite; and I was there for forty-two years. You've got to have the will power. If you set out to do anything, do it—don't just talk about it—or forget about it. I got this job and I stayed in it. See, if you don't have any responsibilities, you don't have to live up to what you promised yourself to do. If you've patience and want to accomplish something, stay with it.

EDWARD LAMB

Successful Toledo attorney; key legal counsel who defended strikers and their supporters.

I was born April 23, 1902, in Toledo. I have always lived here. My mother was English, my father was a fisherman on the South Shore Lake area. He was a commercial fisherman, and I grew up on the beach and fishing grounds. I am one of ten children, and the last survivor of the ten children. And my educational background was through Toledo schools. Then, I went to Dartmouth College and Harvard Law School and graduated from Western Reserve Law School in 1927 and became a lawyer in Toledo. I was assistant city law director when I started, for just a year or so, then got out and started practicing law. And 1929, I had a very substantial practice, for a young man, and by 1930 or 1931, I represented several successful corporations. And then, as the depression heightened and I became more interested in social problems, I became very active in the New Deal group. I was Republican and was offered a job in the Internal Revenue Service under the Republicans in 1929, 1930. I then became interested in the cause of labor and various civil liberties cases. Labor wasn't organized too much at that time, certainly in the mass production industries. So, one of the first cases that I had was in the Electric Auto-Lite strike case in Toledo, Ohio.

The depression had really become total at that time. Unemployment was vast and starvation and poverty common around this community of Toledo and probably every other community in the United States. Our people were being dispossessed—the farmers were having these really violent dispossession proceedings around mortgage foreclosures, unemployed labor was being thrown out of its house and, yet, being misrepresented by some very, very corrupt old AFL leaders. And one, the principal person in Toledo, a labor leader, was an old man by the name of Francis Dillon, who had been sent here by the president of the AFL, William Green. And Dillon was an old-line trade unionist, and he was really a sell-out artist to the labor people; I'd seen him try to force really outrageous settlements. And there was tremendous opposition to him. And so, finally, the thing just exploded.

Many of the owners were my friends. Clem O. Miniger, the president of Auto-Lite, of course, had been a very, very close friend of mine. He was the president, a very rich man here, and I had originally represented that group until I started representing these workers. And then, of course, all my corporate clients disappeared.

C. O. Miniger came from Fremont, a self-made man who made a fabulous fortune quickly. And he got a little armature plant down there on South Church Street, and it started supplying parts for Willys-Overland and finally got parts business for Ford and later Chrysler. And he just made a fortune, he made a fortune fast. And he acquired many other companies. And he was a local hero. He was "Mr. Big," an awfully nice guy. C. O. Miniger was a great guy. I knew his family, his daughter, and all the rest of them. He was a very good community citizen; he was the president, Chamber of Commerce and Manufacturer's Association, and on the trustees, and director of banks, and a symbol of total success. His stocks had gone crazy, and a lot of people in Toledo had made fortunes out of Electric Auto-Lite stock. I've forgotten what it went to; maybe it was 187 or something, I don't know. And so, there was tremendous local pride and interest in the Auto-Lite company stock. He was the success story.

Another very great friend of mine, Ward Kennedy, who later had trouble in the Willys-Overland Company and sold it, he was very heavily into Electric Auto-Lite. And several other people in Toledo. Byron Fayhe, who later became a friend of mine, happened to be the foreman of the department at Auto-Lite that I worked in as a kid. And he was the guy that charged me for a tool that someone else stole from my bench. He later became, I think, president of the Electric Auto-Lite Company. Very rough, free enterprise guy. Anti-union guy. And when I represented the union, of course, many, many personal friends of mine became personal enemies of mine, or they thought I was an enemy of theirs for being connected with the union. But the feelings were really on one side or the other, and there were very, very few people on the labor side in this community at that time. Certainly, in the mass production industry, such as the automobile industry and its satellite suppliers of the automobile companies.

Auto-Lite was a very large company, six thousand employees, at least. They made not only all the spark plugs, or a large percentage of spark plugs, but they made other automotive equipment. A very vital supplier and a very reactionary company. But conditions became so awful that this fermented into a condition where we could get recognition of an outside union. They had first to overcome the old AFL chains, and they could only probably do it through this violent explosion. And I do emphasize violence. It could not have come any other way, I'm sure.

There was a new breed heading the union. Tom Ramsey was a good progressive outsider. These young men weren't guerrillas. These were all good, honest, progressive young people that really had to overcome these sell-out artists from the AFL, old skilled craft unionists who were selling them down the river. The AFL had very strong restrictions about bringing anyone into the fold. They were not organizing the mass production industry. This was just the beginning of it.

Then they didn't know where to turn except to strike, just stop working, and face up to the individual landlord who was throwing them out, the employer who was throwing him out of his job, the grocer who was cutting him out. So, he'd move out and sleep on the streets. And those were the conditions for these six thousand people working for the Electric Auto-Lite. The newspapers were saying, "Well, aren't they lucky they got jobs? Who are they to complain? Look at all the people who don't have jobs." So, these people had to face up to this atmosphere and criticizing, because they had jobs at the Electric Auto-Lite.

But the depression: people were hungry, they didn't know where to turn. This was a country of tremendous storehouses of surplus food—and yet burning the food—and people starving and actually camping out on the courthouse lawn, on streets, selling apples. These people had no hope. There were really hundreds and hundreds of them out on the courthouse square and other places all over town. They were thrown out of their house, they couldn't pay rent, they couldn't move. So, you had the explosive condition that was necessary to create this catalyst to bring about the recognition of an outside union.

3

The Auto-Lite Company

As one of many producers satellite to the major automobile assembly companies, Auto-Lite began to grow in the teens under the leadership of its president, C. O. Miniger. He had secured patent rights to an electric starting motor, which replaced the hand crank, and production and distribution of that starter motor increased Auto-Lite's business dramatically. From that product, Auto-Lite branched out into other lines, concentrating mainly on electrical equipment for automobiles. Initial contracts with Willys-Overland in Toledo gave Auto-Lite a boost, and a contract with Henry Ford in the late twenties led to major expansion. Auto-Lite also established a worldwide network to distribute replacement parts for components used in the initial assembly of automobiles. As long as automobile assembly companies used Auto-Lite parts as original equipment, the replacement parts business remained lucrative. However, the position of satellite in auto production proved precarious, because assembly companies like Willys-Overland, General Motors, Chrysler, and Ford would purchase from companies like Auto-Lite only as long as they could supply parts at the lowest cost. As soon as the assembly companies could purchase or produce these parts cheaper, they would do so; thus, Auto-Lite's days were numbered. If it lost a major account, particularly after expansion, it could be devastated. Auto-Lite nearly collapsed in the early thirties when Ford cancelled its contract and began to produce its own electrical components.

C. O. Miniger held the presidency of Auto-Lite throughout the strike. Although a very wealthy man, he had a reputation for the common touch, at least among the workers around him in the office. His reputation as a kindly, considerate man appears consistently in our narratives. His paternalistic style proved attractive and effective. After the strike, he stepped down from the presidency as the result of a merger with Moto-Meter Gauge and Equipment Company, a merger which brought with it a large contract with Chrysler.

Our narrators in this chapter held managerial or skilled positions. They recall their relationship with Miniger and recount the impact on Auto-Lite of the depression and Ford's cancellation on Auto-Lite.

CLARENCE FOSTER
Assistant manager in the service parts division at Auto-Lite.

I started to work at the Electric Auto-Lite Company on the 13th of June, 1915. I was doing clerical work in the office.

INTERVIEWER: *What was Auto-Lite engaged in doing in 1915?*

Well, of course, our business was making electrical equipment for automobiles, tractors, and trucks, and that sort of thing. Such things as generators, starting motors, and lamps, cutoffs for Detroit Rotors.

INTERVIEWER: *And you rose to . . .*

Assistant manager of the service parts division.

INTERVIEWER: *Did you notice any immediate impact on operations there from the depression, from the market crash?*

Well, sure. Naturally, the work volume wasn't there, so people worked either short hours, or they were laid off temporarily. They tried to take care of everybody they could with the volume of work that was available. A lot of it was short hours or short weeks for some people. I would say, offhand, that maybe 40 percent of them were women. Maybe it wasn't quite that high. But there was a lot of women there. Of course, a lot of it was light work, too, you know. We had established throughout the country, in fact throughout the world, authorized service stations to repair and service our product. Now, these people had to have service parts. We served them through the service parts warehouse.

INTERVIEWER: *Was there any conscious attempt to recruit women that you know of?*

Not that I know of.

INTERVIEWER: *Were there any women working in your operation?*

Well, in the office, yes. I would say that 50 percent of the service personnel in the office was women. We had women in our packaging department, but that was about all. At that time, I don't think we had over a dozen women in the service parts warehouse. Oh, some departments were all women. Women were employed as armature winders and so forth. There were certain kinds of jobs that actually women were so adept at with their fingers, faster, they were entirely women, oh, maybe with the exception of a clerk or checker or maybe foreman, assistant foreman, etc. Some departments were, you might say, 98 percent women.

RAY GARBERSON
Supervisor in Auto-Lite's cost and budget division.

INTERVIEWER: *What was it like to work at Auto-Lite in your department?*

During those days they worked longer hours, from 8:00 a.m. to 5:00 p.m. and 5:30 p.m., sometimes 6:00 p.m. During the strike time, not the strike necessarily, but during that period, we were working at least forty-eight hours a week and some overtime. Forty-eight hours was the scheduled work period.

INTERVIEWER: *How many were you in the department?*

At that time, I would say there were about twenty-five in the cost department; perhaps, three, four thousand, if my memory is right, in the Champlain Street plant.

INTERVIEWER: *Did you have much contact with the factory part?*

A great deal. I knew mostly foremen or salaried people. My contact was with division managers, departmental managers and heads, superintendents, assistant superintendents, and so forth, regarding supply costs mostly.

INTERVIEWER: *Was Auto-Lite doing fairly well—able to stand on their own two feet at the time?*

Well, no. I would say no. At one time we got into the manufacture of electric clocks just to augment our loss of business due to the recession; and, at the time of the strike, Auto-Lite and Moto-Meter Gauge and Equipment Company merged. The head of the Moto-Meter Gauge and Equipment Company, Royce Martin, was related to the Chrysler family; and I would assume that, for that reason, he got the entire Chrysler electrical business, which was a godsend to Auto-Lite—all their starting motors, generators, coils, lamps, equipment. I think that saved Auto-Lite. I understand that Royce Martin was the brother-in-law of Walter Chrysler.

I knew Art Minch; I knew C. O. Miniger. Mr. Miniger was one of the finest men I ever knew—very common, ordinary. He'd come in in the mornings and nod and speak to the people as he went through with a big smile—wonderful. Naturally, being in one big office building, I knew them all. I didn't have too much personal contact with them, but very good speaking acquaintance.

ELIZABETH FRITSCHE
Stenotype operator and secretary to the manager of the service parts division at Auto-Lite; worked during the strikes.

INTERVIEWER: *What was Miniger like?*

Clem Miniger? I always called him an old sweetheart. He was nice looking, an old man with snow white hair. I only met him two or three times through my boss. I started there in March—and the following Christmas we had a Christmas party, and, of course, one department would go in among other departments, and that's the first time our group went into the main office to meet Mr. Miniger. What I knew about him, he was mighty nice—and a good president of a company.

CLAUDE W. POUND
Production manager at Auto-Lite.

We tried to operate all through the depression and did, too. Of course, our orders passed way down. So they started building clocks—electric clocks. They kept a lot of people working through the depression years. From then on the production started up again. That was in the latter part of 1933 or 1934. Then, of course, we run into that strike in

1934. I was production manager there at the time of the strike and went through all of it. That was pretty rugged. The guards was in—killed two or three of 'em—that was a pretty rough time.

INTERVIEWER: *What type of person was C. O. Miniger?*

One of the most wonderful men that ever lived. Yes, sir, C. O. Miniger. He did everything in the world for his town and got a lot of abuse for it. Well, he couldn't help it. This strike came on and everything was all in a mix-up, and they turned against him. Not the town itself but the people, the gang that lived down there. But he was a wonderful man. He built a couple of hotels on Madison Avenue and Fifteenth Street—the Hillcrest. He was always doing things for them. Made all kinds of contributions for charity and things of that sort. He was a very, very good man. He was not the plant manager—he was the boss, he was the president.

INTERVIEWER: *What about Mr. Art Minch?*

Well, I resented the thing up through the years, I can say that little bit. He was, in one sense of the word, my boss. There wasn't an official affair, but he was really taking charge of it.

INTERVIEWER: *Was he a good man for the position?*

Oh, that's a pretty hard question. I don't think any of us could have filled it too good.

INTERVIEWER: *Who was the plant manager?*

I was—practically. I had the title of production manager. I guess you'd call it plant manager.

INTERVIEWER: *Could you explain a little bit about your job?*

Well, improving production up until the time that this strike came. After that it was a good deal of negotiating with unions and supposedly running a plant. That's all it was.

ROBERT A. CAMPBELL
Auto-Lite machinist and MESA member; continued to work during the strikes.

INTERVIEWER: *Do you remember anything about the company higher-ups like Miniger?*

Yes, Mr. Miniger was a very nice man. I know I started the Auto-Lite in December and didn't have a paycheck coming; and he come around personally and—five dollars in those days was quite a bit of money— and he personally would give everybody a five dollar bill at Christmas time and shake your hand and wish you a Merry Christmas. A wonderful person. So, I had no ill feelings for the company. I was always treated good, very good. But other people had other ideas, I think, and production workers—I can't say—they probably had their reasons for starting the union, without a doubt. But as far as my end of it in the skilled divisions, why, we were always taken care of in very good fashion and treated right.

INTERVIEWER: *What about Mr. Minch?*

Mr. Minch was a very nice man. I knew him personally. He was one of the original starters with Mr. Miniger. Those men started the Auto-Lite plant. And the Auto-Lite plant started over on Cherry Street; and from there, they moved over on Champlain and they had a small building there.

When John N. Willys started Willys Motor in Toledo, why then they started making the starting equipment for Willys Motors. That was their first customer. And so, they developed real fast. And then the Ford Motor Company was one of our big customers. That's when we built a new plant to make their equipment. Then Ford Motor Company decided to make their own, so we were in trouble until they got the Chrysler business. When we got Chrysler business, we were in good shape again, and we tooled up for that. I remember that was a big job.

INTERVIEWER: *But everybody in the model shop belonged to MESA?*

MESA, yeah. We were all toolmakers by trade. That was more of a skilled trade in the model shop because we had to make all the original samples for approval. At this time, we were making all the instruments for the car and all the instrument panels and all the accessories from heater motors to windshield wipers.

GEORGE KESSEL

Accountant at Moto-Meter; crossed picket lines to work on the merger between Moto-Meter and Auto-Lite.

My two superiors at the time, Mr. Royce G. Martin—he was president of Moto-Meter Gauge and Equipment—and Mr. Walter B. Flood, who was vice-president and comptroller, they were the type of individuals that wouldn't walk into anything unless their eyes were fully opened and they had formulated plans that they thought could work. And at the time, Auto-Lite had lost their ignition equipment contract that they had with the Ford Motor Company. Ford Motor Company was the main vendor with Electric Auto-Lite Company for starting motors, generators, distributors, and other parts of the electrical system in an automobile.

INTERVIEWER: *Why did Ford pull out?*

They felt that they were going to go into the business themselves and save money, which they did. So, they made their own equipment, which left Auto-Lite in a precarious position at that time because Ford represented about 70 percent of their original equipment volume. So, this was an ideal situation for us to come in because our president, Mr. Martin, was very, very close with Walter P. Chrysler—the old Walter P. Chrysler. Chrysler was buying their electrical equipment from General Motors, and this was not a position that they liked very well. They would rather deal with an independent company like Electric Auto-Lite.

INTERVIEWER: *The merger itself was in the air during early 1934?*

I don't think it was in the *air*. I think it was being discussed between our officers and probably Mr. Miniger and his confidants, but it wasn't open publicly. It was in the stages of Auto-Lite determining if a merger with Moto-Meter Gauge and Equipment would be advantageous, and likewise, if it was going to be advantageous for Moto-Meter to merge with Auto-Lite. Now the whole thing hinged on the acquiring of a big automobile account to fill these facilities that Auto-Lite lost by reason of Ford Motor pulling out.

INTERVIEWER: *So, the friendship with Walter P. Chrysler is really the leverage that Royce Martin had?*

He had this in his hands, right, and Mr. Miniger, a very, very able gentleman and a very good businessman who put his heart and soul into the Electric Auto-Lite Company, he wanted to leave this world knowing that he had done the right thing by his people who had worked for him for years, that were still left.

INTERVIEWER: *Through negotiations he was concerned about keeping the plant open and keeping the people on. . . .*

Absolutely, keeping his workers—not talking about staff. He was also very much interested in the people who were in the nucleus of putting that company in the position where it once was. The battery divisions of Electric Auto-Lite Company, the foundry division of Electric Auto-Lite Company, and the ignition equipment plant of Electric Auto-Lite Company, plus its far flung after market service station set-up all over the United States, was out of this world. The replacement business created your big profit margin.

FRED C. [WHITEY] HUEBNER_____
Management in Auto-Lite's time study department.

I was in charge of the time study department at the Toledo plant of the Electric Auto-Lite Company in 1934.

INTERVIEWER: *And what did your job consist of?*

My job consisted of overseeing the time and values put on the factory operations in the plant and setting measure of time for each operation to be performed. So, I was very close to all the workers in the plant at that time. Then we started in the manufacture of generators for Chevrolet, our chief customer, if you can imagine. As it developed, they were entirely separate and really antagonistic to Auto-Lite, because we were closer to Chrysler than we were to General Motors. My entry into it was from the standpoint of industrial relations, time study, and format.

4

Working at Auto-Lite

W ork has a social as well as an economic dimension. Attitudes toward work frequently depend as fully on relationships with fellow workers and with supervisors as they do on the intrinsic qualities of the work itself. Of course, skilled workers, such as the tool makers and machinists in the model shop, could not be easily replaced and thus enjoyed significant security. Organization of these skilled workers into MESA, a union unaffiliated with the AFL, generated little hostility from management. In general, however, Auto-Lite workers had little security. At Auto-Lite, as in industry overall, the relationship between foremen and workers proved the most delicate and potentially the most disruptive. Workers found themselves trying to please foremen to protect their jobs. Even supervisors and foremen felt some insecurity, since they had to keep production rates up. But foremen had the power to reward and to punish, to favor some and to harass others. That power was, from the point of view of the workers, final, because foremen had the power to hire and to fire. Consequently, in this time of massive unemployment, good relations with the foremen were essential to workers' security. The uncertainties of the times thus magnified the uncertainties of human relationships in the shop. This held particularly true for the unskilled or semi-skilled worker at Auto-Lite.

The favoritism found under such a system rankled deeply. Workers took pride in their ability to do their jobs and felt cheated when less skilled or less experienced workers displaced them. That violated their basic right to their jobs, an injustice exacerbated by the personal indignities the workers were forced to endure in order to keep their jobs. Under observation even into the toilets, workers found themselves sneaking a bite to eat or a puff on a cigarette, aware that they would be fired if discovered. Favoritism toward relatives, cronies, or those who did favors for the supervisor also debased the process. The foreman's exercise of his power to select workers for jobs appeared arbitrary. The worker had no way to enforce open and equitable evaluations of work beyond appealing to the person selecting.

In virtually every department, a supervisor had the unrestricted power to choose the workers to perform the jobs available that day. The most vivid symbol of that power, the bench, stood along the wall in the punch press room. There workers sat until the supervisor chose them to do a specific job, and they returned there when that job was finished. There they sat until chosen again. They earned no money sitting on the bench. The only virtue of the bench in the punch press room was its safety. One can often identify punch press operators from this era by the joints, fingers, or other pieces missing from their hands.

Low pay proved less a problem than the dangers and uncertainties of the job itself. The wage scale differentiated on the basis of sex and many jobs were classified effectively, if informally, "women's work"; but even the "men's jobs" paid poorly. Mixed with shortened work weeks and sporadic employment, these low wages provided scant fare for the table. However, a few workers made out fairly well when they worked, because Auto-Lite employed a piecework system that placed a premium on speed. The young and agile could sometimes make comparatively good money, but Auto-Lite's system of time study set standards or quotas to the workers' disadvantage. When workers consistently exceeded original standards, standards would be increased, thus generating less money for the workers.

The Bedeaux system, named after its creator Charles E. Bedeaux, an American industrial engineer, held out the possibility of a bonus to workers who exceeded quotas set by management. Supervisors would set the quota on a particular operation according to its difficulty. A worker would be expected to meet a standard rate of production on that job. Should the worker be unable to meet that standard, he or she could expect disciplinary action. That was the stick; the carrot dangled on the other side of the quota. Should the worker produce above the quota, he or she would earn additional money. For example, the standard quota on a job might be set at a thousand pieces an hour. A worker who met that standard would earn the hourly rate—at Auto-Lite about forty-five cents. Should the worker produce two thousand pieces in that hour, a bonus would be earned. Thus, the system provided an incentive to speedy workers.

However, the Bedeaux System had a catch to it—a catch which escaped no worker. In the above example, one would expect that the worker would receive ninety cents for the two thousand piece production. Since the first thousand pieces were worth forty-five cents, the second thousand pieces should logically be worth the same. They were, but the worker did not receive it all. The second thousand pieces earned the worker only a portion of the additional forty-five cents—perhaps half or less. The remainder was divided among the supervisory personnel who oversaw the worker's production. This provided them an incentive to see that the worker produced more than the standard. Of course, if a worker consistently produced more than the quota, he proved that the quota had been set too low; and the supervisor raised it. Pressure to produce more created a truly satanic cycle.

That pressure inevitably would result in an oppressive work pace, less bothersome to the young and agile but exhausting to the average or slower worker. The pace of work at Auto-Lite is clear in the recollections of our first narrator in this chapter.

JOHN SZYMANSKI
Auto mechanic, self-employed during the strike; later, Auto-Lite machinist and union supporter.

Well, in 1929, I worked at the Auto-Lite. And working for the Auto-Lite at that time—naturally, I was only nineteen years old and strong as a bull, you might say, able to work hard. I was mechanical-minded, because when I was fourteen I went to an automotive school, and I learned a lot of things about automotive and machinery and things of that nature. And factories were looking for people who were capable of operating machinery. But in working for the Auto-Lite, I found that my sympathy always went out to my fellow worker, especially if I was working with an older person.

I'll tell you frankly. I worked with a guy from St. Mary's, Ohio. He was working on generator frames, starter frames, and he was counterboring internally, see. He had to file them and get the burrs out. And I'm thinking that guy sure is—he's really something, you know; he's really fast. And there I am; I'm counterboring the outside and sanding the outside frame and popping them into an automatic machine that would tap them and would drill and then it would tap these holes out. Why, you were bouncing around like a rubber ball. And this guy's doing the same thing. He was feeding them to me, and I was the final end of the line. The beads of sweat on that guy would be as big as my little fingernail. Gosh, this guy.

There was no such thing, at that time, where you get a five-minute break for personal time. But every time something would go wrong with our machines and you had to shut them down, you know, I used to say to him, hey Dad, why don't you run over to the restroom and rest up a little bit, and we'll do the best we can for you. Because whenever a machine was broke down, especially if it was heavy—then behind you, you could accumulate these frames, you know; you'd stack them up in piles and so forth, and that would give somebody in the group between us a chance maybe to pick up this guy's operation for five, ten minutes or something of that nature. Because fixing these machines never took too long, because if it took too long, boom: they sent you home.

So, this poor devil, I thought he was going to collapse one time. He was just hopping around there like a jumping jack. It so happened on one occasion we were eating our dinner. Most of these guys, elderly fellows, I suppose, relax as much as they can without moving around too much, see. So, on this one occasion—I believe it was raining outside or something—and I stayed inside. And that poor guy, he's trying to eat his lunch and he's still a-twitching and, you know, moving around. And I says to one of the fellows, what's the matter with that guy? Did he get hurt? I never seen anything like this stuff in my life. He said, "The guy has got Saint Vitus's dance." I think you'd still say the same thing. I suppose it's palsy or something like that now.

You felt sorry for these people though. They had a gripe because the Auto-Lite was an unusual company. They employed people, but they had a tendency always to drive and drive hard. They had guys in the employment office all the time. And the guards over there were awful tough, too.

INTERVIEWER: *The company guards?*

Oh, yes. They'd push you around, pop you in the head with a billy if you'd mouth off or something like that. Oh, well, I mean if you got out of line and tried to speak up on behalf of somebody. At times, they would just take you out of the place bodily. They'd come in and take you out, and that would be the end of you. You worked there no more.

And then again here was another brutal thing about working for them. Supervision—they had a habit. Say, for instance, if you brought them butter, eggs, chicken—you know, invited them out to your place if you had produce and all that jazz—well, you got good, cushion jobs, you might say. They kind of looked after you.

They had other evils, too, and I wouldn't even want to say over the air because to me it was very—I imagine if the company would know what some of those guys were doing, they'd probably even fire them because they were unethical. Well, it was bad. The reason why I say it is this. If you're an investor, you want profits. If you're a manufacturer, you have to manufacture and make profits. So, what happens? You're going to get the guy to work for the least amount of money you can so you can make bigger profits. If you become injured or hurt or something like that, well, there was nothing wrong with you getting a slip saying, well, you're laid off. Maybe you walk fifteen feet away from the machine; already they're putting another guy on, see? Get the point? Now, today working, because of labor organizations, you have a system now where if a man is injured or hurt, they try as much as they can to help you, based on the wishes of a doctor, to give you some type of work where you can get back on your feet again. Now see, they don't pay the same rate of pay, but at least you got a job and you can eat. It ain't like then. You were out on the street, see.

MARY ABERLING _____
Production worker at Auto-Lite; supported the union and honored the picket lines.

When the depression was on, they didn't have too much work at Auto-Lite; but I did get to work one or two days a week making electric clocks, at that time. I worked there for twenty cents an hour for a short time.

INTERVIEWER: *Twenty cents an hour and on top of that only a few days a week?*

Yeah. It did keep the wolf away from the door, anyway. It was rough. It was very hard.

Then I got to work on piecework, and then I made a little more money. I always worked on production. I never wanted no day work. That way you couldn't make money. Where you worked on piecework, I had the speed; so I made as much as I could. You had to make so much to make out, and then after that you made the bonus. Then the hourly rate went up. I think it was thirty-six cents at that time, for the women. Thirty-six cents an hour, all hour. You made certain amount that you had to put out.

They timed you, you know, by the pieces. They did time study, taking the time while you was working, with a stop watch. Of course, the faster you worked, the more you put out; so, you couldn't have a lot of speed at that time, because you didn't know how that work was going to go. So, the longer you worked on the job, the faster you could go. So, once he timed the job, it stayed that way; and if you were a fast operator and put out the pieces, then you made a little more money.

At that time, I was working on one of those little drill presses putting threads in brush holders at forty-seven cents a thousand; and I put out ten thousand a day, so that was four dollars and seventy cents a day. That was good money at that time. I was a fast operator. I could put out work fast, and a lot of the girls didn't have the speed, you know; some were faster than the others. So, every chance I get, I'd make as much as I could—put the speed on it. This was just a woman's job. The men had different rates than the women, higher rates always. The men always got higher rates than the women.

INTERVIEWER: *Was that particularly bothersome, or was that just the way it was?*

Not really, it was just the way they set it up, and that's the way it worked. That was 1925 at the time. I was working on assembling regulators. Just women assembled the regulators.

INTERVIEWER: *Was there much turnover at Auto-Lite, new faces around all the time, or was it pretty stable?*

Well, they'd quit and they'd hire in. They would only keep the good workers really at first, because when I worked what they called the New Building, when Ford come in in 1928 and, like I said, went in 1930 again, well, I was winding motors and the forelady would come around and say, "Mary, put on some speed because we're going to have a layoff, and the only ones they're going to keep are ones that produce." So, the more you could put on, well, that's the one they would keep and not lay off, because at that time there was no union, you see. They'd lay off anybody they wanted to. So, with me, I'd never get laid off, because I always produced; and that's the kind of people they wanted working there. Wouldn't dog around and just go in there and put in their time. During the depression, I was working full weeks.

Sometimes, maybe we would work two or three days, but usually I worked a full week. I was never laid off. Only vacation time, I'd take my two weeks after they had organized.

INTERVIEWER: *There were no vacations before?*

Oh, no, God no! Not then. Then, you'd better be working every day or they wouldn't keep you because they wanted somebody they could rely on.

INTERVIEWER: *How would you know when not to come in?*

The day before they'd tell you before you went home not to report the next day; and if they didn't tell you, you was in then. But like I say, you had to be a good worker or they wouldn't tolerate you.

INTERVIEWER: *Did you have a sense of permanence about the job?*

Yes and no, because you never knew whether they was gonna keep you or whether they wasn't. That's the reason that I worked fast, just to be able to hold a job. I liked to work there, I really did, for the simple reason they had the piecework, and I could work faster and make more money. Yeah, it was a good job for me.

ELIZABETH NYITRAI
Production worker at Auto-Lite; crossed picket lines and worked during the strikes.

Every morning, gosh, I had to leave home about 5:30 to walk that distance to get there on time. Sometimes, I had to half run because I'd stayed out late, and then I didn't want to get up in the morning, and so I'd be late, and I'd get in the gate just as the whistle blew, so sometimes I'd skip breakfast, you know. Well, good heavens, about 10:00 you'd get starving, you know. You weren't allowed to walk off the job or even eat an apple on the job. Oh, no, not with that cranky boss. "This isn't no restaurant. This is no place to eat. You're supposed to work. This is your job. You're supposed to do your work. This is no place to eat."

I remember one time I got a bad case of diarrhea, and I had to go quite a distance, way to the other department, to the restroom; and I was shy and I got sort of embarrassed running back and forth. I'd no sooner get back to my job than I had to go again. So, I went up and told my boss, you know. And he says, "Keep running to the bathroom, but just keep on working." Do you know, he wouldn't let me go home? I spent a miserable day. He never even mentioned to me that we had a nurse downstairs; go downstairs and have her give you something. Nothing. He'd look at those girls and I'm telling you. You'd look around and there'd be tears. They were afraid of him, you know. He was so nasty mean.

One foreman I worked for was sort of a pompous person who felt that he was big and important; and, of course, he had this friend of his who was a forelady, and there was rumors that they had an alliance, girl friend, anyhow. And she was all dolled up. Her fingers were always covered with rings. Her pets would give her something, and she was good to them. Well, I didn't have any rings. So, if it wasn't him going around, "Get the rag out," and "We gotta get this work out in a hurry; step it up, step it up," you know; then he'd leave, and she'd make her rounds. And they all quit one by one, and I stuck it out because I had to help my mother and dad support my brothers and sisters.

Well, we were working on ignition coils. Did you ever see one? They're pretty heavy and the cast iron pans or steel pans, they're about two feet wide and they held about twenty-five coils, I'd say, and the pan itself must have weighed about ten pounds, because they were heavy. And, of course, then, we'd have to stack them up; and, as your stack got higher, you know, you'd have to lift that way up. Nobody give a darn. You'd have to do it yourself, you know. Later on, why, as work slacked up, you'd take them out of the pans and do it. But you had to keep up because it's piecework, and you can't hold up the other girls.

You never knew if you had a job the next day. Like some of these women would buy the forelady gifts, hankies and whatever she liked, cologne and stuff like that. Well, I couldn't afford to do that. Then we had a couple of younger bosses, like the one that used to be a machinist. He knew that I had to work, so he'd lay off some of the other girls, you know. He always hung onto me until the last minute. Of course, you're used to doing piecework and working fast and I'd finish it up in a hurry; and he'd come around and he says, "What'd you do? You're on day work. You're not supposed to work fast. Sit around and talk, and if you see a big boss or a big shot from downstairs come around, why, get real busy."

There's always a lot of rejects. A lot of these girls would slip it through because you had to sign your card how many pieces you had in there. Well, this southern girl was real fast, and she'd always make more money than I did; but I'd solder mine all the way across, but she'd just tap it and run it through. I was a perfectionist.

JACK C. LATHROP_____

Foreman in Department Two at Auto-Lite; crossed picket lines and worked during the strikes.

INTERVIEWER: *What did your job consist of?*

I was the foreman in the pressroom. This consisted of two things; being a foreman was still work with the planning department—we were given sheets of orders for what we had to make. Each and every one had a part number. And ours were all punch press and drill press. Anything that consisted of parts that were made for distributors and your motor parts like coils, they were all made by the punch press. My partner was Arthur Ryder.

When they put in this piecework system, you hung a card on the punch press and the name of the part and how many pieces—your time card. The checker then checked your meter, turned it back. At various times the card might call for an odd job or something, and we would use it in a different press. But in doing that, after piecework went into effect, you would have to pay an allowance because the job could not be run proper and with the proper speed that your standard was set for. Therefore, you would be given a difference.

INTERVIEWER: *Do you remember which ethnic groups were predominant in the Auto-Lite? Were there Poles, Germans, Hungarians—ethnic groups?*

Oh, I'd say, Polish.

INTERVIEWER: *Mostly Poles down at the Auto-Lite?*

My department was 80 percent. See, we have a lot of Polish here, I'd say 100 thousand out of the 300 thousand.

INTERVIEWER: *Do you remember if there were any blacks employed in the plant?*

No, they wouldn't allow them the light. In fact, they never were approached until after the union organized. It wouldn't have done them any good. I mean, it just was "we ain't got nothing for you," and that was it.

INTERVIEWER: *What was Minch, the vice-president, like?*

He was the anti-labor man of the organization. Finally wound up being transferred to Port Huron, Michigan.

INTERVIEWER: *Because of the strike?*

Well, I wouldn't want to be quoted as saying that, but you can draw your own conclusion.

Now, Art Minch himself was a nice guy, personally. In fact, he's the one I went to work for. He had charge of the clerks and timekeepers at that time in the cost department. Claude Pound himself, who was the vice-president, was in a position where he pretty near had to be strictly a company man and live that way. The job demanded it.

When you're the foreman of a line, let's say—maybe you've got a dozen operators—it's up to you to get production. You get the orders and that's it. So, I tried to the best of my ability to pick who I thought was a capable man and who had had experience. I picked who I thought. It was like I told Claude Pound, I said, what the hell, if you want pieces, and if I get ornery with them, you ain't going to get your pieces. Think about that, Claude. And he used to be a foreman. He said, "Yeah, but under the conditions." I said, conditions, so what? That's it.

NORVAL HISEY

Electrician at Auto-Lite; crossed picket lines and worked during the strikes.

INTERVIEWER: *When did they recall you at Auto-Lite?*

In 1934, just before the whole shebang out there. I didn't even have enough in the house to feed my two kids. It was rotten, boy. I'm telling you, it was rotten. Everything closed up, everything.

I would say, at least 72 to 73 percent of the workers were women. I'll tell you why. You see, they wanted armatures, generators and that, coils, or circuit breakers, and that was all woman's work. Now, the men's work was on the automatics, running out shafts, and setting out laminations for your armatures, but the women did most of the wiring. They had these fine coils to wind, and it was more of a woman's job, the real touchy wiring and that stuff.

ROBERT A. CAMPBELL

Auto-Lite machinist and MESA member; continued to work during the strikes.

I was at Auto-Lite during the depression, and we managed to work three days a week; and, of course, it kept food on the table for my father and that was very fortunate. I was just a young person and I'd never worked in a plant before, and I personally thought the conditions were all right. I mean, you had the condition where the foreman, if he didn't like you, if you did something, he could fire you immediately without any questions asked, so you more or less did your job. You couldn't have any coffee breaks like you do today. You worked nine hours a day and five hours on Saturday. And, of course, in those days apprentices did a lot of dirty work that they don't do today. And every Saturday morning was our job to clean the whole shop. We took brooms; we scrubbed the floor. It had to be clean before we left on Saturday, the machines cleaned. And today, they have men that do this now.

But I enjoyed every bit of it. It was very nice; there was a bunch of nice men working there. There was the start of a union then—a machinist's union—called the MESA, that was started by a man by the name of Matt Smith, and our dues was only fifty cents a month. But up until the sixties, MESA was still in force at the Auto-Lite in the skilled trades; the drafting room, our tool divisions, and our machine shop was all controlled by that union. See, we actually had two unions after the strike of 1934.

STEVE ZOLTAN
Set-up man at Auto-Lite; stayed out with the strikers but did not picket; later became a plant superintendent.

Seniority didn't mean anything in those days. You either had to do something for the foreman or you wasn't working. I knew a foreman that whenever he needed his home painted, he would lay off two or three operators, then offer them the job back if they painted his home. At the Overland of Toledo, for instance, I knew a foreman that used to get a cut—10 percent—from their wages. But it was that way because the foreman did have the power to hire and fire, and they did as they pleased.

I remember very well, when I was married in January 1923, the company had notices placed throughout the plant: "This plant will close for seven months." I was off for seven months. That was life. They closed whenever they pleased; didn't recognize seniority. If you had the ability, you had your job; if you didn't, you just didn't work.

I become one of the best job setters in the Auto-Lite, in the company's opinion. Any short order or mail order jobs that were tricky, I would get and got paid by the hour. I think my high wages as machine set-up man were seventy-five cents an hour. We had to buy our own tools, but once you bought your own tools and you wore them out, broke them, the Auto-Lite would replace them, but only like say, screwdrivers, maybe a chisel. But micrometers or any measurement tools you had to buy yourself. They did replace hammers, screwdrivers. They did supply the gloves. That was the extent of the company's replacement—gloves, screwdrivers, hammers.

ALBERT ABERLING
Punch press operator hired into Auto-Lite during the strike.

I started work at the Overland in 1916, during the first World War. I stayed there about two years, and then I went over to the Libby Glass. Then I went back to the Auto-Lite back in 1923. I was on punch press, Department Two. I stayed there until 1926, and I think I was out to Timken Bearing; then I went to Detroit in 1930, and I worked there. I was there for a year, then I come back to Toledo again. The work in Detroit casting truck transmissions wasn't so good. It wasn't paying good, and all that cast iron dust I had to breathe wasn't any good for me, so I left there. Then I went over to the Auto-Lite after they walked out on the strike. I went over the next day.

When I was at the Auto-Lite in 1923, we were talking union then, about having the union shop if we could. A lot of the fellows said, "Well, you couldn't do that in the factory 'cause there is always somebody to take your place. You don't have to be a trade." And I said I don't know, that you could probably form a union. Then still, when they walked out that time, then I went in, but I didn't want to. But, I had to work; I hadn't worked for a long time, and I needed the money. I'd never go through that again.

I tried to get a job there way back a couple of months before that, but they said they weren't taking anybody. They got enough people there. Then, I kind of heard something about there was going to be a strike over there. They are going to walk out. Then my wife told me, "When they walk out you'll have a chance to get a job," she said. "They'll have to hire somebody." I went over there. If I'd had someplace else—a job—I wouldn't have went over there. I'd awent over there on the picket line with them guys.

I worked in plants in the Overland and in Detroit and them places when they didn't have no union, and I knew what working conditions were. Why, you was nothing but a slave in those places. They had nothing, no wages or anything else. The Auto-Lite paid what, forty cents an hour for the men and piecework you made seventy cents. If you made over that, why, they'd cut you.

MARY ABERLING: He worked on motors, generators.

ALBERT ABERLING: Yeah, starters. Some of the jobs there wasn't heavy, but they preferred men on them instead of women.

INTERVIEWER: *What was it like to work there? I'd heard some people say it was a dangerous place in some jobs.*

MARY ABERLING: Well, the punch presses, yeah. Course, they had safety guards on not too many at the time.

ALBERT ABERLING: They had a guard on mine. When I was there in 1923, it took part of my thumb off. It had no guard, and they changed the die and shortened the die instead of shortening the wires. That's how I happened to get it.

INTERVIEWER: *Did that happen often?*

ALBERT ABERLING: I remember one fellow. The assistant foreman was showing the state man, you know they come in to check, showing him how that happens and I'll be darn if he didn't get his nicked off. He got his'n off, too, the same as the fellow before him.

MARY ABERLING: I recall one time one of these machine operators, these automatic machines that used to cut the pieces off for the motors; and the rag got wrapped around the machine, and he had his thumb in there and he couldn't pull it out. And that machine pulled his whole thumb out. They brought him into the hospital, which was right there where I was working. Even that cord that was part of his thumb got pulled out, and that was a sight. They had his hand wrapped up. He lost his whole thumb and, you know, occurrences like that happened. The girls used to get their fingers clipped off, and after that, I wouldn't take a job on a machine. I'd have assembly work because there was no danger of getting hurt.

CHESTER DOMBROWSKI_____
Punch press operator in Department Two at Auto-Lite; union organizer.

To begin with, it was kind of tough about the depression time. I remember I was laid off about fifteen months before I got called back.

A lot of guys would come in in the morning. And, if you were a favorite of the foreman, you worked; and if you weren't, you were sent back home. We stood there like a bunch of soldiers at attention, and the foreman says, "You stay here 'til I look around." If he had anything open—like on presses—well, he'd say, "You come on with me." He'd put them on the job. Johnny J., myself, and quite a few of the guys in the locker room—he'd say, "You guys go over there and sit down on a bench, and if I have anything," he says, "I'll let you know."

So, we used to sit there anywhere from 7:00 in the morning until 11:00 or 12:00 noon. We paid streetcar fare out of our own pocket. We rang our cards, but we didn't get no money for it. We sat there in that corner 'til the foreman would come around, and he'd say, "Well, fellows, come back tomorrow. I don't have anything for you." That went on for I don't know how long. Then maybe for a couple few months—then he'd finally come out and say, "Well, I'll call you when I need ya." So, we just went out and walked the streets. I didn't have a job for fifteen months.

I've seen guys bust the die. Home means just as far as you go—you set the machine center, and it hits home as tight as it can. Now if you put two pieces in, that makes it twice that thick. Now that don't have anywhere to go. When that hits, something has got to give and that die splits wide open; and if you do that over there at the Auto-Lite, man you got fired so fast it wasn't funny. I've seen guys get out of there, they put their coat on, and they didn't even tell the foreman. They put their coat on and rang the card, run home.

Being there awhile, you know, you have to tell your stock. I mean the thickness, whether you had a mic [micrometer] or not. I was so good at it, I could tell it by the eye. Some of it was thirty-eight and forty-two—you could tell the thickness—if it was ninety-five thousandths, thirty-eight thousandths, twenty-five thousandths, whatever. Once, after Ryder, the foreman, walks away I said, we can't run those pieces—that stock is mixed up. Somebody was running thirty-eight and forty-two stock on that. So, I looked at Steve, and Steve looked at me and said, "We better tell them; we'll get the blame for it." We did. We got the rest of the week off on the street.

You couldn't go to the toilet. You couldn't smoke. If you got caught smoking, you would have been fired. If you'd get caught eating a sandwich, you'd a been fired. If you'd get caught going to the time clock to ring your clock like they do today—they give you ten or fifteen minutes to wash up and stuff—you'd have been fired. I saw a guy get fired for just walking past to see what time it was.

If you broke a punch, that was it. It didn't have to be your fault. I've went around with a foreman who was going to put me on the job. I've seen him break three different punches on three different dies that he wanted to put me on. Now if I'd have done it, I'd probably gotten fired. I've known a guy to give a salami sandwich to the boss, just practically every day. We used to call them "little red apple" days.

We had this in our noodle all the time, you know, saying so and so, that pot licker, he's working, he's making fun of me; he's laughing at me, but he's working and I've got more seniority. Maybe I got the guy the job, he's laughing at me and I got him the job. You know, you don't like that, that don't sit so good. Especially when a guy starts showing his teeth, you know, when he starts laughing at ya.

I remember keeping a sandwich behind my shirt, and I'd see the foreman going up to one end of the building or up to the department. You'd get behind your shirt, quick take a bite, and shove it back; and if you were nearby him, you'd be chewing, and he'd see your mouth moving. Boy, that would be it.

So, you'd get forty-eight cents an hour, and in five days you had to make out—they had what they called the Bedeaux system. This is more or less piecework. Sixty minutes was sixty B's. This is the truth, now. You have to make out five days in a row to stay out of the red. They had a big sheet on a bulletin board, and they had everybody's name on there. And each one was marked each day what you made— sixty B's or one hundred B's or ninety to one hundred (you might as well keep that out because in those days you couldn't make a hundred). If you did, you had to be a suck hole. That's what we used to call a guy that would be a suck hole around the boss to get the best jobs them days. So, you got a raise to fifty-four cents an hour if you made out five straight days in a row.

We didn't dare ask for a time study; because if you asked for a time study, you were walking the street. So, nobody ever asked for a time study if you couldn't make out. All you did, you were putting your pieces in there as fast as you possibly could. I don't know how many weeks it took me to make these five days. The last day would be on a Friday night. Maybe, I'd miss out by a few pieces or so. I couldn't help it, nobody could help ya. But I finally made it by a penny a day or two cents a day or, you know, a few pennies a day, because I wasn't one to know the foreman or, you know, suck hole around him, see. I was on my own. So, I finally made it with fifty-four cents an hour.

Then, another thing is this. For the first hour, suppose you had to run a thousand pieces to make your hour. That was for the company.

And if you made fifteen hundred pieces an hour—or suppose you could make two thousand pieces an hour—for the first hour, say, you got a dollar or, say, fifty cents, or whatever it was. For the second hour, you wouldn't get the full amount. You would for the first one; but for the second one you should have gotten, say, another dollar for that, you only got a half, maybe less than half. The rest went for the foremen and all. They would get a bonus. I remember someone saying that our foreman got a bonus of three thousand dollars through the year. That is because he pushed the men. If you were in red when the foreman would be passing out the checks on Friday, he had your record that you were in red; two or three days a week, he'd say, "Let's see if we can't do better next week."

CARL LECK_____
Stockroom worker at Auto-Lite; union supporter.

INTERVIEWER: *You started at Auto-Lite when?*

1928. My brother got me the job. Barney was there a year and a half before I was. And, as a matter of fact, Marie's husband worked there at the time. He got Barney on. But when that depression hit, I still remember Red Vollmer coming around saying, "Carl, how much you making, sixty-five cents an hour? Starting tomorrow, fifty-five cents an hour." A month later, "Carl, you're making fifty-five cents an hour, tomorrow forty-five cents an hour." Just like that.

INTERVIEWER: *Was there any way to object?*

No, no way, no recourse or nothing. Take it, or out. A lot of men were waiting for your job.

Old man Pound, he was a production manager at the time. I've seen him walk down the line and hear somebody over there putting the gear on top of a generator taking a steel hammer and hitting them like that, instead of protecting it. No way. He'd just walk over, tap him on the shoulder, "Get your time right now, you're done." Maybe the man wasn't properly instructed, that made no difference whatsoever. "You're doing it wrong. Out! Right now!"

INTERVIEWER: *Did you know of people being fired for being too old?*

That wouldn't be because they were too old. No, you can't say that. Some economy engineer says we can do better to lay off all the men in the stockroom and move directly from the receiving dock up to final assembly and let them take care of it. We used to have at one time thirty men in that stockroom. When they wound up, they had one man. And these older men, that were too old at that time, where would they go for a job? They couldn't get a job.

INTERVIEWER: *Did the company try to get them back in the operation there some way?*

No, no way.

ELIZABETH SZIROTNYAK_____
Production worker at Auto-Lite; crossed picket lines and worked during the strikes.

Women were paid less than the men. The men always had a higher base rate, they called it. See, I started at twenty-four cents. I made at the start nineteen dollars a week. But we didn't always work full weeks. See, I never made more than twenty dollars a week. Then, of course, that was supposed to be pretty good. That's nine hours a day and five and one half days.

They'd try to have all the safety devices and things that they could; but you know, when something's developed new, there's always some things that need improvement, see. And half the time, the only way they found something to improve it was after somebody had a finger off or a hand off or burned. Oh, we used an awful lot of naphtha. Then, when somebody got their hand off or burned or something, then they got these efficiency experts over there; and in no time, they had a device, a safety device, all rigged up. Well, maybe they didn't know how it would occur, and after they found out how it would happen, then they could remedy the problem. But it almost always would cost an arm, a finger, or a burn or something like that. And then, of course, you had to push them into any kind of benefit to you.

Miniger, every year, (he was president), every Christmas, all of us would get ten dollars. Now ten dollars was almost a week's wages, a ten-dollar Christmas gift. And he did that all on his own. Then when Miniger stepped down and Royce Martin came, well, he didn't give us the ten dollars anymore; but he was nice otherwise.

JOHN [J. J.] JANKOWSKI_____

Punch press operator in Department Two at Auto-Lite; union organizer.

Working in there was the biggest cause of unions to be born any place. The only place you could smoke was during noon hour on the steel stairway going down to the next floor. They wouldn't allow you to smoke anywhere in the toilet. The foreman walked in and smelled smoke, he'd check you right away, see if your stool meant anything. Sitting down there with nothing but your pants down, he'd run you out. If you do that once too often, he'd can you. So, we used to sit on that stairway.

A lot of these guys that started in there when they was fourteen, fifteen years old. Them days it wasn't required to be a graduate of high school; you didn't have to have no education at all. If you were big enough, they'd hire you. So, they hired these kids.

Wages was terrible. Press operators went down as low as twenty-seven cents an hour. That was our wages. And in a couple of weeks there in a row, I took maybe one day's pay home; some guy took in only four hour's pay home. They could send you home any time they didn't need you.

The biggest thorn was that big bench across the windows there, where the lockers were out in the open. Nothing was in closed rooms. Maybe you run out of pieces, you'd be done. He says, "All right, go over and sit down." You'd ring out the space that you wasn't working, and you'd sit there and wait an hour, an hour and a half, two hours—until they got another job. When they got another job, he'd say, "All right, come on." Point a finger at you, you'd come up to him, ring in and start working again. Now, you were there eight hours, you actually worked maybe only four or maybe five or three.

Part of it is you had to produce. They had a chart on the wall. Once a week the clerk would bring it out and hang it on the wall. Them days, they didn't have thumbtacks; they had one of them little hammers. They used to put a tack in it. He'd bring that chart out, spread it out, and all these men that worked around there would get a chance to go look at it. And across back of your name would be the chart for the whole week. If you didn't make the percentage they wanted for that day, they'd put you in red ink.

INTERVIEWER: *How would they determine that percentage?*

The production come through that you made that day. If you run that job all day and didn't make the quota they wanted you to, they'd have a record of that, see.

INTERVIEWER: *They had a standard that they set?*

Yeah, they set the standards, oh yeah. Price standard on each order card. It was hanging on the press. When the set-up man got the job, he'd get the card and he'd hang it up there. The set-up man would get an okay from the inspector. He'd hang the okay for inspection, that the job was okay to run. Then, the checker would come to check you in. He'd take the order card, put the standard on and the name of the part and the number of the part, and he'd mark it on your time card. Then at the end, when you finished the job, if you dogged around a little bit or something like that, you finished the job, he'd have a record, off the meter, how much you made in that hour. There was meters on every one of them machines. If you didn't produce—if you only produced eighteen hundred when you was supposed to produce two thousand— he'd mark that up: how he was on the job five hours, he was supposed to produce ten thousand pieces, he only produced five thousand. That's red ink. See what I mean?

Every week they'd come in, they'd hang the chart up, and those fellows used to go around and look at what you done. Now, if you were all black across there, you were all right, not too high up. Some a little higher. But if you were in red here and there, the foreman would come around, maybe about two, three hours after that chart's hanging. They'd usually hang it up on a Friday morning. He'd come around and say, "Hey, you were in red two days last week," he says. "What goes, what goes? You don't improve yourself," he says, "I'll have to let you go." That was it. And if you didn't improve, you went. They kicked you out. They wouldn't have nothing to do with you.

There was a lot of guys coming in and out all the time. You see what they done, the personnel that worked there, the boys that I worked with together, all good Catholic, religious men, some of them were, and they were churchgoers and everything; but they got so riled up about being treated like animals, that that's what caused them to join the union. You'd come in in the morning, he'd say, "Go sit down. Ring out, go sit down on the bench." You'd go that week, all week, to that shop, every morning. Well, you'd sit on the benches over there. "All right," he says, "I can use you, come on; ring in." You had to ring in, then go to work. Maybe it was 9:00, 10:00 in the morning. You've been there since 6:30. Then your pay would start at the time you ring in. Add up the hours throughout the week, let's say forty-eight hours. They worked Saturday most of the time. It was straight time. Forty-eight hours—maybe you'd only bring home a twelve-hour pay, or eight-hour pay throughout that week. Some of these "red apple" boys that he had, like friends of his, personal relations of his, they were getting full weeks. They were the ones that were so bitter against having the union. That's why it was so hard to crack.

Women didn't run punch presses in them days. That wasn't allowed. No, no punch press are female operators. They sorted a lot. For instance, some guy would run a machine and maybe the punch would break. He wouldn't know it; he'd run a bunch of them—maybe a couple thousand pieces—with a hole missing. Well, the girls would get them and have to sort it out, see.

The guys that was on the beginning as committeemen, they only wanted to get the recognition of the union and get the conditions for a human being to operate under. That's all we wanted. We didn't give a damn too much about wages, because you got seventy-five cents an hour; the guy across the street—another factory—got seventy-five. That wasn't it. It was the conditions that you were under. You had to be like Gestapo. Stand in line, be checked every morning. That was your conditions.

5

Organizing at Auto-Lite

Organizing production workers at Auto-Lite began in 1933, partly—perhaps predominantly—because of conditions our narrators have just described, and partly because of workers' movements in the auto factories in Toledo. At Willys-Overland, Bingham, Spicer, City Auto Stamping, Logan, and other small auto-related factories, workers, including some who once worked at Auto-Lite, decided to form a union. Semi-skilled and unskilled workers, with no claim to sponsorship by a particular craft, sought support from the AFL, which eventually responded by chartering an Automobile Workers Federal Labor Union Local 18384.

In Local 18384, workers found structure. In addition, the National Industrial Recovery Act appeared to bring the federal government's blessing to workers' efforts through Section 7(a), which affirmed the right of workers to organize unions of their own choosing for purposes of collective bargaining—a right disputed during the previous decade. In both instances, support proved more spiritual than material, but it was enough to encourage the active and aggressive to make the attempt. Chances for success rested squarely upon the skill, energy, and persuasiveness of the men and women who worked in these factories.

Many factors augured ill for successful organizing at Auto-Lite. The concept of a union, although formulated in the United States even before the American Revolution, lacked clarity, particularly in mass production industries. Our narrators express uncertainty and some confusion about the nature of a union and what it could achieve. How would a union fare in a confrontation with a management holding unchecked power over the workers' economic lives? The danger of dismissal, and with it the loss of dignity, stood bold and clear before the workers. Some would not take the risk, and others waited to see which way the wind would blow.

A few saw clearly the gains a union could bring. It could end exploitation, assure that workers would reap more of the wealth they produced, and establish workers' rights to grieve without fear of reprisal. It could mean the end to the bench and to the petty rules that assaulted the workers' dignity.

One's point of view on the union clearly reflected one's relationship to management. Managers and those who worked closely with them found organizers to be uncouth, ill-mannered, and disloyal. Disreputable and destructive, these agitators divided an otherwise harmonious enterprise. Virtually by definition, they were outsiders who had never been true members of the Auto-Lite family. Organizers' charges exaggerated conditions and stirred up a satisfied work force. At the opposite pole, workers who identified with each other and with the organizers saw in management a heartless, conscienceless force exploiting them of their earnings and dehumanizing them.

Complicating that struggle at Auto-Lite was the Auto-Lite Council, an "independent" or company union. It purported to represent Auto-Lite workers to the management. One cannot date its origins precisely, but it seems to have appeared in late 1933, attracting to its ranks workers who more clearly identified with management. Unaffiliated with any existing labor union, the council met with management apparently to discuss working conditions; but it brought forth no contract, if it even attempted to negotiate one. From the point of view of union supporters, the Auto-Lite Council was beneath contempt because it undermined worker solidarity and deflected workers' legitimate demands. It raised a false loyalty to the company in place of the true loyalty of worker to worker.

This clash of loyalties was easily resolved by some, but the uncertainty at the time is clear in the narration of Norval Hisey.

NORVAL HISEY

Electrician at Auto-Lite; crossed picket lines and worked during the strikes.

Auto-Lite had what they called a union of their own. Mr. Lyons was supposed to be the head of it, but it never proved out successfully. He was in charge of all sanitation in all of the buildings. I wouldn't say he was the president of the Auto-Lite Council. We didn't elect him; he was a spokesman I'd say, that's all, for the company union. But there was very few belonged to it because there was nothing to look up to. There wasn't enough majority to do anything. When the UAW tried to get in, they raised hell about it.

INTERVIEWER: *What did you think of the union at the time?*

It wasn't a decision to make at the time because you didn't know anything about it. We didn't know what the hell they wanted to offer or nothing.

The man that really caused all the trouble, he was a bull-headed pot licker; that was Art Minch. He's the one that wouldn't even listen, wouldn't even talk, wouldn't even consider. Well, that's something that then and nowadays you should do to a certain extent. He was the plant manager. They wanted a meeting; this Minch wouldn't allow even to talk or anything else. And that's what provoked them, and they started tearing things up.

Mr. Miniger, the guy who started Auto-Lite, was one hell of a swell fellow, but he had too many obstacles to overcome. He was the president, but you know, when you get a gang against you, you ain't got much to say. But he was one hell of a nice fellow.

ROBERT A. CAMPBELL
Auto-Lite machinist and MESA member; continued to work during the strikes.

At Auto-Lite we had a union in the plant that was trying to get started, and the company had a union of their own; so there was two factions that were sort of fighting for recognition. The AFL was headed by a man by the name of Ramsey. Like I say, I wasn't too concerned. I could see Mr. Ramsey out in the street, and he had a loudspeaker, and I couldn't hear all he was saying because it was too far away. But he would get up, and he'd have a congregation of people around. And he was instructing them what to do even the day of the strike. I mean, he was telling them what to do. So, it was very obvious who the leader was.

INTERVIEWER: *What do you remember about the Auto-Lite Council?*

I know some of the people who belonged to it. And they were nice people. Of course, everyone has their ideas of how they're treated. I don't know who was back of starting this AFL faction, but the Auto-Lite Council—I think they both started about the same time. When the company knew there was a union, then they probably got some of their friends to start this Auto-Lite Council. I wasn't in either one of those unions, so I couldn't tell you. I never went to any of their meetings or anything. The only meeting I ever went to was MESA.

INTERVIEWER: *What did MESA do during the strike in 1934?*

During the strike in 1934, we really did nothing. It was not an official strike as far as we knew, and we did not observe their picket lines. They had a gentlemen's agreement later on if one of them would be out, that the other one would observe their picket line.

STEVE ZOLTAN_____
Set-up man at Auto-Lite; stayed out with the strikers but did not picket; later became a plant superintendent.

C. O. Miniger was a feeling person. It wasn't Miniger that was so tough, it was the other part, and some of the names that I forget. They were all dollars. They were all profit. Oh, to heck with the guy in the shop. There has got to be that profit. Miniger was a different kind of man. He was no different than the employee. He used to walk through the plant, talk to people, imagine a man—a chairman—but the others were just high-hatted. That's the reason they started organizing. They wouldn't respect you as an employee at all, but Miniger did.

INTERVIEWER: *Do you recall anything about the beginning of the union—you know, like 1933 to 1934?*

We had at that time Mr. Rigby, Mr. Byrd; there was quite a few of them. They began to get the employees together and talk to them for maybe four or five months, hold meetings in different places. Finally, they all said they'd join the union. Then, of course, we began to organize. I think it was two dollars to join the union and fifty cents dues. Then, when enough money was collected, they rented a hall on Huron Street. Then, more and more people began to come in. When the leaders of this organization felt that they had enough people behind them, then they requested a meeting with the company. Of course, the company wouldn't recognize the union, and they told them so.

RUTH LYONS UNFERDROS_____
Daughter of the president of the Auto-Lite Council; observed the strikes.

I'm Mrs. Ruth Unferdros, and I'm the daughter of Nelson D. Lyons, who was president of the Auto-Lite Council. He was born and raised in Toledo and I was also. I believe at the time of the Auto-Lite strike, he was a guard at the plant and he was elected president of the council. I don't know how long my father was out of work until he got this job at the Auto-Lite. Well, I'd imagine that it would be around 1932 or 1933. And they had this election and the council won out, I believe, by quite a large majority. Now, as far as the council being concerned, up until the strike, I don't believe it was in effect much more than a year. It wasn't very long.

INTERVIEWER: *What kinds of things did the Auto-Lite Council do before the strike?*

It wasn't functioning that long to do anything. I mean they hadn't had any meetings with the company for negotiations or anything, because this all came up so fast that there was never anything like that done. Now, it was not a company union. Of course, mainly for one reason: because it hadn't been formed long enough. Possibly in time, it could have been something that would have been considered a company union, but it wasn't. I don't believe it was even a year before all this trouble came up. So, they had no opportunity to do any negotiating with the company over anything. So, you couldn't call it—it was just a separate union.

INTERVIEWER: *How did your father get interested in the council?*

My father was a union man. He belonged to the plumbers' union for years. In fact, while he was at the Auto-Lite, he gave up his plumbing trade during World War I and never went back to it, but he kept a withdrawal card. So, my father was, even until the time of his death, a strong union man in his way. But after the strike and everything was settled, then my father eventually went into supervision; so, he never belonged to the union.

INTERVIEWER: *Was the Auto-Lite Council connected with any other particular union group?*

No. It was a union by itself. And it wasn't called the Auto-Lite Union; it was called the Auto-Lite Council. And possibly someplace along the line, why somebody will say possibly that my father was like working for the company, which wasn't true, I mean as far as unions were concerned. I know after the strike, after he was guard for awhile, he became like a maintenance man. Well, even up until 1939, his wages weren't large enough even to make a thirty-dollar-a-month payment on our house. All they could do was pay the fifteen dollars a month interest. In 1939 then, he got a better job with the company. So, it was hard and, like I told you, my main reason for contacting you was to protect my father's name in case anything would come up because someplace along the line someone will tell you, no doubt, that he was a company man and he wasn't.

INTERVIEWER: *How old were you at the time?*

I was twenty-two, twenty-three years old. It seems to me not too long after the [union] election, the Auto-Lite Council was formed. About the only function that they had was an Auto-Lite Council picnic at Toledo Beach. And I can remember Mr. Miniger, the president of the company, coming to the picnic. And a Mr. J. Arthur Minch and his wife, a vice-president, also came for awhile.

ELIZABETH FRITSCHE
Stenotype operator and secretary to the manager of the service parts division at Auto-Lite; worked during the strikes.

And I remember one man in particular; his name was Tom Ramsey. He was one of the business agents for the union. He was the strict rabble-rouser. He'd just get these people so worked up and shout and scream and frenzy. And that Ramsey would stand up on a truck every day and just loudmouth about the officials of the company. "Open up the trap and let the rats out" and—just ornery.

I don't think that there was too much dissension among the Auto-Lite Council, but there was a lot of agitation on the part of this outside organization to break up company unions. It was really disgraceful to hear those people on the street corner when the plant let out, talking about the company, talking about the officials of the company. And I heard a lot of it, because my office happened to be on the second floor, right opposite the corner. And it was really disgusting. And they had people that, well, I can't help feel that they were just born agitators. They were not employees. All this agitation on the street was not by employees of the company. It was outsiders.

TED SUSKA

Auto-Lite production worker and early union supporter.

INTERVIEWER: *Did you help organize it?*

Yes, I was helping, but I was not one of the boys up front that was organizing it. But I was a part of it.

INTERVIEWER: *How would they go about organizing?*

Well, there was a few of us, you know what I mean, they would sign up for the union, see. A fellow by the name of Ramsey was the business agent at that time. We'd go into the factory and talk to some of the fellas we could trust a little bit; because if they found out that we were organizing, they'd fire us. So, we got in, started organizing and signing them up, and first thing you know we had so many pledges and cards.

INTERVIEWER: *What were they saying to get people to join?*

Well, they said: do you want to work for conditions that existed at that time? You know, the conditions were bad. It was all company. It was so bad that you were afraid to move or do anything. They just paid whatever they wanted to, and they shoved you around; and some of these fellas had the guts, you know, like Thompson, Rigby, Stucker, quite a few of those guys, they had guts enough to fight for these things. So, they'd tell everybody, "You want to be pushed around like you are? Is your job safe?"—which they weren't.

CLAUDE W. POUND

Production manager at Auto-Lite.

INTERVIEWER: *What would be the workers' complaints back around 1934?*

I don't know. I don't know what the complaint was. I think they just group organized and spread out. They claimed we was starving everybody to death and all that kind of stuff, but that's normal.

CHESTER DOMBROWSKI_____
Punch press operator in Department Two at Auto-Lite; union organizer.

It was during the summer months, I remember, we used to go outside
and sit in front of the building. We were just a bunch of young fellows,
we'd sit out there, you know, in the summertime. We were on the first
floor—we would walk outside the gates—we had badges—we'd walk
outside the gate and we'd sit there in the sun, sunning ourselves during lunch hour. Here comes some guy along the street, you know. We
don't know him from Adam. So, he's standing there across the street
and sit down on the ground, you know. It was a parking lot. He'd just
sit there, and he must have been an organizer. Ask me his name, to
save my soul I couldn't tell you, but I can picture him still today. He
called us over. He said, "How are you fellows doing?" and stuff like
that. So, he said, "Say," he said, "you know there is a law now that you
can organize," he says. "You can join a union and," he said, "you don't
have to be afraid." Well, one fella looked at the other, I looked at one,
and the other one looked at me, and we all looked at one another. We
were scared, naturally, because we never heard of any such a thing.
But I do remember. I think there was something in the paper. We were
scared because we knew that if we did anything in the shop that we'd
get fired one by one so fast that we wouldn't know it. But the first thing
you know, it gets from one thing to another.

He said, "Say, you know you fellows ought to join a union and you
could get organized." He said, "You don't have to worry about getting
fired. If you get fired," he said, "you can be backed up by the union."
Here, we didn't even have a union. So, we were a bit leery, you know.

The next day, he come back again and he talked to us. Then he kept
on, you know these organizers, little by little, because they're kicked,
too, sometimes, you know. So, he kept talking to us; and you know the
way things were going in that department and throughout the shop,
we thought, heck, we were getting only forty-eight cents an hour and
you had to make out so much before you'd get to fifty-four. He mentioned seniority rights, he mentioned guys working there and guys
probably laid off, you know. He asked questions like that, see. He said,
"How would you fellows like to have seniority rights and all that? How
would you like to get a little raise?" I'll never forget that guy at the
Auto-Lite because I know, I was one of the first fifteen in there, so help
me God. That's the honest to God truth.

So, we kept going and seeing this guy. I mean every noon, lunch
hour, we'd go out there. There he was. Then first thing you know, he

says, "There will be a meeting over to the Moose Hall." I forget what we paid. We used the hall only for an hour or so. It wasn't too long. We didn't have no money. It was just a little room, just a few chairs, that's all. I'll never forget that. We just sat there, we didn't know what to expect. We just sat there listening to the guy talking, he kept telling us things about organizing and getting this and getting that. That's how these things started.

From the beginning, we didn't have anything—we didn't have a dime. We were on our own. I remember Eddie Szymanski, he's dead now, but he brought up a union. He says, "You know, fellas—look, we run one thousand pieces, we get so much for it." He says, "We run two thousand," he says, "we get thirty-eight cents for that one, instead of getting a dollar for them. Who gets the other? The boss and the big shots get it all." That don't sound so good. After the union, we got everything that's coming to us. There was no foreman that got three thousand bucks a year for his bonus, and all the executives in the office got theirs in their pocket. We got what was coming to us. If we run two thousand pieces an hour, we got paid for running two thousand pieces.

JACK C. LATHROP_____

Foreman in Department Two at Auto-Lite; crossed picket lines and worked during the strikes.

INTERVIEWER: *You said that they began organizing for the union in the department where you were foreman?*

They was playing around there for four or five months working on it, yeah.

INTERVIEWER: *How did you feel about that at the time?*

As far as I was concerned, I was absolutely for it. Of course, it caused a lot of dissent; but the minute that they seen what it meant, well, it meant the difference of—let's say thirty-five, forty-five, to fifty cents an hour.

Another thing that came up. They started out with what they called B's. You could make so many B's—we'll say one hundred twenty B's an hour. Well, some of them started to get hungry, and they kept pushing and pushing when they got to piecework. They wanted to make the most they could make, and along with that there was proof then that we better re-time this job. It must have been timed wrong, or you couldn't be making that kind of money; and that caused dissension and cutting and what have you.

INTERVIEWER: *What was the atmosphere like in the department when they were organizing?*

What was the atmosphere? That's a hard question in a way. You had several that was on the fence. They couldn't decide whether or not that was what they wanted. That pertained to a lot of the older ones who, well, they didn't know whether this was going to do us any good or not. Then, it pertained to the other one who would be the younger one who had only maybe been there a year or so and figured to himself, "Well, this ain't going to do me no good. Look where I'm going to wind up. I'll be way down on the bottom. They'll set it up on seniority; I'll wind up taking whatever I can get." But there was never no real hard dissension. In fact, I'd say they went about 80 percent. There was only possibly maybe 20 percent that stuck around and attempted to cross the picket line and started to go in and go to work.

I'll say this, salaried help in some departments who were not too well liked by their own men got a little rough time. But I seemed to get along with all the boys. In fact, Claude Pound said to me one day, he said, "What the hell, somebody told me you were over at the corner drinking with the gang." I said, sure, why not? They work for me. "Well, that's true," he said, "but don't you think that's a funny picture?" We both laughed about it. Which was true. What the hell, they all worked for me. I live there. I built a brand new home right out here in a Polish neighborhood.

HILDAGARDE & WILLIAM LOCKWOOD_____
Office workers at Auto-Lite; crossed picket lines and worked during the strikes.

HILDAGARDE: I was in the factory time office. We took care of the factory payroll. He was a checker in the plant, in the factory, and I was in the time office.

WILLIAM: What they termed as a piecework checker. You recorded the part number of the job, the operation number, the rate of pay on that given job, the amount of pieces that they produced, and this was recorded on a long duplicate time card. Each individual job that the employee performed during the course of the day was recorded in the succeeding space and also any idle time that they had due to break down of the equipment or lack of assignment. And any other job classification that they were required to do had to be recorded separately. That was then handled by the office clerk, extended, and then sent to the time office for figuring.

HILDAGARDE: That's where I come in. At that time, our office was in the factory.

INTERVIEWER: *Where you were working nobody went out?*

WILLIAM: They did, down in Department One, where I was working. That's where I was checking, but we were not considered eligible for the union. Because we were considered office employees, because we handled the payroll.

HILDAGARDE: We weren't even thought of at that time. As far as the union—the factory people—was concerned, the checkers were not considered a part of the factory. They were more or less considered in the office. The company held that the timekeepers and clerks, handling as he did the count of the pieces that the employees would turn in and so on, they were considered—as Mr. Martin, who was president of the Auto-Lite at that time, said—the cash registers for the company.

WILLIAM: We handled the purse strings, in other words.

INTERVIEWER: *There was another group other than the union?*

WILLIAM: The Auto-Lite Council. The company formed that union. The company was responsible. It was their people. That was done in 1934, part of it possibly in 1933—the nucleus of it.

HILDAGARDE: It was probably done to offset the union.

WILLIAM: That's right.

HILDAGARDE: It was a company union.

WILLIAM: Now originally, when the automobile workers started out under the AFL, if William Green had had his way, there would have been a separate union for the pressmen, one for the electricians, one for the millwrights, one for the sweepers, one for the truckers—there would have been fifty different unions within that one plant. Craft unions, is what they were classified under. That was the purpose of the formation of the CIO: to break down those lines and put them into one union. That was one of the fallacies of the AFL.

I felt organizing was justified because I had seen over the course of my employment where discrimination had existed. In fact, during that period the company ruled that only one person out of a family—I mean a man and a wife out of one family—could work there. There could be brothers, or an uncle and a brother, or an uncle and a son for that matter, if they were separate households. But that was the attitude of the company at that time.

HILDAGARDE: If you had been working there and they wanted to bring in one of their people, you were laid off. That was the unfairness. In the beginning, when that first started out, I was company—strictly company. It took me a while to see, but he always saw the union from the very beginning.

WILLIAM: Another thing that existed. You were a commodity as far as the company was concerned. You would go in to go to work and the boss would tell you, "Well, you wait up in the restroom. If I need you, I'll come and get you when I need you." You might wait 'til 10:00 in the morning, and he'd say, "Well, I don't need you today." So, you go home and you didn't get paid, even though you were on the premises.

FRED C. [WHITEY] HUEBNER
Management in Auto-Lite's time study department.

INTERVIEWER: *Do you recall the organizing in the plant?*

Yes. It was a slow thing. It went on for weeks before the so-called blow off. You got acquainted with the people; some were belligerent, some of them were very decent and mannerly, but the thing operated in pretty good fashion until the one famous day in 1934 when the lid blew off.

The major point of the whole strike was focused on one issue and that's the representation of the UAW. It was not common at the time. This was the thing that the company saw fit to battle. We didn't want to be the first one to knuckle in to a union and then admit partial domination of our business; and that was the dominant thing.

INTERVIEWER: *So, that's where the conflict originated?*

Yes. The representation theory emanated from about five years before at the start of the depression—five years, 1929, yeah—five years before. People were hard up. They didn't have any money. Business was very poor, and these people were working for thirty-five cents an hour. And this created a little animosity and a little bit of ruckus between the management and the people. They felt that they should get more money, and some of the practices that had been prevalent were odious to them; and one of which was perhaps—take this properly now—we had one department which was the punch press department. Why it is, I don't know, but you will find that three-quarters of the operators in punch press departments are Polish people. This was so in our place, and we had some excellent workers in that department.

We had a practice of letting the people come in to work and not paying them unless we furnished them a job. They had a bench, and there they sat waiting for a job; because there were so few jobs and so many people that they took turns, and if a fella's turn came, he went over and did the job for whatever length of time it was and was paid for that length of time. Well, this was obviously something that later on would be laughed at by both industry and unions, because later you had the feature of paying a person from the time he entered your plant until he left your plant. Might not pay him as much, but you paid him, at least.

INTERVIEWER: *Wasn't there a company union?*

Yes.

INTERVIEWER: *When did that originate?*

That originated before the strike; and it was a factor in the settlement of the strike, because we had to make provisions for this union—so-called company union—to be protected when the thing was over with. They represented people, so if we recognized UAW, we recognized the independent union in the same fashion. And we had to keep a level there that was proper. We wouldn't dare throw the company union people over our shoulder just to settle the thing, so we did not. Yes, there was a company union. It finally wore out. I mean it just sort of faded away.

INTERVIEWER: *Did it offer as much as the other union?*

The company saw to it that what the UAW got in the way of grants or gifts went for the company union as well.

INTERVIEWER: *Would it be safe to say that the company union originated because of the organization of the UAW union?*

Yes, yes, it would be a safe statement to make, because you have to go back and try to orient yourself to the situation of that time. The unions were rather a strange thing, and we had had experience with the Overland strikes that had happened prior to ours, which were not in the same category but started people thinking. At that time, probably just as many people resented the union as there were people who stood up for the union. I think that it would be safe to say that there were perhaps more people at that time who resented unions. All it did was give the worker another boss. Where he had only the company and his family to look out for before, now he had the company, the union, and the family to look out for; and he had to divide his loyalties, and he had to pay for that privilege.

EARL MOORE

Auto-Lite worker and union supporter; went out on strike.

INTERVIEWER: *When was there first talk about the union?*

I would judge around the year of 1933, middle part, during the summer, somewheres around there. It was quite a mixed affair to keep things straight, you know what I mean, so you could tell which way the wind was blowing. Because of the company's attitude towards a person who was working, you had to watch your foot, because you might have overstepped. And if you did, you was out, because you had no protection whatsoever.

6

Organizing the First Strike

Organizing workers confronts its own share of ironies. When the organizer points out the uncertainty of the job, the precariousness of the worker's hold on his place, he argues that the worker has inadequate or even no control over his economic life. He does so in order to persuade the worker that a union is necessary to restore mastery over the future. The irony occurs because the organizer also thus evokes the worker's insecurity, itself a serious barrier to supporting or joining a union.

The strongest weapon against that insecurity was personal loyalty. When a series of personal loyalties link, they create solidarity, the underpinning of successful unions. At Auto-Lite, personal loyalties among punch press operators created the nucleus of organizers essential to build a successful union. And they were few, perhaps even fewer than they themselves understood at the time. Though few, their trust of each other reinforced their determination to stick together.

The test of that loyalty came on February 24, 1934, when these few workers struck Auto-Lite. Coordinated by Automobile Workers Federal Labor Union Local 18384 with strikes at four other auto parts firms in Toledo (Spicer, Logan, Bingham, and City Auto Stamping), the strike at Auto-Lite found fifteen workers walking the picket lines, supported by another fifty or so workers who simply stayed home. Some supporters remained at work.

The strike lasted only five days, resulting in a temporary thirty-day "settlement." Workers at the other four plants refused to return to work unless the Auto-Lite strikers were reinstated. The Auto-Lite settlement—more accurately the truce—reinstated the strikers and nominally recognized Local 18384. In fact, Auto-Lite merely recognized the existence of Local 18384 but refused to bargain with the union, thus, virtually assuring a second strike. Both sides began to prepare. Auto-Lite increased hiring in an attempt to dilute the strength of Local 18384 and to assure continuous production even if another strike occurred. The leaders of the strike redoubled their efforts to sign up workers for the union.

In one sense, the February strike resolved nothing. In another, it resolved a great deal, for the reinstatement of the strikers emboldened others and added credibility to the organizers' appeals. Clearly, united action, even by a few, could successfully challenge Auto-Lite management. The risks seemed to diminish, and the future opened on hope. The solidarity of workers in Department Two, the punch press room, proved inspirational.

In this chapter, our narrators recount developments leading to that strike and results stemming from it.

CARL LECK

Stockroom worker at Auto-Lite and union supporter.

INTERVIEWER: *In 1933, there began to be some interest in organizing. Was there much before that?*

Nope. It was all on the q.t. then. Before that, you didn't hear much about it, until President Roosevelt come out and give us the right to organize. When Spicer went out on strike, we went along with them. That was one month before the 1934 strike, in February. But like I said, there was five of us in final assembly that went out. And throughout the plant there couldn't have been over fifty, plus Department Two.

INTERVIEWER: *And Department Two?*

Practically 100 percent. They went out solid. Rigby was the one that was the big organizer. I think we met at Memorial Hall. When Spicer settled, they gave us a thirty-day contract. We knew what was ahead of us. They figured after thirty days we got them beat. We didn't get nothing. Just that they would recognize us for thirty days.

INTERVIEWER: *Were you out on the picket line in February?*

I certainly was; and when I went back, my time card was still in the clock. I rang it in. The other four, no time cards—this is true, no time cards. They had to go back down and hire in all over again. So, an hour later, Red Vollmer, my buddy, comes back and says, "Carl, you've got to go back and hire in, too." So, I had to go back.

INTERVIEWER: *How come your card was still there?*

'Cause Red was covering for me, that's why. He was the foreman. He was the one that hired my brother back in. Of course, in that thirty days, they hired everybody and his brother they figured would stay in. Yes, sir. They hired—I don't know how many hundreds they hired in that thirty days.

INTERVIEWER: *More than they needed?*

Oh, you better believe it. They knew what was coming.

INTERVIEWER: *Well, what did they do with these people?*

Put them to work.

INTERVIEWER: *So, they increased the production during that whole period?*

They didn't increase the production, but they kept them working there 'cause they knew they had a strike coming up in thirty days.

INTERVIEWER: *Where did they get these people?*

Primarily through their straw bosses. All their friends and everybody else. Come in, we need them right now, bring them in.

INTERVIEWER: *How did these new people react to the idea of the union?*

Well, they had thirty days. You couldn't get any reaction out of them. Course, in that thirty days, we're busy organizing. We knew. Now I'll tell you this, when I went out on strike the first time, when this Department Two went out, and the five of us went out of final assembly, all these gals on the circuit breaker line were all lined up to ring their clocks and go out with us. Freddy Bernard and Freddy Techmeyer, they sat there and had a little chat with them, and they all went back to work. They were straw bosses. So, they talked the gals out of it for that first strike. The second strike, they didn't talk them out of it.

It was touch and go. I think the Auto-Lite figured they had us beat all the way, see. "We'll give them a thirty-day contract, and when they come back, we'll beat their brains out; they haven't got a chance." We talked it up for a month there; and when we went out, we brought about 50 percent out with us.

JOHN [J. J.] JANKOWSKI

Punch press operator in Department Two at Auto-Lite; union organizer.

In the meantime, Spicer's was organizing; they were shaking the boat in regard to unions. Maybe around 1932, 1933, there, when the depression was started. So, us guys in February of 1934, the nine of us, saw that Spicer's was out. That's in 1934. We were members, when we were trying to organize in the plant. That's why we were watched so close. We were watched by spies because they knew that the union was starting to raise there. We used to pass out membership cards underneath the toilet bowls. You know, here's your card and give you the dollar. That's all it cost then. That was AFL, see. Thirteen of us got together: Alex Donachevsky (I can't spell their names; don't ask me to spell their names), Alex, Charlie Rigby, Al Schreader, Bill Collins, Walter Moore, Lester Byrd, and, uh—there's quite a few guys, and I don't remember them all. Some of them are almost dead. Donald, he was another guy in another department. But all of us, we called ourselves "the unholy thirteen" at that time, just between ourselves, see. Well, we went out on that strike in February. Spicer's was out, too. That's what caused us to jump out at that time and walk out on Department Two only. "Let's walk out," 'cause Spicer's was out. That give us like the yen to go out 'cause they were out. "What the hell, let's go out." So, us thirteen or fourteen of us, I guess about fifteen—a couple of sympathizers—walked out.

We walked out in front of the plant like kids was going out of house, you know what I mean. We stood there, started picketing the place, made our own picket signs out of cardboard. Walked the picket line for a week in February, one week. We were out there, to tell you the truth, stealing bread. These bakeries years ago, they used to put the bread inside the doorways; and the grocery man would open in the morning—he would have his fresh bread. So, we used to go in, open the box, and have a couple loaves of fresh bread, slam the door, and we'd go around the stores and beg for food, anything they could give us to keep us going.

That's in February, the first one. Logan and Bingham, they fell in after the Auto-Lite strike. They become members after that. But Spicer's was the only one that was out on the street at that time. So, we went out, and they sympathized with us. They come over back and forth and helped us on the picket line. They helped us get some pup tents, you know, canvas. We had a little fire going out there. They was stealing the coal from the railroad, and it was given to us by the brakemen on the railroad. And one thing about it, too, the railroad men wouldn't go into the company, in the yard. The railroad unions, no, the engineer, no, or the brakemen. They wanted a car pulled out of the Auto-Lite property, they wouldn't do it. So, Auto-Lite started hauling by trucks. They'd haul them out someplace down around Union Station, I guess, and then they'd transfer them into the trains. The trainmen wouldn't come in there, the freights, they wouldn't. They were sympathizers. They were union way before I was born.

Others sympathized with us. Everybody around the town knew what a tough spot it was to work in. Of course, there was some still worse than this one. There was about twenty-five, twenty-eight of us, about twenty-eight men working in Department Two at that time. A little over half, about thirteen that I remember, were really loyal. They walked out. There was a few sympathizers walked out, but they went right straight home and never came to the picket line. That's in February 1934.

You see, a few of them women, when we walked out in February, they was sympathizers, but they stayed right in the plant and worked. They were sympathizers after work. Some of them used to come over to my house and bring some food over, so as to see that we weren't short. And they were 100 percent, but they were scared to say anything. Everybody was scared.

These watchmen just told us to get away, and they tried to get the police. The police come over and says, "We have nothing to do with that. They're not harming anybody." They was good; they wouldn't do nothing about it, you know.

Spicer, they agreed to go back to work. They had the contract settled; they would go back under one condition—if Auto-Lite boys go back. "If Auto-Lite boys don't get back," he says, "we're not going back." So, what happened? C. O. Miniger, that's the big shot of Auto-Lite, met Dana of Spicer's, probably at the Toledo Club is where they used to get together, you know, to chat. Well, maybe their house, I don't know where they met. But they must have. "Look, C. O. Miniger, you put them men back in there because I can't start my plants because these guys won't go in." So then, the pressure come from us miserly few handful of men. Pressure come. Auto-Lite thought, "We'll get 'em in and working." In other words, we got our foot in the doorway as the union. Just our toes in in the Auto-Lite.

A lot of people in the Auto-Lite at the time were laughing at us thirteen. Said we'd never make it. They were laughing at us.

INTERVIEWER: *What did they expect?*

We were going to get back and we were going to get canned, see. But we was Local 18384, AFL. They were a little bit scairt. They were a little bit scairt to fire us; but they watched us, that we wouldn't expand any further. And they tried to nibble on us a little at a time to see if they could catch us doing something wrong, breaking a die or something like that, so they got a reason to fire us. But in the meantime, when we come back in, there was a lot of people in there that was against the conditions so rotten that they had there, that they themselves started saying, "Well, I want to join, too. I'll join, I'll join."

We just took the fear out of some of them. Not all of them, but some of them. Which is quite a bit. Then in 1934, that's in April of 1934, Spicer's was already working with their new contract. We come back in there just to be recognized as a union. And in April, we had quite a bit of men already.

INTERVIEWER: *Were you doing any negotiating between?*

The company only says that we recognize the union, period, and that's all there is to it. They recognize the union. That's the only thing they recognized.

Charlie Rigby was the chairman at that time, and he had to negotiate after working hours. He couldn't go there during working hours and talk to the big wheels. No, no. He had to come in there after he's done his day's work. Went in the office, and he'd wait until they'd make up their minds to talk to him or not. That's how they'd negotiate. The first contract we made with Kapurski and Rigby, Walter Moore and Bill Collins. We're the first ones that was in that office. That was after working hours. That was in February, in Claude Pound's office. He was a plant manager, and Art Minch wasn't there. He was over in his main office. He paid no attention to the union at that time. That's in February, I'm talking about.

ELIZABETH NYITRAI_____
Production worker at Auto-Lite; crossed picket lines and worked during the strikes.

We got slack, so I got transferred to the condensing room where they made condensers.

[Reads from Diary] "Everything going strong at Auto-Lite. It looks like depression's over. I feel like an old woman. I get so tired."

This is February 15, 1934. It's on a Thursday. "I slaved as usual."

This is the next day. "Too tired to go out, and besides, where could I go?"

Oh, broke up again. Then I had a new baby sister again. "Had to cook supper. My mother is confined. When I got home so darn disgusted with my job, I wish I didn't have to work." Yeah, it wasn't fun.

Now, February 27, 1934: "Five percent of the Auto-Lite is out on strike for more wages. I'm sticking to my work with the rest. They took a vote and some went out, and I didn't want to go out. My buddies didn't go out. I couldn't afford to go out because my parents needed the money and so I stayed in—I'm a scab. I caught a cold in the meantime. I'm just about dead. The strike is still going strong. I feel so cheap going in past the pickets. Went to auto workers' union. It was interesting. Girls persuaded me to join, and I did. What next?"

I joined the Auto-Lite Council.

WILLIAM LOCKWOOD_____
Office worker at Auto-Lite; crossed picket lines and worked during the strikes.

Actually, I know some people who were involved in the formation of the UAW in Toledo. Now, they had to meet secretly, and they met in Ottawa Park. If you were known to be a union member, you were fired. There were no unions. There was no recognition. They met at night, as a rule. This was in, I'd say, 1933. There was no discussion of unions around the Electric Auto-Lite. The majority of people knew nothing of it until very early 1934. Most of them found it out when the first strike occurred, and that was in February of 1934 and there were twelve people that walked out of the plant. In Department Two, in the pressroom. It certainly was a surprise. In fact, people at that time knew little or nothing of unions, especially the younger people because they had never been subject to it. If you were from the mine areas or the steel industry, something of that nature, in the teamsters or longshoremen, around that activity, then you had some idea what a union was. But most of these people had no idea what a union was other than a name.

See, during that strike, too, February, March, and April, there were approximately one thousand people employed that were brought in during the strike. They were taking the place of the people that were on the outside. Another thing about the thousand people, they couldn't come in and take an employee's place and expect to get the production out of that new employee that they got out of the old employee. In a good many instances, they had to double up—two for one, or one and a half for one, because that new employee couldn't produce the way the old employee did.

CHESTER DOMBROWSKI_____________
Punch press operator in Department Two at Auto-Lite; union organizer.

I'll be honest with you. At the time, we didn't know what was going to happen. Our department was the only one that walked out. We were the only ones that started organizing. There was fifteen of us. I think there was Johnny J., Charlie Rigby, Charlie Brown, Tony Kapurski, Joe Cheney, there was fifteen of us. The first meeting we held was up to the Moose Hall on Cherry Street, undercover. Undercover, understand, this was undercover. Nobody said anything; we knew we could trust one another. We didn't know how many others we could have trusted in the department then; but little by little, whoever we could talk to, we mentioned it. But at the same time, we wondered what was gonna happen if the foreman would get ahold of it. If he's get ahold of it, we don't know what would have happened. It was 1934.

A guy by the name of Ramsey was our first business agent. We elected a committee—Charlie Rigby was on a committee, I think Tony Kapurski was on a committee. The fifteen of us went back in the shop after this first meeting, then we had to get some more members. I mean, we had to start to talk to people in the shop, in the factory. We tried to convince them. Well, the Spicer Corporation organized, too, and we went out on a strike with Spicer. Old Man Dana himself—boy, he had a lot of nerve—he was a good old guy, though, I can say that much for him. He come up, I think the civic auditorium or someplace. He talked to the people himself, in person. Now, you've got to give that man a lot of credit. He was a good old guy.

Our department, that's Department Two, the pressroom, was the only one that walked out and when we walked out, we set a deadline. The management was told that we were walking out on a strike. All we were asking for at the time, I remember, was recognition. We wanted recognition first. That's what we were told, to ask for recognition first. After we were recognized, then we would go back and ask for more. We formed a committee. Then, after the first strike—we went out for four or five days—we got recognition. Just the Auto-Lite alone then.

To begin with, on the first strike they hired whoever. I don't know if they were out of town, but some of them were from Toledo, right off the streets. Then a lot of people, I guess, heard of this strike; and so they probably come from wherever, and some of them were hired. People came from Bowling Green or from Prairiesburg or around in this area or wherever.

We were trying to make them understand that we were doing this for ourselves and for them, because someday it will do them good, too, besides us. They wouldn't listen. But I suppose, you know, the depression, the belly is empty. When a person is hungry, he's liable to do almost anything. I thought about that lots of times. I said, well, we've got to fight this thing out now that we've started it.

Finally, the committee met with Art Minch; and Tony, he come out and he says, "Old man Minch," he says, "he called us a bunch of Communists." I said, he did? How is that? He said, "Well, for getting organized." Minch was a high official there. He was pretty mad at the time. That happened after we got a foothold there.

When we first started, we didn't have nothing. We didn't have no building, we didn't have any money, we didn't have nothing. When we stood there—it was in the wintertime—we had a drum, we had some guy bring in wood. I don't know where he got it, out of the dump somewhere, in order to keep warm and stay on the picket line. We didn't have nothing to look forward to. We got box lunches or you carried your own sandwich or somebody made a pot of coffee, whoever from, I mean from the public, even the public. I mean, they'd come out there and say, "You fellows want some coffee?" They'd make coffee for us. I mean, that's all we had to look forward to.

After we got recognition, I think the committee went in and told the company they wanted this and they wanted that, little things like safety, that had to be right. If the machine wasn't right, and it was dangerous to work on, they asked to have the man come out and fix that up. Just little things from the beginning. Just something to start with, see.

ELIZABETH SZIROTNYAK_____

Production worker at Auto-Lite; crossed picket lines and worked during the strikes.

There was a *lot* of them, men as well as women, that were out of jobs and did have to pull that little wagon for their food. And so, naturally, when a chance came along like that, "Oh, boy, they're hiring. Let's go!" And they didn't have no trouble getting people. But when the first strike came, why then I stayed on. I thought, well, I'm going to work.

7

Crossing the Picket Line

C rossing a picket line is, at best, a risky business. The picket line represents the union's ultimate weapon. Stopping production forces the company to negotiate and settle differences, for without production there can be no profits. Auto-Lite attempted to remain in production when the second strike occurred on Friday, April 13, 1934, and encouraged workers, both newly hired for the strike and old workers, to cross the picket lines to work.

Many workers did cross picket lines and remained at work. Members of the Auto-Lite Council, who identified with management, remained at work, of course, as did managerial personnel in general. From management's point of view, the strike was unconscionable and violated their right to run the company as they saw fit. And union organization did imply an end to that right. It asserted explicitly that the worker had the right to a voice in determining working conditions, and, thus, to end management's autocracy.

Some workers crossed the picket line because their jobs fell outside the jurisdiction of the union. Local 18384 sought to organize the production workers, so some workers were not eligible for membership: skilled workers in the model shop, for example. Others, who held clerical positions or who kept records—those who were not engaged in actual production—had no union of their own but were not eligible for membership in Local 18384. Production workers also crossed the picket lines and in significant numbers. Many had been hired since the February strike and had not identified with the union movement. Often, they had been unemployed and felt lucky to be working. Some who had been employed at Auto-Lite longer felt the hand of hard necessity and could not bring themselves to join the strikers, even though they might sympathize with their efforts. Reasons for crossing the picket lines ranged from ideology to whimsy, from uncertainty and confusion to defiance. Some saw in it an adventure, a dare, a demonstration of courage.

No matter what the reason for crossing the picket line, union supporters viewed it as a hostile act. All who entered the plant were called scabs, but feelings ran highest against the newly hired who took strikers' jobs. During the early days, the strikers expressed those feelings largely verbally, if sometimes roughly, and they were effective. Some scabs were outraged, some intimidated, and some felt guilty because people they knew and, as importantly, people who knew them marched on the picket lines. They could not ignore the pickets nor could they evade the social censure that followed this violation of community norms. To this day, members of the working class community remember who crossed the picket lines to work. Perhaps as a defense mechanism, responding to the censure they experienced—the social snubs, the insults—our respondents often recall outsiders rather than acquaintances on the picket lines.

Those on the picket lines spoke when workers entered and left the plant, imploring them to join the picket lines. As the strike lengthened into May, speeches gave way to catcalls and insults, yielding finally to pushing and shoving. Auto-Lite then began to transport some workers to the factory, picking them up at their homes in cars or trucks in the morning and returning them home at night. Frustrated in their attempts to confront the strikebreakers directly, union supporters began to rock the cars as they left the plant, overturning some. As the strike wore on and Auto-Lite remained in production, a successful outcome for the union seemed to fade, and the strikers became more aggressive. Those who crossed the picket lines became increasingly anxious and reluctant to do so.

ELIZABETH SZIROTNYAK_____

Production worker at Auto-Lite; crossed picket lines and worked during the strikes.

During the second, the big strike, a few of us did go in, we stayed. My husband—he wasn't my husband at that time—he didn't approve of it.

He was furious. My sister worked with me, but she wouldn't come in. She stayed home. But, of course, at the time and being young, I didn't think that much of it, but I certainly wouldn't do it again. I mean, I didn't realize what I was getting into until they started throwing those bombs and shooting at me. And they'd tip the cars over and burn them, right on Champlain Street. It was terrific.

INTERVIEWER: *Were you the only one in your family who broke the line?*

Yes. My sister was hired in before the strike, but my sister didn't go, although we both lived together at home. And then, I don't think I'd have gone either had my friend not insisted. I got hell all the way, you know, from my folks, and from my husband-to-be.

I had a lot of reasons for doing it, you know. I had logical reasons: I was out of work all that while. And then I was the type that was never idle. I didn't mind. I worked hard all my life, since I was about ten years old. And I just didn't like not being able to earn my own way. And it wasn't a bed of roses at home, either, with seven of us, and so when I got a chance to go back, I went.

It was like we went in and we dared. That's what I mean. Cocky. I dared to go through the line. Even after we were in there, it didn't bother me that I was in there. Every day it was tougher and tougher to get in, 'cause more would stay out, and walking through the line you took a lot of abuse. They hollered things and, especially, there were an awful lot of women and men right from Birmingham. They walked the Ashton-Sall Bridge. And all those kids that grew up with me, if they didn't work at Libby Glass across the bridge, then they worked at Auto-Lite, because it was walking distance.

Even then, you'd walk around, be seen somewhere, you go to a gathering of some sort, why there were slurs and things at you.

INTERVIEWER: *Do you remember what it was like to be inside the plant?*

Yes, I do. As time went by, you know, you sort of lost your cockiness. It would be sort of like in a conflict, a war or something. We were the good guys (laughter).

HILDAGARDE & WILLIAM LOCKWOOD

Office workers at Auto-Lite; crossed picket lines and worked during the strikes.

HILDAGARDE: The company union stayed in.

They were consistently hiring people to take the jobs of those who were out on strike; and that's why it was such a bitter fight, because people were going in there and taking the others' jobs.

It was the people that went in and took the jobs, hired off the street, that they were bitter against. They didn't bother the people that already worked there and had stayed in.

WILLIAM: Then in April when the second strike was called, I think it was April 13, the whole Department Two went out, and then it progressively got larger. The next department involved was probably down in Department One. That was in the frame department and automatics and Bullard, Brown and Sharp Machines; Warner and Swazey; modern Johnson equipment that made the frame for the generators or motors.

I recall several instances where people got beat up, and I know of one instance where a girl got off the bus; and she was walking down from Elm Street towards the plant, and they tied her dress above her head. But I knew of a lot of instances where different ones got beat up. It was more or less isolated. Of course, the longer this thing went— from April until well into May—well, the more heated it became. And these people that were on the outside were observing people coming out of the plant that had gone in and taken their jobs, so naturally there was a lot of bitterness in that respect. As I say, they didn't bother the people that had worked there previous to the strike. They said little or nothing to them. In fact, the people that I knew, I had no difficulty with. In fact, I talked to all of them. It was the new people.

They called them scabs at that time. That's actually what they did. They went in and took somebody else's job that was out on strike.

HILDAGARDE: Well, I think it was just building up, and they had taken just so much and this was it. That's the way it appeared to be. You know, there was a breaking point; and I suppose they were probably just getting desperate that it was going on so long, and they had to use some drastic means. That's the way I figured.

WILLIAM: Well, there were also some people that were imported at that time to man these picket lines, and just who they were I just can't say for sure.

HILDAGARDE: At that time, you must remember that Communists were very active. Particularly trying to get ahold of labor unions. It has been admitted on both sides that they were really the destructive elements in it.

WILLIAM: It's possible that there were some imports. I don't have much doubt in my own mind that there were some. I know that there were some miners that were brought in, that is, coal miners which were union members. Everybody who was on a picket line wasn't a Communist.

HILDAGARDE: Oh, no, no. But I mean they were a destructive element in there, and they were Communists.

WILLIAM: You had building trades and everybody else out on that picket line. Helping these automobile workers. In fact, in 1937, there were about one hundred fifty to two hundred of us that were sent to Flint, Michigan, on the General Motors strike. I was up there for what, about three or four days, I think.

INTERVIEWER: *You said you were sympathetic with the strikers from the beginning. Did others in your department feel the same way?*

WILLIAM: Oh, yes.

HILDAGARDE: Many of them.

WILLIAM: There were people in the plant, too, that had been working there that were sympathetic with them, too. But a good many of those people had just gone back to work a short time before, and they'd been out of work since 1929 or 1930; and they were tickled to death to get a job. The other thing, too, as I say, their knowledge of union was almost nil. It wasn't distrust. They didn't have any knowledge of what they were, other than the fact that they were bound together. They had never seen any actual examples of what the strength would mean to them, I don't suppose. I suppose, too, there was a certain amount of distrust among them. But I do know that a lot of people that were in there were sympathetic to the union. The men responded first. Some of the female departments were some of the last that were organized, that is, where they had almost 100 percent female help, and they were some of the last that were organized as departments.

INTERVIEWER: *But there were both men and women striking and on the picket lines?*

WILLIAM: Not on the first strike but on the second strike. There might have been two or three on the first one, but that's about all.

HILDAGARDE: That walkout. You call it strike. You mean walkout. On the second strike in April, there were a lot of women involved. But the majority, I believe, were men.

ELIZABETH FRITSCHE_____
Stenotype operator and secretary to the manager of the service parts division at Auto-Lite; worked during the strikes.

Well, what I remember first—I think it started in February. They had their grievances and started picketing in February; and I know it was cold, because they had salamanders outside with coal in them to try to keep warm.

INTERVIEWER: *What are salamanders?*

Big old drums, empty drums that they put coal in, and they make little outside stoves. Yeah, they picket around those to keep warm.

I always rode with the man that I worked with, an older man; he has since passed away. He lived nearby; and my husband would drop me off at his home in the morning, and we'd go to work. And he'd bring me out to his home, and my husband would pick me up. And they hammered through his windshield one day on our way out. Fortunately, it didn't cut us, but they could very well have. But we had to go through that every day. You didn't know when you were going to get it. And quite a few of the people would go out at night, and their cars wouldn't start. They'd raise the hood and pour sand over the whole engine block, down in the ports, and in the gas tank and, you know, that's expensive to get cleared out. So, there was a lot of that. I think they did a lot of damage to cars, and finally it got to the point where they'd overturn them. They'd just push them and rock them until over they went, with or without people. Didn't make any difference. It got real critical. And they'd rock them to scare you to death and maybe not tip, but you'd think any minute you're going over. I hated to go in, really, but still I went. It was my job, and I had to be there.

RAY GARBERSON_____
Supervisor in Auto-Lite's cost and budget department.

INTERVIEWER: *What was it like going through the picket line?*

Well, like I say, personally, I had no problems. They knew who I was, and the office people were not involved; therefore, they didn't bother us at all. And we drove in the yards. Of course, that was all that was allowed in the yards anyway was the office people, salaried people. The open parking lot across the street and around in various places was wide open where the factory employees and a good share of the salaried employees parked; however, only a certain few were allowed in there in the administrative offices. The foremen and so forth, some got in and some didn't. They had room for so many and, based on your seniority and your job, why you would be assigned a parking place; so, I was fortunate enough to be inside the yards there where we were protected to a certain extent. And we were assured of our usual parking place.

ROBERT A. CAMPBELL
Auto-Lite machinist and MESA member; continued to work during the strikes.

INTERVIEWER: *Were many women involved?*

Yes, there was women that worked there. About an equal number stayed in as went out, I imagine. I'm not sure. I know there was women who held office in the Auto-Lite Council. And I know one of the men that worked in the model shop. Going out one night, the pickets got a little rough, and they dumped him over—the man who worked right in back of me. His name was Clarence Mallick. They dumped him over in his car. He didn't get hurt. The police kept our cars moving real fast until we got a couple blocks away where there was not too many people; because once you stopped in the traffic—this was when they would come to your car, and so we would just keep moving. You wondered whether it was worth it to go into work or not.

CLARENCE FOSTER
Assistant manager in the service parts division at Auto-Lite.

The trouble started when the Auto-Lite Council people stayed in and the others stayed out. Then these outside agitators, of course, worked with other people and created problems.

They tried to intimidate these people. They were threatening to overturn cars; they were threatening to fire cars; they were threatening to manhandle people, and it got pretty hot.

INTERVIEWER: *Weren't there any police around?*

(Laugh.) They couldn't do anything.

FRED C. [WHITEY] HUEBNER_____
Management in Auto-Lite's time study department.

This thing was building up for a long, long time. But I came to work every morning, and I went home every night and got a little verbiage from the pickets outside, a little kidding back and forth. I recall there was one woman that we called "Apple Annie." And every time I came in or every time I went out, she'd say, "Wait, give me a dime. I want a cup of coffee." I'd say, all right, Annie, and I'd give her a dime, and she'd turn right around and give it to one of the pickets, you know. She was very, very rough. She said some things that I wouldn't repeat.

During the time that we were having this strike, we were having a Russian delegation visiting us. We had a contract to provide them with know-how for certain operations that they were going to perform in their country. So, one of these fellas—a little, short Russian fella— didn't know what to do, because he had been caught in the factory before he could get out—the mob was there so you couldn't get out— but anyhow, he was a lost soul. I could speak a little German, and he could talk German, so we could communicate. I said to him, what would happen if this happened in your country? He says, "Oh, this could never happen in my country. You know what would happen? They would call the soldiers, the captain would step out and say, 'You go home or we shoot.' " And he was serious about it, and it was an honest answer. It was what would happen in Russia if the same situation prevailed over there. Many things you look back and find, if it only could have been done over again, you would have done so many things differently than you did. I don't favor shooting. Far from it. But I do favor law and rules of conduct, and certainly the rules of conduct and the law broke down in this instance to beat the band.

KATHRYN SCHIEVER_____
Stenotype operator for Auto-Lite management; crossed picket lines and worked during the strikes.
&
MARGARET JACOBS_____
Payroll department worker at Auto-Lite; crossed picket lines and worked during the strikes.

KATHRYN: All the office was still working. We'd go like we always did, but they'd kick us and spit on us, call us names.

A thing like that is infectious, I guess, if you're a certain type of mentality. You see somebody doing cruel things, mean things, some people want to do the same.

MARGARET: I know that some of those people that I had seen for years, come and go, wouldn't do anything like that ordinarily. You know, monkey see, monkey do. But do you know that I got kicked? They knew I worked in the office. They knew all of us girls because they'd see us. And there was a policeman standing right there and everything. I said, he kicked me. He said, "Is that so? I didn't see it." And he watched it. They were scared to death, too. There were rats that they would tie around the strikebreakers' necks. The police were very inadequate.

Another thing that made it so very difficult was even the people that were not involved in the strike came down to sightsee. It was packed for blocks, hundreds of people, and that made it even worse. It's a funny feeling to get out of a couple of cars and go through this line and have them yell at you and spit on you. They knew we worked in the office.

INTERVIEWER: *What were they saying to you?*

KATHRYN: Not nice things. Not nice things at all.

INTERVIEWER: *So, you would always have to go through these masses of people?*

KATHRYN: Yes, yes, and as I say, they had no respect for anyone. Even the officials of the company, and they knew we had nothing to do with the strike. We couldn't have belonged to the union even if we wanted to.

NORVAL HISEY
Electrician at Auto-Lite; crossed picket lines and worked during the strikes.

At the beginning, they didn't have any pickets or anything around because they tried their best to get an interview with the company first, see. But then when Minch got so nasty about it, well, then they got nasty, too. They started fighting and tearing things apart. And the gang that was doing all this wasn't even employees of the company. They come from Detroit—hoodlums. Never even was on the payroll or anything. But this Ramsey was going to organize this thing, and he brought his own gang with him. I don't know what his first name is, but that's the guy that came from Detroit and tried to organize the Auto-Lite.

INTERVIEWER: *Wasn't there anyone out there in the picket area that you'd recognize at all?*

Nobody that I knew. All total strangers to all of us. Whether he was sent down or came on his own hook, I don't know. You know, years ago, your unions were rougher than hell, boy. You really had some goons. They was paid for that, too. The unions years ago didn't have a very good name until they got Reuther in there. He straightened a bunch of them out.

RUTH LYONS UNFERDROS
Daughter of the president of Auto-Lite Council; observed the strikes.

Well, the way I look at it, the union just politely—even though they lost out—they sent their goon squad in from Detroit to break the council, which eventually they did. Of course, my father's life was threatened, and the company did provide us with a guard at our home. The guard was at our house for a month, from 6:00 a.m. to 6:00 p.m., from 6:00 in the evening to 6:00 in the morning.

GEORGE KESSEL
Accountant at Moto-Meter; crossed picket lines to work on the merger between Moto-Meter and Auto-Lite.

My first visit was when the picket line was there. The fellows and the gals that were parading around there figured that I was part of the negotiating team and that maybe I might be on their side; but I don't know whether they made inquiries or whether they just got it in their own minds that I had nothing to do with it, and that's when I started to get some pretty callous treatment and bad remarks—cursing and swearing, jostled about a couple of times. In fact, one of the gals spit in my face one day. Now, most of the pickets at the time I went through to go into the main office were, I'd say, 70 percent females. I'd say at the time I went there, maybe twenty to twenty-five pickets just walked up and down. And then sometimes they'd stop and talk with each other.

INTERVIEWER: *Did they have signs?*

Well, they had some improvised, hand-painted signs, but there weren't too many in evidence right around the main office.

ELIZABETH NYITRAI
Production worker at Auto-Lite; crossed picket lines and worked during the strikes.

Now, I can't understand this.

[Reads from Diary] "April the 16th, 1934—On another strike. Will it ever be settled? I'm so afraid I'll get a beating. I hate to sneak around the way I do."

"Tuesday, 1934, April 17th—I called the Auto-Lite and asked them to call for me because I'm taking no chances. I want more of life."

This is the next day—"I feel grand riding to and from work in a green Nash. Rode home in an Auto-Lite mail truck tonight, and a carload of pickets followed us. Were we only scared stiff."

That was fun.

This is 1934, May the 1st. "I wish this strike was over so I could be in peace. I don't dare go out alone anymore."

Well, quite a few girls lived a few blocks away from me. One was a striker, and she was out to get me. And she was a heavyset woman, so I didn't dare go out at night. I had to stay home because they swore they were going to beat the daylights out of us. Every night, they'd bring us home in a different car—a mail truck or like a Nash the next day, try to sneak us out, you know, and then they'd pick us up in the morning. Well, this one time a whole gang of cars followed us all the way to where I used to live. The plant was across the river, and I lived on this side in Birmingham.

"May 14, 1934—Wish this darn strike would end so I could relax and enjoy working again."

You see, I didn't enjoy working, but I did it because, like I say, I had to. Then, the pickets they were out there and then, of course, I was ashamed of it, too, because I should have went out with all of them; but, well, some of them were married women, and their husbands were working and they could afford it where, my gosh, my mother needed the money.

This is May 22, 1934. "This darn strike is still going on. If I get out alive, I'll be darn lucky. I'm so darn nervous."

8

The Curious and
the Concerned

The Auto-Lite strike attracted the curious, the concerned, and men and women whose profession took them there, such as police and news reporters. The initial weeks of the strike saw relative calm on the picket lines; but increasing confrontations, reported in newspapers and communicated by word of mouth, brought hundreds of spectators to Champlain Street. One measure of the strike's growing attraction appears in complaints of movie theater managers whose ticket sales slumped as confrontations at Auto-Lite increased.

Many who found themselves on Champlain Street during May had serious business to tend. For example, police had a duty to keep events under control, to prevent injury, or to aid the injured. In many ways, they found themselves quite literally in the middle. People who lived or worked in the neighborhood inevitably became involved in the concerns of their neighbors, as did activists in labor unions elsewhere in the city. Members from the Central Labor Union gave moral support, sometimes joining the picket lines. Speakers from a number of political groups, such as the American Workers party—followers of A. J. Muste, who founded the Brookwood Labor College—attracted adherents from Toledo and other midwest cities as they offered their analysis and advice from street corner and soapbox. Their level of involvement varied with the depth of their concern. And news reporters, competing with each other and with other newspapers, sought copy for their readers, hoping to inform them about this major event in their city. Freelance newsreel photographers even staged events to bring the action and drama of the Auto-Lite strike to both a local and national audience.

During May, the Auto-Lite strike spread into the courts of Lucas County when Auto-Lite sought an injunction to end the strike. Auto-Lite's counsel tried to convince the court that the strike was an incipient communist revolution. To counter this claim, Local 18384, its counsel, and the American Civil Liberties Union insisted that the strike was led by patriotic American workers who demanded only freedom and justice. The court compromised by granting an injunction that limited pickets to twenty-five. The injunction assigned responsibility for enforcement to the Lucas County sheriff's office. Mass arrests followed and Edward Lamb, attorney for many of the strikers, found himself called to defend them. The work of a number of leftist political groups, such as the Workers League and the Communist party, expanded as well. These confrontations produced a class consciousness that brought thousands of workers to Auto-Lite's picket lines in support of Local 18384 and, thus, materially affected the outcome.

EDWARD LAMB

Successful Toledo attorney; key legal counsel who defended strikers and their supporters.

They met in my office, a little group met surreptitiously. They knew that there were spies. They knew that the chowderheads were being brought in with their guns from out of state, which was perfectly legal at that time; anyway, it was practiced all over the country. But this was the beginning. This was just plain, unadulterated, unorganized development. No theme, a lot of preachers here, a lot of theorists telling them what to do; but these guys didn't know any more about revolution than anyone else.

I remember Ted Selander and Sam Pollock. They called themselves the Workers League, at that time. Fine young fellas. And they were having meetings at the gates, pleading with people to stay out, don't go in that scab operation, and really legitimate picketing and organizing. It wasn't possible too easily then. In the first place, they had the chowderhead goons, the strikebreakers, all over the lot, including the police and the unofficial police, all over the place. But they were down there and did get groups to depart and stay out. And this went on for several days.

INTERVIEWER: *What were those men like, their personalities?*

All of them were in the unemployed workers movement. I think they were idealists, clean-cut young fellas. I think they were also terribly ambitious to get their own movement started. I think they were basically motivated to help these people, and only differing interpretations of Marxism, I think, caused them to have different theories of how to go about it. One group would think that mere disruption was the element and do anything except let them get totally organized. I have my own opinions about this, but that was prevalent; in the first place, get trouble started. And they did get a lot of trouble started. It's very easy to get a mob disorganized, start throwing bricks and so on. And that's what, I think, they did. I don't think they had any firm notions of getting a mass organization started. This is my feeling now, years later, that I don't think they really wanted to get a united auto workers union organized; I think they wanted to get a revolutionary condition created.

I believe that the Communists, on the other hand, would have liked to have seen a strong, mass-based trade union movement actually organized. Whether they could get in it or stay in it or get control of it is a subsequent question. But I think they really and sincerely wanted it.

There were some other people, Socialists. These were generally school teachers or intellectuals. A lot of them moved in from around the country, just to see this show, I think. And many teachers were there. Now, they didn't really get into the rough stuff of picketing or getting arrested; they were observers. But I would say those young members, Ted Selander, Sam Pollock, those Workers League guys, really wanted to get turmoil and rioting and violence started, to see what would happen. My own feeling is that the Communists, obviously all of them, were taking advantage of this, that they hoped for a revolutionary condition, to advance their own case.

Incidentally, Arthur Garfield Hayes came in as an attorney for the American Civil Liberties Union. He was a much older, and probably wiser civil liberties lawyer. He wanted to get these people out of jail. And we didn't always see eye to eye. I really wanted to see the workers organized. And so, we would have our own pre-trial discussions. He wanted it tried just on the law, and I must admit that I would like to have seen this strike result in a mass organization, a legitimate union of all the industrial workers. So, we did have basic tactical differences. But we ironed them out without any arguments. I think he arrived a day or two after the case started; but, anyway, he was a very calm and very able, very experienced lawyer in civil liberties. He was the general counsel in the American Civil Liberties Union. But he was always warning against letting these various groups use this platform as a stage to where they build themselves an audience or a following.

My own inclinations were to let the working conditions be brought out in the light of day and to let the need for a union be apparent. And also, to show this continual sell-out by these old AFL racketeers. This was the major problem of getting a legitimate union started. They couldn't get off the ground because these AFL people joined the corporation and let the company bring in these thugs and knock off their opponents. It was done then. And these poor people didn't know what had hit them.

And so, these young people who came in deserve a lot of credit, 'cause they ran great hazards. I mean these militant strikes now are nothing compared to the danger, the individual danger they ran; because they didn't have anyone to help them, protect them, and they needed help to take the first step getting an industrial union organized.

There were several little strikes around here, but the big one broke loose in the Electric Auto-Lite in 1934. They tried to organize, they had an old-line AFL group organized. Dillon was here to try to further their interests. It was really a company union that, as I remember, was called the Automobile Workers Union. It was something thrown together, really, to sell-out the Electric Auto-Lite workers. And Dillon had several meetings with them and couldn't get the workers to swallow his go-back-to-work routines.

There was another group trying to organize; in fact, several of them. And so, finally, a fellow named Tom Ramsey, who was sort of the rebel among the auto workers, tried to organize and did organize a group called the United Auto Workers Local 18384. Several people were assembling; there were sporadic walkouts and, finally, the whole thing exploded. And then the company tried to get an injunction against picketing.

All hell had broken loose by this time. There were shootings at the gate, tremendous violence. But, through it all, anarchy. No one really knew what to do; there was no line, they just wanted to prevent Dillon and the old AFL leaders from selling them out.

When this injunction proceeding started, the company was actively joined by this old AFL craft union under Frank Dillon. And they brought this action against the employees, trying to terminate the picketing. Now, this proceeding came to a head after a lot of fooling around. They couldn't get a judge, really, to want to sit on it, it was so loaded with dynamite. But all of the judges passed it around, and, finally, there was an effort to get all of the six common pleas judges in Lucas County to sit in back and hear this together. But even they wouldn't all go for that, so it finally resolved around having the trial scheduled before Judge Roy R. Stuart, who was quite a character and old-line judge, but also quite a drunkard—as a matter of fact, alcoholic. I knew him very well, but this thing had gotten so much publicity and excitement that poor Roy Stuart didn't know whether he was afoot or horseback by the time the trial arrived.

Outside the courtroom, in this state of the depression, there were many hundreds of people sleeping out on the courthouse lawn. Employees weren't being paid their wages, even by the city. The city employees were being given scrip, which they'd take to some of the stores and get food for. But there was total anarchy; no one knew where they were going next. This was the type of crisis that certainly bred revolution. And people recognized all over the country that here was the type of violence that might be the beginnings of an overthrow of the American government; a real workers revolution. And that's why many, many people descended on Toledo. And so, with these people descending on Toledo, there was a lot of people of different political faiths.

The Communist party was not very well organized itself at that time. There were many people who came in who were called Communists, and there were various shades of Communists. Louis Budenz, who I guess at that time was a Trotskyite and not a Communist, he later became a functionary in the Communist party and edited *The Daily Worker*. Even later, you know, he became a professional witness against Communists. In fact, he was one of the principal witnesses against me in my trials before the Federal Communications Commissions in the fifties under Joe McCarthy.

INTERVIEWER: *How well did you know him?*

Well, I knew him very well, because I defended him. I defended all of the people in the Auto-Lite strike, all of them, irrespective of what their shades were; they could be Communists or they could be Trotskyites, they could be Musteites. Reverend A. J. Muste was here. And all of them were trying to get a foothold in the revolutionary movement; each one of them would start their own little movement, or try to.

They wanted to get arrested. So, they'd get up in the courthouse grounds and they'd be making speeches, "Down with this and down with that," and "Let's hang the sheriff, let's go in and knock off Judge Stuart, the drunken so-and-so." But all these people were making speeches; it was a very revolutionary condition. Ted Selander and Sam Pollack and Art Preis, all of them became leaders in the Trotsky movement later. But Robert Lymer, who was a Communist—he was one of the few who admitted he was a Communist functionary, party member—was a cartoonist and a very successful one on the St. Louis *Post Dispatch* and then he joined the Communist party. He was a very, very effective guy. He was here.

But in the meantime, too, there were really dozens and maybe even hundreds of reporters came from all over the country. Heywood Broun was here and stayed here. We became very good friends at that time. And I kept him supplied in whiskey, and he kept me supplied in good stories. But a very wonderful character, colorful character. This became national news and a very important crisis in the organization of the labor movement. I think the violence called attention to it. Heywood Broun and other reporters recognized that here, in the middle of the depression, a revolutionary condition was being born. No one knew what was going to happen; but whatever was going to happen, Heywood Broun and the other reporters wanted to be in on it, wanted to see the show.

And there was a successful resistance to court-mandated restrictions against picketing. These people said, "We don't give a damn what your court order says, we're not going to abide by it." If it could happen here, it could happen any place. It was just an accident that it happened here.

Law and order—they certainly couldn't get any law and order from the sheriff; he didn't know where to turn. In fact, he couldn't even control the crowds in that courtroom. They just threw up their hands. The workers said, "Sheriff, we'll throw you out of here." And they were going to throw the judge out, too; and they would have.

The workers knew that Judge Stuart was drunk. There were a lot of oaths of obscenity and a little bit of kidding. It was too serious, though, because they knew that they were going back and picket, and it was going to be a test of strength between the law and themselves. And here was this judge: very red-faced, white-haired, looked like a judge. And this fellow was very quiet. He had been a Republican, very active Republican party functionary during all his life, and assistant prosecutor, and then he was elected judge here. And he sat up there, and he'd take a load of whiskey before every session. And, you know, I have been in the court chambers when he did it.

In the morning, we had these arguments on the injunction; and the mobs were in there, and you could hardly squeeze through. And there was a lot of yelling, and these fellows like Louis Budenz and A. J. Muste, they were yelling at the top of their voice right in the courtroom. And remember, I wanted to give these guys a forum. I wanted to let A. J. Muste get on the witness stand and say what he had seen, because he could have put on a pretty good show. But Arthur Garfield Hayes opposed it, and so we didn't put them on the stand; but they didn't hesitate to interrupt any witnesses or anything else in making their speech. There were a couple of deputies, I think, and the sheriff made statements, and they called them goddamned liars (laugh). There really was turmoil, and the judge sat there. Then he said, at 10:00 a.m., "I'll give you the decision," and he'd come back at 2:00 p.m.

Well, all hell broke loose in the meantime with people fighting to get back in the courtroom. They had a real time getting him back into the courtroom. I remember several people helping him up on the chair. He said something about the law ought to be respected—it was all equivocation—and that, while he knew that they had the right, they were good citizens, and so forth, yet they really ought not to picket. And he said he would suggest something, that there be twenty-five pickets. When he showed up late, some of the strikers said, "The hell with this," and they just walked out. They were being tried for contempt, and they said, "What do we care about this stinking judge anyway?" So, they got up and just walked out of the courtroom. "We're through, we're not going to stick around." So, they went back to the picket lines.

One of the big problems was the attorney for the Electric Auto-Lite Company named George D. Wells, who was a long-time adversary of mine. I finally represented the workers, and he'd be representing every corporation in town. A real dignified guy, with a morning coat on and eyeglasses, and he'd make these pontifical speeches that were enough to make you throw up.

I have in this book the actual transcript of George Wells, where he said, "These people aren't Americans; they're all Bolsheviks. And law and order have totally disappeared." This is George B. Wells and I'll quote from my book, *No Lamb for Slaughter*, on page thirty-nine:

"George B. Wells, a leading Toledo lawyer, appeared as counselor for both the Auto-Lite Company and for those workers who didn't want to strike. Wells said,"—and this is from the records—"These eight hundred and fifty employees have a Constitutional right to work. They have more rights than these Bolsheviks. Last night we had disgraceful riots. Innocent employees were attacked. A situation of anarchy exists in Toledo. Somehow, this court ought to be able to have its orders enforced by police and deputy sheriffs and the National Guard. We are helpless today. All the forces of order have disappeared. Yet this is not Russia; but fifteen hundred Bolsheviks, not employees, simply Russianized agitators, seek to close this Toledo plant. They are bandits and killers. Already, five hundred tear gas bombs have exploded and already, several picketing mobsters are dead."

Well, at this point, I stopped some of the storm by interjecting: "This strike and this whole situation has gotten out of hand by stupid, short-sighted handling of our fellow human beings. These men are not Bolsheviks; they are our fellow citizens. In the midst of starvation and struggle, these Auto-Lite workers, who have sought simple recognition of their union, are beset with many pains and many troubles. This Auto-Lite Company seeks to go behind the workers' own union and set up illegitimate relationships with certain ousted AFL officials. Now is the time for good-faith negotiations between the responsible representatives of the union and the corporation."

Then I describe "the noisy courtroom was filled with warring factions. The old Automobile Workers Union leaders, under Francis Dillon, urged to stay and stand by for law and order. Then 'new' United Automobile Workers union leaders, headed by Thomas Ramsey, asked the defendants to walk out of the trial and return to the picket lines. A dozen or two of the defendants just walked out of the courtroom, chanting, 'We'll not be railroaded by a drunken judge.' When we went out on the courthouse lawn a few hours later, the crowds were still being harangued by the Reverend A. J. Muste of New York City, Louis Budenz, and three Toledo leaders of the unemployed: Ted Selander, Kenneth Ostheimer, and Kenneth Eggar. 'This is their day in the sun,' my colleague Arthur Garfield had said. 'Each faction is trying to get arrested. Each group wants to get into the act and become a leader of the working class of America.' "

So, that describes the total anarchy, the total disarray of what people were seeking. Basically, they wanted to have their own union. And they were confronted with this action by the corporation, calling all of the workers Bolsheviks and so forth. And then, the old AFL union joined in the company action to restrain these unorganized workers from getting organized. It was a day of great difficulty. People were hungry; they didn't know where to turn. And here they're trying to get a spokesman, and they're really putting their jobs on the line. Many examples of great bravery in these people.

INTERVIEWER: *What became of the suits, the injunctions?*

Well, there was an injunction issued, sort of a wishy-washy thing that no one paid any attention to. And that's the great significance of this, that the workers successfully resisted this injunction, which is the first time this was done. And then the efforts for mediation took over. And so nothing was settled by the injunction; everything was settled by the mediations. They sat around the table over here in the old "C" court and worked out a settlement. First, that the workers were going to be allowed to choose their own representatives; this, in itself, was important.

INTERVIEWER: *But Selander and those people didn't go to jail?*

Oh, no, not as a result of the injunction. They were in jail as part of the mass arrest, but they'd get them out pretty quickly. All of them went to jail, all of them. Generally before and during the trial. This went on for a week or so.

Now, this Ken Eggar and Ken Ostheimer, whom I mentioned, were a different faction. They were Communists. Eggar was the local Communist leader here. I lump the names in that other particular grouping with Ted Selander and Arthur Preis and Sam Pollack. They were Trotskyites. But Ken Eggar and Ken Ostheimer were well-known Communists here. But all of them went to jail just by being picked up at the gates or even out on the courthouse lawn. Not many people were picked up on the courthouse lawn, because the sheriff wouldn't have been safe going into that crowd. This was before the day of mass gassing and so forth.

INTERVIEWER: *I was also wondering about the Chamber of Commerce and the Merchants and Manufacturers Association. What did they do in relation to the strike?*

I don't recall that the Chamber of Commerce or the Merchants and Manufacturers Association came out too prominently. Things had gone too far. When this mass rioting around the plant was going on, no one was appealing by advertising to people to be calm or anything. I mean, they were undoubtedly in touch with the governor and screaming for the National Guard. The governor was on the spot. I know they got the guard, and they came in with great fanfare about 3:00 or 4:00 in the morning. But there was total anarchy, and things didn't calm down just because the National Guard was here. It was out of hand, and no one knew where to turn. And that's why this mediation was helpful.

INTERVIEWER: *Why did you become involved in the strike with these radicals?*

I think I was searching for some fulfillment of ideals. I could see this poverty, lack of planning, lack of theory. I'd visited the Soviet Union and many other places, written books on Russia and the nature of planning. I could see our own lack of planning. So, I don't think that the strike was a challenge that, somehow, we're going to get a better world out of it. I think that I saw it as an opportunity. The people might get the masses organized, where it would be a spreading of the resources of the wealth of the world among large numbers of people.

It was not a totally defined philosophy any of us had. We were searching; we knew that there were people hungry and there was no need for it and that there must be, first, a recognition among the largest number of workers that, somehow, they would have spokesmen. And when the New Deal came in, they were doing many, many things to give us security. One was the recognition of the right of the workers to choose their own bargaining agents.

I was accused many times, of course, of being Communist, because I defended Communists. But I also defended plenty of capitalists. And it didn't make a bit of difference to me what they were, what their social or ideological attachments were. If they needed help, I always took a certain pride in extending a helping hand to them. I still will.

LYNN G. WATERS
Toledo policeman; on patrol at Auto-Lite during the strike.

INTERVIEWER: *You were down at the Auto-Lite strike?*

Oh, yeah. We were working sixteen hours a day.

INTERVIEWER: *The policemen who were down there, like yourself, had been on the force for quite a while?*

Oh, yes. At that time, there weren't many men put on the police department. I was at the Auto-Lite. The Auto-Lite is what really, really—there was quite a lot of Communists mixed in that. On Saturday night there would be maybe one hundred fifty pickets from Detroit would come down here, and they would really make it bad. Communists were pretty strong in here at that time. People were ready for anything. They were so disgusted and broke that anybody that offered them a little sympathy, why, they would fall for it. The Communists used to have a paper that they put out daily during the Auto-Lite strike.

INTERVIEWER: *What were the pickets themselves like?*

The pickets weren't bad at all. I mean the thing would quiet down, and then there was quite a number of special deputy sheriffs who were sworn in, too.

INTERVIEWER: *From where?*

Well, from Lucas County here. The sheriff had special deputy sheriffs. Well, they had no experience in police work. Things would quiet down, and then one of them would shoot a tear gas. That wasn't too bad, but they'd commence shooting vomiting gas and that was tough. You'd get a couple of breaths of that and you'd had it. God. Oh, man, that was awful.

INTERVIEWER: *What did strike duty consist of?*

Patrolling up there sixteen hours a day. You could spot trouble, of course, and you'd try to get it quieted down and usually could. There is always one or two people on the strike or on the picket line that has power. We got along with them, always have. They're the ones that say, "We won't," or "We will." All strikes in Ohio you have to read the Riot Act, that's the law. They all know the Riot Act better than we do. Where the fighting starts is when some guy, a deputy or sometimes the National Guard, would stick a guy with their bayonet, you know, and tell them to get back and stuff like that. That started them up again. It didn't take much to start them. They were mad anyway, of course.

INTERVIEWER: *What made them mad?*

Well, being out of work that long, you know, living on nothing. You couldn't get relief if you were on strike.

INTERVIEWER: *There were some people inside working?*

Oh, yeah. They were kept in there by the company, of course. There were a few workers, but there were mostly supervisors; and they caught one of those supervisors coming out there one day, and they tore all his clothes off except a necktie and marched him right downtown to Superior and Adams. Right in the daytime.

It was pretty busy taking guys to the hospital that got slugged by somebody. Well, on a Saturday night, we usually arrest maybe one hundred, a hundred and fifty; and 90 percent of them were from out of town. Just came down to see the fun and start all the racket they could. That was Saturday and Sunday nights, and Friday nights.

I think we had some men that never did recover from that vomiting gas. They had to take an early pension, especially one that became chief for about two or three months. He died, and I actually believe it was—he was an older man, and with the vomiting gas, that was awful. Fellas in the wagon would start to the hospital with injured people, and maybe they'd have to stop along the way—the driver and, as we call him, the back-in man, would have to vomit for ten or fifteen minutes.

INTERVIEWER: *So, you weren't especially happy when the deputies arrived?*

Any time that you—these special police, there isn't too much love lost between a regular policeman and a special officer.

INTERVIEWER: *Did you get along all right with the people? Was there a lot of tension?*

Oh, yeah. Well, there was enough tension; but as long as you can keep the drunks out of the way, you aren't in bad shape. The average striker knew that we had a job to do and, of course, we tried to do it. Most of them, I'd say 95 percent of them, they're all right. But they just didn't have a job. No money. The tension.

Houses up there at that time were pretty close together, little houses. They would take an inner tube, cut it in half, and nail it on the corner of two houses, between the houses; and they would get ahold of a brick, and about four men would pull that thing back about four feet and let it go. If you were in the way, it would take your head off; it would go right through those metal things over the windows. That was dangerous, not only for us but for everybody, even the strikers. The outside of the windows all had screens over them, heavy screens. They'd get right through the screen, these bricks. After the sun goes down, of course, there is no light. They'd, of course, broken all the lights—the street lights.

INTERVIEWER: *Were there any kids around?*

Well, no, not many kids. We had trouble one day—the Tom Mix circus was held here during the strike. We had a little trouble then keeping the kids out and away to keep from getting hurt. They wanted to get in. Kids—you can't tell them—they would play hooky from school or told their parents they were going out to Tom Mix's circus. Instead, they came over to the Auto-Lite. They'd just stand around, you know. We tried the best we could. I think we done a pretty good job. There was only one kid hurt that I know of. Somebody shot a tear gas on top and just skinned his head. He didn't mind the getting hurt, but he was wondering what he was going to tell his parents when he got home. We took him to the hospital. He was a nice little kid. Felt sorry for him.

INTERVIEWER: *Were many people hit by tear gas?*

Well, yes, there were quite a few. The shells are about eight inches long, about an inch and a half in diameter. If the wind was blowing, they have a lot of gas in one of them things. And as soon as they fire them, they get hot; you can't pick them up. When I first went with the department, we had the tear gas bombs. They were bombs like grenades. You pulled the pin, and you hold your thumb down when you throw it. It can take three or four minutes to heat up. But those that I'm speaking of get hot right away. You pick them up, and you can burn your hand off.

INTERVIEWER: *This was a very unusual event, then, in a policeman's life?*

Oh, yes—oh my, yes. I went on in 1928, and I never had anything like that.

INTERVIEWER: *I wondered where all these bricks came from down at Auto-Lite.*

They would get them from around these houses. Some of those houses didn't have many bricks left in the foundation after that strike was over. The ones across the street were small houses. They had a pretty good supply of bricks to last three quarters of an hour. Then they'd go to the next house and start tearing at the foundation.

INTERVIEWER: *Didn't the people in the houses complain?*

Didn't do any good. Sure they did. They were crowded clear up to those houses, clear back behind them.

INTERVIEWER: *In other words you were just sort of there, and helped clean up?*

That's right, that's right. We were so outnumbered—you'd have maybe twenty-five or thirty policemen out there where you'd have five to six thousand strikers and sympathizers. It wasn't just the strikers, of course. Their families, their wives, and friends came over there and tried to help them out. I would say that in that neighborhood over there, north of Cherry Street at that time, that 75 percent of the working population at that time were working at the Auto-Lite.

WILLIAM H. STONER

Toledo policeman; worked in the police department's bureau of identification in 1934.

INTERVIEWER: *Do you recall the attitude on the police force about the strike?*

Well, the attitude towards the strikers? They were against it, very much against it. But there was nothing we could do about it. They were not in sympathy with them, you could say that.

INTERVIEWER: *The police were not in sympathy with the strikers?*

No.

INTERVIEWER: *How come, do you think?*

Because it caused too much trouble, I think. They would have been more in sympathy with them if they would have just picketed the place and not destroyed property, see, and beat up people.

SEYMOUR ROTHMAN

Newspaperman just entering the trade in 1934; reported some events during the Auto-Lite strikes.

The strike itself, as far as my own experience is, was pretty much that I went out there. I was on the outside. And basically my job, when something happened, someone got hurt, was to get his name. I do know this. There were two things that struck me. If you were two blocks away, you had no idea of what was going on. It was simply you didn't have this sense. If the wind was right, then you could smell the tear gas, and you would know something was wrong; but basically, you could be going down one of the adjoining streets and not really know something was going on. Of course, once you got on the site, you were well aware of the fact not only that something was going on, but that it wasn't really a laughing matter. These guys were throwing half bricks; and when they come down, they're heavy. It is amazing that more people weren't seriously injured.

Reporters were not too popular then. You had to be a little careful, although there was usually someone around there calm enough to say, "Well, he's only doing his job." So at least you'd escape with your life. But the other thing was you did have to watch out not to get hit. You could get accidentally hit just as easily as you could get hit deliberately.

It was a little difficult to do because it was very simple. As soon as you'd tell someone that you were from the *Blade* or from the *Times*, they'd say, "That son-of-a-bitch paper—get the hell out of here." Then, you'd have to decide if you wanted to get the hell out of there or stay and get the information; and I'd say invariably you'd stay, as a matter of pride. You couldn't let anybody drive you off. I couldn't because, in the first place, I wanted to get into the business. But, even then, someone else would be there and say, "Aw, they're only doing their job," or some guy would want to get his name in the paper anyhow. It was a completely disorganized thing. Sometimes, you'd just turn your back on the guy who decided he wanted to make a speech about how bad the paper is and how tough he is and talk to someone else. Matter of fact, you kind of got used to it during that period.

Photographers were in the same situation as the newspaper people except that they had to get close. In those days your equipment was much, much different than it is today. You'd carry a big four by five Speed-Graphic instead of that little thing, and you put your film on what we call plates—film holders, which were fairly good size. They had to be big enough to hold four-by-five-inch film; and you carried a good size suitcase with your equipment in it, so it really wasn't made for moving around fast. If someone wanted to make a target of you, they could. And, of course, some guys didn't want their pictures taken, and some didn't mind it as much. But it was pretty difficult, as it would be today, to take pictures with those bricks flying around.

At the time, they must have still been using glass plates instead of the film they use today; and one of the photographers, after he took the shot, put the plate holder and film holder in his pocket. He was struck in the pocket with a brick, and it cracked the glass plate. He was still able to develop it, and he ran it in the paper with the crack in evidence. Strikers are going to be anti-policemen, anti-newspaper. We're not now talking about leaders. We're talking now about the guy on the picket line.

The strike was the most important thing in town. Basically, in those days you had competitive newspapers, and you had to battle not only for the best story but to have it first. So naturally, this took bigger battalions of reporters. And also, you played local news. That would have been a good story any time, you know, but also the tendency was to play local news greater.

One of the big problems there was to avoid tear gas—you'd learn soon not to walk into the wind with the tear gas coming. It was a simple thing; you could tell from where the people are where to go. They'd all naturally get on the windward side of the gas so that it'd be blowing away from them, so that's where you'd go. You'd come back in the office, and your clothing would smell from it for a long time; but again, it was just part of the fun and excitement. It was adventure in a sense. See, we never touched the real issues.

You took it for granted there was going to be a Socialist party around, there was going to be a Communist party around, and neither of them would ever get strong enough to ever make a serious bid for anything; but you also had the Young Communist League, which was active. As the union itself took form and gathered some momentum, these guys simply were shunted aside. They were mostly intellectual types, but no one needed their intellectualism. I don't think most of the guys that were on those picket lines really cared about the form of government. This wasn't what they were looking for. These guys wanted a contract that would let them eat better. They just wanted to get the factories running; and they wanted to get paid, and they wanted to feed the family. It was as simple as that.

AUGUST DANNER

Metal polisher; union representative to the Toledo Central Labor Union, which supported Auto-Lite strikers in 1934; he did not work at Auto-Lite.

I was the representative of the Metal Polishers' Union to the Central Labor Union. And the Central Labor Union had what they call the steering committee composed of twenty-one various representatives from various unions who were not directly involved in the strike at the Auto-Lite to try to raise money for them, keep them on an even keel, and things of that kind. We supported them indirectly.

At that time, we couldn't raise very much money. You know, none of our members were working. And the organizations themselves had very little money. We didn't go out and solicit funds. But we done what we could—which wasn't very much. None of the leaders of the Central Labor Union ever appeared on the picket line, to my knowledge.

Top: A picket line forms in front of Auto-Lite factory during the first strike. (Late February, 1934.)
Bottom: Twenty-five pickets allowed by injunction. (Late May, 1934.)

Left Top: Police peacefully arrest a picket on the corner of Champlain and Chestnut streets. (Assumed date, late May, 1934.)

Left Middle: Tension builds as sympathizers watch the allowed pickets. (Late May, 1934.)

Left Bottom: Picket (possibly Alma Hahn) injured by a projectile in front of Auto-Lite factory. (May 23, 1934.)

Right Top: Police aid man injured in sporadic fighting. (Late May, 1934.)

Right Bottom: Strike breakers use water hose from factory to disperse pickets.

Toledo • Lucas County Public Library

Toledo • Lucas County Public Library

Top: Special deputies throw tear gas, antagonizing the pickets. This lead to a siege on the plant in late May 1934. [Clarence Bailey saved this print, even though the glass plate he carried broke when he was struck by stones.]

Bottom: Man with submachine gun stands inside the Auto-Lite office building during the siege.

Top: Pickets are pushed back from the Auto-Lite factory by the National Guard at the onset of the Battle of Chestnut Hill. (May 26, 1934.)
Bottom: During a charge up Chestnut Hill, a storm of bricks and stones fells a guardsman on the sidewalk.

Toledo • Lucas County Public Library

Toledo • Lucas County Public Library

Top: A guardsman is carried to safety after being stoned.
Bottom: A picket (probably Frank Hubay) is seriously injured by a National Guard bullet.

Above: A young guardsman stares through the broken glass of the guard house as calm returns to the Auto-Lite factory.

Toledo • Lucas County Public Library

Above: Local 18384 became Local 12 C.I.O. and sent its delegation to the 1937 U.A.W. convention. William Lockwood is first person on the left on second step. Next to him is probably Charles Rigby.

I don't know whether they were directly involved. They didn't have any of their members working over there, I know that. The people on the Central Labor Union were generally older than I was, at the time. Probably most of them were in their fifties where I was in my thirties.

The manufacturers and the business people were definitely opposed to organized labor at that time, very much so. I think what organized labor meant to them was they had to pay higher wages, they could make less profit.

INTERVIEWER: *When other people were organizing new unions, did they come to the Central Labor Union for help?*

Oh, yeah.

INTERVIEWER: *What kind of help would you give them?*

Mostly advice, I suppose. Nobody ever had very much money. You couldn't give them any financial support, but we would try to assist them in getting members by talking to different unorganized people in the various factories where the men worked. I mentioned the fact that the most of the union people were tradesmen, like myself. Metal polishers, machinists, millwrights, and electricians work in these factories. The bulk of the employees were unorganized. The main support that we probably gave them was talking to the unemployed, unskilled help. We had enough trouble keeping our own members in the organization at that time because nobody was working. Nobody could pay any dues.

INTERVIEWER: *I understand there was almost a general strike during the Auto-Lite situation.*

I don't think it probably was as close to being a general strike as it might have been assumed. I don't think there were any plans of any kind being made for a general strike. Probably talked about by some people but don't think there was any specific plans made.

The Central Labor Union done what we could to organize the unorganized and educate them. That was our main purpose as a labor union, educating them in terms of organized labor, what organized labor could do with an organization.

Better working conditions were more important than higher wages at that time. You could get fired for nothing. If you wasn't the right nationality or wasn't the right color or something like that, you could get fired and you had no recourse.

DOROTHY MATHENY

*Teacher; organizer and member of Toledo Federation of Teachers; witnessed
Auto-Lite strike events.*

I was teaching English in Woodward High School in the North End in
1934. It was right in the midst of the auto production places. During
the Auto-Lite strike, we had surprisingly very little absence because
they were warmer in school than they were at home because some of
them didn't have heat in their homes. We did set up a little soup line,
sort of, at noon; and that, sometimes, was the only food that many of
those youngsters had.

INTERVIEWER: *Who set that up?*

Well, the home economics department prepared the food, and I, for
one, picked up material from over at our grocery store. He would put
out his wilted lettuce and vegetables, which weren't as fresh as they
ought to be to be put back on the shelves. I'd pick them up in the
morning and bring them over, and she would use that. Other teachers
did the same thing. We would bring contributions to put in the soup
pot. That was what they ate.

INTERVIEWER: *You don't believe that a lot of the students skipped school
to go to the strike?*

Not skipped school. I think their parents wouldn't have allowed them
to do it. In those days the parents ran the show, not the children. They
wanted them to have an education. They themselves come over here
with not too much. They come from a working class in Poland. They
wanted their children to be educated, and they saw to it that they came
to school and stayed there.

   I did have an experience with children fainting on the floor—which
was pretty devastating—because they were hungry. But they hadn't
complained, and I think that's one reason why we didn't talk about it—
because they preferred not to. There was too much of it at home, and
they wanted to get away from it.

THOMAS PROSSER

Toledo policeman; on patrol at Auto-Lite during the strikes.

INTERVIEWER: *Most of the police, then, that were working down at the
Auto-Lite, were older, experienced men?*

Oh, yes, yeah, because they had laid off all the young ones.

INTERVIEWER: *And you were working?*

Twelve-hour shifts. No days off. It was over a month. We were all wore out by the time it was over.

I think that if it had been confined to just the people that worked there, they wouldn't have had any trouble. But a few outsiders came in, and, you know, 'course there's nothing easier to lead than the mob. I used to go and pick the leader, and that's the guy I'd pick on. And if I could get him straightened out, the rest of them would go along. But you had to go in there and get that leader. The union brought in a bunch of goons from Cleveland.

INTERVIEWER: *How were they identified?*

I don't know.

INTERVIEWER: *Did they give speeches or that sort of thing?*

Well, they got the information that these goons were in here from the men that worked at the Auto-Lite factory. They told them that these goons were being brought in by the union leaders. And, of course, there was rumors flying all over at that time. But I know that there were some brought in by the union because some of those that were arrested gave their address as Cleveland.

JOHN TOCZYNSKI_____
Toledo resident; never worked at Auto-Lite but went to observe strikes.

I never worked at the Auto-Lite. But when the strike came on over there, well, I just went down there to see what was going on. It was more or less a chance for people to go down there and see a little excitement. I would say most of the people were spectators. In fact, I know because I would estimate myself that there would be at least five thousand or more people in the crowd. And I know they didn't have that many people employed there.

So, as far as the strike is concerned, why, I used to go there after work. In fact, I helped throw a few bricks in the windows myself, you know. (Laughter.) Just like anybody else. We used to go down there then just to pass a little time; and after awhile, we'd begin to feel, well, we're all fighting for a cause, we're all working people. And we felt, at least I felt, that by going down to help throw a couple bricks out at that building and join the crowd that we were all fighting for a cause, which was the working man's cause. And we figured it was about time that the working man had something going his way, instead of always the other way.

9

Besieged

Six weeks after the strike began, fighting erupted between strikers, strikebreakers, police, and special deputies in front of the Auto-Lite factory. The company's ability to remain in production threatened the strikers, for should the strike fail, Auto-Lite would certainly replace them permanently. The injunction attempted to shrink the picket line to assure easier access for strikebreakers crossing the picket lines to work at jobs the strikers felt rightfully belonged to them. The resulting frustration and anger boiled over into a full scale battle late the afternoon of May 23, when strikers and sympathizers besieged managers, foremen, strikebreakers, office workers, and members of the Auto-Lite Council in the plant. Lucas County Sheriff Dave Krieger's attempt to enforce the injunction by arresting hundreds reduced the issue rather simply to a test of power and will.

Encouraged by Auto-Lite management, Sheriff Krieger made the fateful decision to augment his force of deputies by recruiting special deputies from the area, including some supervisory workers from Auto-Lite as well as some members of the Auto-Lite Council. These special deputies had a strong emotional investment in the outcome, and Auto-Lite agreed to pay their salaries. Auto-Lite had prepared for confrontations by purchasing and storing in the factory tear gas from Federal Laboratories. It is difficult to document what other weapons they had on hand.

The picket lines in front of Auto-Lite grew dramatically during the week as news of clashes between sheriff's deputies and strikers spread across the city and country. Members of the American Workers party and the Communist party joined the pickets, as did hundreds of sympathizers and the curious. Discipline on the picket lines broke down under the rain of tear gas thrown by the special deputies. Rocks and stones flew through the factory windows, some propelled by slingshots made from rubber inner tubes. Even random sniping with guns occurred.

The siege apparently was planned, but the planners remain unnamed and the full dimensions of the plans uncertain. The plan may have been nothing more than a message spread by word of mouth to prevent the scabs from leaving the plant. Whoever initiated the plan, it resulted in hundreds outside the factory joining in it, raining bricks on the factory from a pickup truck that "conveniently" broke down nearby. Characterized by some as a small war, the struggle lasted through the night; those inside seeking refuge in the upper stories in the back of the building. The events of that night burned into the memories of those besieged in the factory. Some were bystanders, in a sense, eager simply to escape, and others were angry combatants.

Rumors flew inside the plant as the din of battle rose and fell outside: truckloads of goons had come from Detroit, hired to beat up the strikebreakers; cadres of Communists, bent on destroying the factory and fomenting revolution, lurked in the crowd. Many inside feared for their lives. Such rumors were not wholly unfounded, but they were certainly exaggerated. Undoubtedly, union sympathizers came to help from Detroit and elsewhere; but it is unlikely that they were hired to come by a union unable to provide financial support for its own members. Political groups from the left instinctively supported this workers struggle and helped picket, undoubtedly seeing in it a revolutionary potential; but they did not create nor lead the union. Had the pickets been successful in entering the factory, someone might have been killed. Therefore, such rumors had credibility, which added to the terror of the night.

In the face of these rumors, people inside the factory armed themselves with makeshift weapons like sticks of solder or blackjacks made out of heavy wire. The bravado of some only served to heighten the drama and the danger of the situation, thus reassuring no one. Some undoubtedly felt deep commitment against the union, but most simply hoped to leave safely. Curiously, it was possible, though dangerous, to leave. The Auto-Lite factory site ran three blocks along Champlain

Street. Behind the factory ran railroad tracks and an empty field. Few apparently took advantage of this despite the fact that the pickets and their supporters crowded around the main plant entrance at the foot of Chestnut Hill. The pickets covered only a portion of one block. That proved to be enough.

However nightmarish the experience was, it appears that few on the inside sustained physical injuries. The tear gas often drifted back into the factory or canisters were thrown back in, filling the factory and choking its occupants; but the preponderance of injuries befell those outside. Those inside suffered from hunger, which was eased late in the night by lunches sneaked in from Homemade Box Lunch. Fear and uncertainty etched that night deep into memory.

RAY GARBERSON
Supervisor in Auto-Lite's cost and budget department.

They let me in up until the last day. I had no enemies on the union committee; they were all friendly. But the last morning I went into the plant, one of the committeemen walked up to the car and he said, "Ray," he said, "you better not go in today," he said. "You won't get out." I laughed and says, aw, you're kidding. He says, "Nope." I said, aw, come on. I went inside the yard, you know, and they closed the gates, but he was right; I didn't get out. That was the day that the real riots broke loose.

Of course, rocks were being fired all the time, bricks. All the windows were broken; they even broke the windows in Mr. Miniger's office and broke some of the equipment in there, like typewriters. At that time, it was quite common for officials to have plate glass tops on their desks; other people didn't. And, of course, all those were broken.

My car wasn't scratched at all. We had two rows of cars along the end of the office building with a drive in between, and they just seemed to pick certain cars. This drive was down an incline, so there was a stone wall up on top, and they'd get big rocks and drop them down on top of the cars.

INTERVIEWER: *Could you see what was going on?*

Oh, yes. You could get up on the upper floors and look all around and see what was going on all the time, as long as you didn't get out on the street when the shooting was going on. But I think most of that went on at night, 'cause it would be too easy to see where it was coming from perhaps. I understand later on that there was a certain house or houses where they were up in the attic up on Michigan Street; and they were shooting across through the Auto-Lite, which was sort of a block away. I noticed twenty or thirty bullet holes. After the windows were broken, there's no way of telling how many shots may have been fired through an open window. Anything they could do, you know, to damage property seemed to be the big thing.

This insurance man just happened to be out at the time making his usual call, and the riot was going on; and his car was parked directly across the street in the visitors' parking lot. It was a brand new Buick, and he watched the gang dump the car over and set it on fire; but I recall he laughed and said, "No problem. I'll have another one as soon as I get out of here."

The rioting went on all day. Normally, we would be able to get in the car and drive out. They knew who we were; we were office people that were not involved in the strike or the argument in any way. This night, there was a mob there and nobody got out. Gates were closed. In fact, they crashed the gates a few times, but continual tear gas kept the mob back. One time they ran out of gas, but the gang outside didn't know it. They could have rushed the gates that time, I suppose.

Sometimes, they'd throw the tear gas out and someone would grab it real quick and throw it back. Then, whoever threw it from the inside would get the worst of it. I didn't get any of it because I stayed back far enough, but the water runs out of your eyes and your eyes burn. You can't see anything, but you doused your eyes with water, and I guess it wears off, no permanent injuries.

None of us had anything to eat all day, the last day we worked, unless you brought a lunch. We couldn't get to the cafeteria; what little food was there, of course, was used up in a short time. Oh, some of us had lunch all right, at noon, but the evening, it was gone. Of course, the cigarette machines were cleared out in a short time, and so we went without anything to eat there at least from noon until the next day when we were able to go home. All the parents and relatives of the employees who were stuck in there all night were worried, including my wife.

INTERVIEWER: *Do you remember the number or placement of the machine guns?*

No, I have no way of knowing actually, with the exception of the one in the office. And what guard manned that one, I don't recall. He was the only one that I know was stationed in the office entrance with a machine gun.

CLARENCE FOSTER———————————————

Assistant manager in the service parts division at Auto-Lite.

Well, boy, those people inside had everything, from bars of solder to armature shafts to everything else. And it would have been a terrible thing if anybody had ever got in there. And, of course, it wasn't improved much by the fact that a lot of curious people started congregating there, too. We couldn't let our people go home. Some of the people had things in their desks they wanted to get, and we wouldn't let them go after them. I know I went in there to the office, and I was going alongside of a glass partition, and a bullet went right over my head through that darn partition. Somebody took a pot shot. They could see the shadow. They must have been up in a tree or a telephone pole. So, I know I personally crawled into the office and got some stuff out of the desks that the people wanted.

They'd take inner tubes and put them around posts and use them as catapults. And those brick bats were coming through the office windows, both through our office and down below. We had pretty good steel filing cases, and they had great big dents in them.

Now, we had people that had been outside; they'd been in Detroit or someplace. And they come home, and they heard about this thing. They got in a little close, and they got mixing with the crowd. And then they'd phone in and let us know what the feeling of the crowd was. They were taking up collections, money to make bombs. They was going to bomb that place. Now, that's the kind of people we were dealing with.

The funny thing, this whole activity was concentrated from the parking lot across the street from the plant. Altogether, from Chestnut down to Bush Street, we had plant area, about three blocks. But the people were all in the area between Chestnut and Mulberry. You didn't see them down below Mulberry very often.

INTERVIEWER: *Why were they there?*

The main entrance was there. Office was there. In the entrance to the office the boys had put big oak tables in front of the door because they was going to come in there, too, and clean house. And we had a couple guys there with guns; so if anybody had tried to come in, why, they would stop them. Some of them were office people. When the fire department would come down there—turn on the fire alarm when you had a fire—they wouldn't let them function. They threatened to cut the hoses or turn the fire equipment over. You just couldn't handle it; you just had a mob.

You know, people react funny when they're in a mob situation. Boy, I don't know how many times we called the fire department that night. They came, but they couldn't do nothing. They had to turn around and go back.

CLAUDE W. POUND
Production manager at Auto-Lite.

Well, I'll tell ya, it was just a young war. They was throwing bricks and everything at us. We used the gas grenades to repel them. Down the street a ways there was one fellow that had a car or he was parked down by a car, I believe; and every so often a flashlight would come on—bang, bang, he was shooting at us. Well, that was all night long.

INTERVIEWER: *What was the atmosphere like inside, with the people inside the plant?*

Oh, they were perfectly loyal, and all right. There were some dastardly things. Things stopped, they just stopped; then when the troops got there, that was the end of the rioting. Oh, there was a little scuffling for a few days, but that died out awful fast.

NORVAL HISEY
Electrician at Auto-Lite; crossed picket lines and worked during the strikes.

INTERVIEWER: *What happened to you the day of the big confrontation?*

The first inkling we got that there might be trouble was when a bullet came through the second or the fourth floor window. It ricocheted around the ceiling and walls for quite a while, so it must have been a pretty good-sized caliber. We never did find the bullet. We looked for that son-of-a-buck for a helluva time, but we never did find it. That was the first inkling we got that there might be some trouble.

INTERVIEWER: *What time of the day was that?*

If I'm not mistaken, I think it was about 2:00 in the afternoon on a Tuesday.

INTERVIEWER: *The deputies must have been there that day. Did they come after the shot?*

After the shot, they was called. The deputies came in. I was right beside the man in the service department—top floor of the office building—that fired the first tear gas shot. I had the shell for years. I wanted to keep it for a relic.

One of my friends lost an eye. We had a lot of people coming down there just for darned curiosity. And a shell hit the pavement, bounced up, cut him across the side of the face, and he lost an eye. His name was Kane.

One incident I won't forget. I remember it was raining that night, and they were turning cars over in the parking lot, burning them up. They shot tear gas over there and, God dang, all at once the damn wind changed and, Jeez, that stuff come back in the factory. You never seen such a sick bunch of people in your life. Oh, boy, puke all over the floors every place you look—laying down, crying, Holy Cripe. I never want to see any more of that again either.

One funny instant, though, was that we was up on the roof and here come a gang down Mulberry Street—stones and bricks and I don't know, whatever you'd want to call it. So they shot a tear gas shell down at them, hit the pavement, bounced up, hit him across the ass, set his pants on fire, and he took off like a scared rabbit up that hill. Oh, I'll never forget that—hollerin', yellin', screamin', beating his pants on fire, the flames flying off it. Gee, that was funny.

We was deputized, all our electricians were, and we had billies made out of four-aught [4/0] wire, oh, I imagine about sixteen, eighteen inches long. And then, we took and peeled the insulation down; and then, we took the strands and bent them over and made a knob. Then, we had them taped to our wrists so we wouldn't lose them if someone tried to jerk them loose from us; but we never had to use them, because nobody ever got inside. Any time anybody even got their nose inside, they'd get a wop on the hand or something; that was it. They tried to get in, but they didn't get in.

Down on the end of one of the buildings on Champlain Street, there was a door that come directly off the street, two steps down, that went into the service office. They pulled the door off of that, and we heard them coming and had been trying to get up to them if we could. God damn—stuck a hand around with a revolver, and there were five shots fired. Three of them missed us like nobody's business. I got the hell out of there. I didn't go back to that corner for a long time. He didn't hit anybody.

There was nobody killed or hurt on the inside. One man was killed on the outside, but they figure it was a grudge case because nobody fired any bullets from the inside of the building at all. It was all tear gas. But this one man in the crowd was shot in the back. Then somebody threw something. I don't know what it was—it hit a girl on the head, and she swore up and down that somebody threw something from the top floor; but we never did. From what we seen, there was nothing. We patrolled that back and forth, and there wasn't one piece of metal that was ever threw out of them windows.

I could roam around, but the rest of them, they couldn't. They made them stay in their own department. But I could move from one part to the other to see what was going on. Well, they didn't mess very much with the railroad because of the railroad detectives. They were trespassing; chased them out of there.

INTERVIEWER: *Were there many people out there throwing these bricks? Could you tell from inside the plant?*

I'd say there must have been twenty-five or thirty in that lot across the street, maybe more than that; but I didn't look long enough to find out because those god-darned bricks come flying. They was coming at a pretty good rate, too. When it hit a window, it would take a whole sash right out, glass and all.

INTERVIEWER: *The other people who were inside, were they regular employees, like you?*

Regular employees. They was all older employees.

Then, another thing at that time was the eating. We had nothing to eat. They had built a tunnel from one building to the other so that in the snow and sleet and everything you could get parts back and forth instead of going outside. And they could get in the Buckeye Brewery warehouse; and by coming through the one door, they could get into Building Fifteen. So, they brought us all a couple of cigarettes, rolled our own kind of cigarette. Milk was the big run because it seemed to settle their stomach in that tear gas. We run out of milk so god-darn quick it wasn't even funny.

INTERVIEWER: *The city police never came then?*

The city police didn't have nothing to do with it. I don't know why. When they started knocking the firemen off the trucks, then I guess they got scared themselves and didn't show up. I thought those two firemen were killed when I saw them knock them off the truck with a brick. The rest of them came down and took them away, and the truck's sitting there. I thought they'd burn the truck up, but they didn't.

You see the mail order department was on the bottom floor of the building on Champlain Street. They broke the windows in there, and then they threw balls of paper in and tried to set it on fire.

The worst part of it was for my family. I had just moved, and the phone wasn't installed yet. My wife didn't figure out what was the matter. Pretty soon a friend of ours come over, and she didn't have the radio on. He said, "My God, they're having a hell of a time over at the Auto-Lite." She says, "Why?" "Well," he says, "they're having a big hullabaloo over there; they're fighting over there." He says, "There are police; they're throwing tear gas, trying to set the place on fire." My God, my wife almost dropped dead then. I couldn't have phoned her because there was no way of getting the word to her. They let us use the phone, but it was no use to me.

When I got home the next morning, that was something. I had my car parked between the buildings because they allowed me to be among the big electricians over there parking between the buildings. The other parking lot was for the others. Well, my car wasn't damaged; but when it come time to come home, going over those bricks out the gate up Chestnut Street, then up Champlain to LeGrange—nothing but solid bricks. Ruined all four tires; the company paid for it. They paid for all the damaged cars, even the ones that burned up.

FRED C. [WHITEY] HUEBNER

Management in Auto-Lite's time study department. [Mrs. Huebner joined the interview.]

The thing started in the early afternoon. I'm speaking of the blow-off now, the blowing of the lid.

INTERVIEWER: *The guards were inside with the fire hose?*

The fire hose was on. They were not guards. They were employees, management employees, shall we put it that way, because they were not punch press operators, lath operators, or fellas who would sensibly be in the union. You find all different types of people in an incident of this sort. There are some of them who will cower back in the corner and be fearful and stay out of the way, if at all possible. Then, there are a few of those who you might call adventurous souls who were doing what they thought was right. They enjoyed the adventure part of it and the danger part of it—the risk. And so, you find various sorts of people to make up a bunch of this sort.

INTERVIEWER: *So, about half of them were caught inside that night?*

Better than half, but that would be probably a pretty good figure. It's pretty hard to separate inside from outside; because those outside not only didn't have any business there, but they had to see what was going on—the great American curiosity. I'm quite sure that you'll find verification for the fact that there were ten thousand people outside.

Then came the other nonsensical part. I guess we had about a thousand that was bottled in the plant that couldn't get out. There were probably about six or seven hundred women; and this was a little bit of a chore, to arrange the thing so that the women had one section and the men had another section so they wouldn't start fraternizing with each other at a time like that. Rules are down, and everything was free and easy.

INTERVIEWER: *When you were caught inside the plant that night, were you given any special instructions?*

We were told to stay away from firearms as such; bullets, guns, there were none as far as we were concerned. But the tear gas, yes.

INTERVIEWER: *Were there any threats to your family then?*

MRS. HUEBNER: No. We worried about that for a while, but nothing happened.

INTERVIEWER: *You were talking about bringing food and ammunition. Did they have a stockpile of ammunition?*

Yeah. I don't know where it was. There was ammunition available from the police department.

INTERVIEWER: *So they brought it in like that?*

They sneaked it in.

INTERVIEWER: *Didn't you have ammunition in the plant before that?*

We had a certain amount, but we ran out about 11:00 p.m. So, that's when we worried.

INTERVIEWER: *So, you were somewhat prepared for the crowds?*

Oh, yeah. I think that if the union had ever known—or so-called union—had ever known the position we were in for that last hour, from 12:00 a.m. to 1:00 a.m., I don't think we'd have made it. I think you would have had many, many more people that would have died.

I talked to the people who were picketing out in front, and they were all very nice to me. Never gave me an occasion to worry or fuss until the day of the blow-off, until that day when I looked down at my car and the windshield was out and the top was bashed in and everything was, oh, battered up. One of the fellas came up to me, and he said, "Whitey"— which was my nickname—"I want you to know none of our people did that. Those were strangers who came in and who didn't know you, otherwise it wouldn't have happened." I was pretty proud of that. The fact that they were concerned about me a little bit, and I was on the other side of the fence to them.

KATHRYN SCHIEVER_____
Stenotype operator for Auto-Lite management; crossed picket lines and worked during the strikes.
&
MARGARET JACOBS_____
Payroll department worker at Auto-Lite; crossed picket lines and worked during the strikes.

MARGARET: I remember about the beginning of it. We went out to lunch; we took a walk. We saw this little truck that picks up clothing, loaded with bricks. One of the girls said, later in the afternoon, "That little pickup of bricks has been driving around here all afternoon." Going around and around and around. And it was nearly quitting time.

They threw something at our windows, and it looked like you know what. We had a receiving office right near us, and there was a boy that worked in there that we thought was kind of simple-minded. He come dashing in and went right to my phone and called his mother up. He says, "Mother, I won't be home 'til the army gets here." We all laughed and thought it was funny. But we didn't get out.

KATHRYN: We didn't. We was there all night. It was something terrible. Rumors about airplanes going to bomb. We were on the top floor trying to get away from all the tear gas and the fires, burning of the cars and turning them over. It was just terrible. What was so frightening was all the rumors. We didn't know if they were going to set fire to the plant, if they were going to bomb the plant, because they were just like a bunch of animals. There is no other word for it.

Before we got herded up on the fourth floor, we'd hide down behind our desks because they were shooting in there. We were afraid after that they would do something to the elevators. They were just like vicious animals. People that you had seen for years coming out of the office and you'd be surprised to see them helping turn over cars and things like that.

It was almost like a virus. It would change an ordinarily nice, comparatively nice person.

My husband was the director of purchases, and he had a sound-proof closet on the sixth floor; and later, we went up there. That was when they brought in some sandwiches. They were delicious.

MARGARET: Of course they were.

KATHRYN: I never did get a sandwich 'til, it must have been, 1:00 or 2:00 in the morning. Of course, there were a lot of people who were locked in the plant who were sympathetic to the strikers. So they were inside and out. But I have nothing good to say about it.

My husband was the only person that got out of that plant that night. He went through Plant Two and through Fifteen. There was some sort of underground passageway to the brewery he knew about and he got out.

JACK C. LATHROP

Foreman in Department Two at Auto-Lite; crossed picket lines and worked during the strikes.

The strikers brought some man in by the name of Tom Ramsey. He was a radical, and I mean a radical. He come out of, I think, Passaic, New Jersey; and he was their first organizer, but he come from New Jersey—Tom Ramsey. Time after time I'd start to walk up to the corner if I didn't want to go someplace else; they'd drive right up, committee-men, maybe one of the pickets says, "Come on, we'll see that you get home and eat. We'll see that you get back. Nobody will bother you." I got along pretty good with the boys.

I tell ya, I don't know whether anybody has told you this one or not, but the biggest laugh I got out of the thing. It was just before dark, oh, around 4:00 or 5:00 in the afternoon. Champlain Street was being tore up. That was the street in front. They had those old time pavement bricks in there. They had taken them up and broken them in two and put them in trucks and hauled them away. Well, there was an old Ford truck and a colored guy driving it. He had this thing loaded with these half pavement bricks. So, these boys had got to him, fixed him up. Anyhow, he come driving this truck right across the street in front of the Auto-Lite plant. So, this guy is going along, and all at once he gets a flat tire. He thinks she's got a flat tire. He gets out, and he plays around. They took an ice pick and, naturally, he got a flat tire. He looks around, and pretty soon he's got two flat tires; so, he left to go get a garage man to get his tires fixed. Well, he hasn't come back yet.

INTERVIEWER: *What was it like on the inside?*

Well, as far as we were concerned, Whitey Huebner, John Archer, Art Minch, the vice-president, Claude Pound, the production manager, and, oh, a half dozen foremen, were all in the office talking. The thing that was bugging most was when were we going to get something to eat. Well, Mose McCluskey, a retired detective captain, had been given a job in charge of plant protection. But in some way or other, McCluskey maneuvered and a wagon from the Homemade Box Lunch got in between them two buildings.

We were deputized. That badge there is what was given to us for protection.

INTERVIEWER: *[Reads:] Special Deputy Sheriff, Lucas County.*

And that's official—you see right on there: Jack C. Lathrop.

INTERVIEWER: *You had full rights as a deputy sheriff?*

That's right.

INTERVIEWER: *You could make arrests on the property?*

Could if I wanted to, but nobody exercised any option. I didn't carry a pistol half the time. They give me a big .38 about a yard long. It was just too heavy to carry that damn thing around.

Dave Krieger, who was the sheriff, he's the only sheriff that I know of that never got out of here without getting a pocketful. You know what I mean, he was strictly a square and honest guy. Anyhow, he'd been out making the rounds, and it was getting tougher to have law. They were knocking the hell out of things and I don't know what all. He come in the office with Minch, I, Pound, Bill Sifke and a half dozen foremen, Whitey Huebner, and god knows. There must have been a dozen of them, anyhow. Dave said to Minch and Pound, "You better call the governor. I can't help." That was it.

ROBERT A. CAMPBELL
Auto-Lite machinist and MESA member; continued to work during the strikes.

When this thing started, the windows in our shop were individual squares—I'd say ten-inch squares—and they were real tall windows, about ten to twelve feet. And the bricks and debris took all the wood frames right out of the windows so there was nothing left on the windows at all. Our tool boxes were on the benches right along the windows; so, to protect our tool boxes, we knew we had to get them out of there. We had tops from our layout tables, and we were using these as shields to protect us from the flying debris coming in; and we managed to get our tool boxes and put them underneath our benches so they wouldn't get damaged. And they were all wood tool boxes, and it would have ruined them, our own private property. And then, we had some delicate instruments that we wanted to get out of the way, so we got things pretty well under cover then. So, we saved a lot of things that way.

So, this afternoon, things kept getting worse; and the Auto-Lite Council, that was the name of the company union, were using the fire hose at the plant entrance and turning on the pickets. The company had brought cases of tear gas into the plant. They anticipated this trouble. The sheriff wanted us to help put the caps on the tear gas, but I had no part of it. I was young at the time, but I knew enough to not get involved in things like this. They were paying sheriffs and policemen to do these things and not me. The sheriff was there to protect us, and we're not there to help protect ourselves.

The only weapons I seen the pickets have was just clubs. They used anything they could throw, from bricks to bottles to stones. Of course, naturally, there's always many young boys that get overenthusiastic in anything like this. So, this added to the turmoil. The young people in Toledo were going down there and having themselves a lot of fun.

LYNN G. WATERS
Toledo policeman; on patrol at Auto-Lite during the strikes.

INTERVIEWER: *That's when they were burning cars, tipping over cars?*

What would you do in a situation like that?

There isn't too much you can do. Let it burn. If you did too much, you would endanger more lives than you'd help. That's the whole trouble. They didn't actually stop the fire department, but they couldn't do too much good when they got down there. Everybody around it, and you take eighty pounds pressure, you'd do some damage with the fire hose.

INTERVIEWER: *So, the fire department came down there?*

Oh, yes. They sometimes had trouble getting down there, getting the people out of the way, but they never refused to come.

HILDAGARDE & WILLIAM LOCKWOOD_____
Office workers at Auto-Lite; crossed picket lines and worked during the strikes.

WILLIAM: Incidentally, on the day of the lock-in, they were singing, "You won't get out tonight," or something similar.

HILDAGARDE: They let us go in, of course. Every morning they let us go in, but that particular morning the pickets chanted, "You won't get out tonight, you won't get out." We didn't think anything of it.

INTERVIEWER: *There were some sheriff's deputies around down there, I understand?*

WILLIAM: Well, they was deputized but, actually, they were employees of the Auto-Lite, because I knew some of them.

HILDAGARDE: They were deputized?

WILLIAM: Some of them were. These weren't plant guards. I happen to know of at least three of them that were deputized; but they were members of the Auto-Lite Council, I do know that. Well, you take the case of a policeman, he's put on strike duty like that, why there is a lot of faces he recognizes, too. So, I imagine that in a good many instances, they turned their heads. I can still see that truck sitting there. A little pickup.

HILDAGARDE: And to think that we sort of joked about it, not realizing what really would happen. The day this happened, we went on our normal duties. It wasn't anything. Of course, there was discussion in the office about them hiring outsiders, and it was rumored around inside the office, because the personnel office was right next to ours, that the M & M—at that time I didn't know what M & M meant but then I was told that M & M was Merchants and Manufacturers—were bringing in these people from the outside, and we didn't think that was right. That much we knew in the office. We had that through the grapevine. But we had a job to do, the factory was running; we had a payroll to get out. We called it lock-in because we couldn't get out because of the throwing the bricks.

INTERVIEWER: *The people inside were angry, too?*

HILDAGARDE: Well, I don't know so much angry as worried—worried as to whether we were going to get out of there alive.

WILLIAM: In other words, if you corner a rat, he's going to fight before you get ahold of him.

ELIZABETH SZIROTNYAK

Production worker at Auto-Lite; crossed picket lines and worked during the strikes.

INTERVIEWER: *Did more men walk out than women?*

No, because I think there were more women. There were more of us, so it stands to reason there'd be more women that would walk out. So, every day more and more would stay out, you know, and join the strikers, until this day when there was just a handful of us. There weren't too many. Not according to how many worked there.

INTERVIEWER: *The people who were inside, were they mostly from Toledo?*

Oh, definitely. There were very few that were from out of town, unless it was Curtis. You know, these small towns around here, Curtis, Genoa, and Parisburg, just close by. But later on, there was some as far away as Tontonganee or Liberty Center. Now that's better than forty miles from here. But we went in. So then, all day long, well, we didn't work. There was so few of us that went in that we didn't do much work. 'Cause we were watching what was going on outside. And it was terrific. You couldn't run a line without all the operators. And then with the disturbances outside, well, it was impossible. So, we just roamed from one floor to the other. Of course, they wouldn't allow us down on the lower floors because there you could get hit with something through the windows. There was yelling all day. And then they kept it up all night.

They didn't leave us alone all night.

We wouldn't even have attempted to pick up anything to protect ourselves because there were too many of them. There were so many of them out there you wouldn't have stood a chance. We didn't actually lay down on the floor and sleep. I mean, maybe you dozed sitting at the table, at the bench or something. But I couldn't have slept. I know I didn't because you were afraid of what might happen. Because like I said, it kept getting worse and worse until morning. When you saw those cars turned over and burning in the middle of the street, why, you had every reason to be afraid.

ALBERT ABERLING_____
Punch press operator hired into Auto-Lite during the strikes.
&
MARY ABERLING_____
Production worker at Auto-Lite; supported the union and honored the picket lines.

INTERVIEWER: *When you came to work that day, was there any indication that this was going to happen?*

ALBERT: I heard something about it, but I wasn't too sure. Someone was saying that, "You're going to go in there and never come back out. Tonight, you're going to stay in there. You ain't coming back out."

MARY: His sister could have wrung his neck, I'm telling you. She said, "Of all things. He wouldn't work when he was at home, and he had to go in there and scab"—and that's the word.

ALBERT: I wasn't going to take much more of that if it kept on, but then they finally closed it up.

MARY: Well, his other wife made him go in there. Otherwise, he wouldn't have.

ALBERT: Yeah, she worked there, see, and she wanted me to come in there and work, too. So, what are you going to do?

INTERVIEWER: *You were there all through April and May?*

ALBERT: Right up to closing time, right through the riot.

MARY: He was in there that night.

ALBERT: Yeah, I was in there.

MARY: There was a bunch of radicals, and it wasn't the people that worked in there either. The women wouldn't get as radical. They wouldn't start it. We picketed peacefully when I went down there.

ALBERT: Well, it could have been that some of the strikers might have asked them to come over to help to give them support, 'cause they didn't have enough there themselves. Like you said, there was only twelve hundred working there, and half of them went out and other half stayed in.

MARY: Well, like I say, we was the ones to see if they could organize Auto-Lite. We were the guinea pigs, that's what I call it. That's why I imagine the bunch from Detroit come down; to give us a hand in helping to see if they could get a contract.

ALBERT: Well, they must have come from all these other Toledo plants, too.

MARY: Well, it could be.

ALBERT: I'm sure they was all giving a hand. They wanted to get a start here. If they organized the Auto-Lite, why then they could organize all the plants.

You know, some people get nosey and like to look out, and all of a sudden a brick would come through the window.

MARY: Well, that was a bunch of radicals that done that, but his wife's son was over there throwing bricks, breaking the windows. His own son.

ALBERT: Yeah, I saw him throwing rocks at the windows.

INTERVIEWER: *Was he a young guy?*

ALBERT: About fourteen.

INTERVIEWER: *Were there many kids like that, young kids?*

ALBERT AND MARY: Oh, yeah, they was having a lot of fun breaking the windows.

ELIZABETH NYITRAI
Production worker at Auto-Lite; crossed picket lines and worked during the strikes.

Oh, they were yipping it up out there, burning cars and upsetting cars.

They had clubs and, of course, we didn't dare look out of the windows because they were throwing rocks and things through the windows, and you could hear glass breaking all over. So, we got orders to move through the covered bridge into the back buildings. So on the way, we picked up long sticks of solder; they're kind of heavy, long sticks of solder that we use for soldering, and we taped black tape on it to get a good grip on it. And they gave us instructions: "When they come pouring in here, you're to hit them in the head."

10

On the Picket Line

To many men and women on the picket line on Champlain Street, Auto-Lite loomed formidable, for it had dominated their lives many years. Because of its prominence in the parts industry of Toledo, it loomed formidable for Local 18384's organizing efforts as well. The executive shop committee at Auto-Lite carried a heavy burden: the hopes of Auto-Lite workers and of all activists in the Toledo union movement. Consequently, leaders and members of Toledo unions offered advice and support on the picket line. Success in organizing the workers there could mean success in organizing thousands of workers in Toledo and perhaps even elsewhere.

Other organized groups, particularly leftist political organizations, saw an opportunity to increase their influence and prestige by supporting the Auto-Lite workers. These organizations, often lumped together by pickets and others as "Communist," joined the pickets on the line. Fine distinctions between Communists, Socialists, and Musteites seemed irrelevant to strikers, and spokesmen for Auto-Lite labeled all strikers Bolsheviks. Many of our narrators note the presence of outsiders, meaning anyone not working at Auto-Lite when the strike began.

The presence of these outsiders made direction and coordination of the pickets difficult, if not impossible. Each group had its own agenda, its own tactics. The support of these outsiders played a crucial role in the strike, however, for it demonstrated a widespread sympathy for the strikers at Auto-Lite among the workers in Toledo and around the country. Union strategy may have foundered on the sometimes spontaneous, sometimes organized actions of sympathizers; but the presence of these sympathizers made clear to Auto-Lite, the strikebreakers, and the authorities that the company could not remain in production with impunity.

The leaders of the Auto-Lite unit of Local 18384 and the Auto-Lite workers who supported them knew full well when the crisis in the strike had come. Sorely tested during five weeks of organizing and picketing, their solidarity had held; but Auto-Lite remained in production. The injunction temporarily reduced the effectiveness of the picket line; but mass picketing in violation of the injunction, followed by mass arrests by Sheriff Krieger, renewed interest in the struggle.

Since the county jail could not handle the hundreds of pickets arrested, they were released soon after booking. This attempt at intimidation only demonstrated the weakness of the authorities in the face of worker solidarity, and the picket lines grew even larger and more assertive. But intimidation by the courts and the sheriff were not the only worries strikers faced. Should the strike fail, the leaders certainly—and their supporters probably—would lose their jobs. Where could a union supporter in Toledo then find another? Only their loyalty to each other and their determination stood between them and disaster. The workers' determination still reverberates through our narrators' tales.

On the evening of May 23, the spontaneous support of strikers and sympathizers swelled behind the siege. For sixteen hours, thousands of men and women roamed the street in front of the factory, pelting it with stones and bricks and returning into the factory the tear gas canisters and shells fired at them. Frustration, anger, and the outrage of an entire community of workers found their focus on the Auto-Lite factory on Champlain Street.

FRANK GRZELAK

Executive committee member of Local 18384 who was employed at Willys-Overland.

INTERVIEWER: *Did you work for the Auto-Lite?*

No, I was on the executive committee of Local 18384 at the time, and I was on the picket line every day.

INTERVIEWER: *Could you tell us a little bit about the organization of Local 18384?*

The organization largely was at Willys-Overland at the time. That was the most powerful part of the organization of Local 18384. And I was an employee of Willys-Overland at the time. And the Auto-Lite had a company union called like the Auto-Lite Council. The employees paid twenty-five cents a month dues; and they had club rooms in the plant, and they had their meals in the plant, and the officers, they were mostly all company people. When Local 18384 started organizing, the trouble really started because the people were joining Local 18384 instead of the company union; and Local 18384 was getting stronger and stronger all the time. Willys-Overland was the backbone of the organization when they were first organizing, and they were organizing Electric Auto-Lite and Spicer-Dana Corporation and other smaller plants in town.

INTERVIEWER: *Did you enjoy that kind of work?*

Oh, at the time I did. I was young and full of pep, and I was active and I was union-minded. Then, too, organization was different from what it is today; because at that time, why, you had your heart in it, see, to get things organized and get the working people to get better working ideas and better wages. We went out there to do the work, and wages was the last thing we thought of for ourselves.

INTERVIEWER: *How was it decided who would picket?*

We had so many volunteers who would go out on the picket lines. They had more pickets than they needed. That was one of the main strikes in the city of Toledo at that time, and they had pickets from all the different plants in Toledo.

INTERVIEWER: *Did that jeopardize your job in any way?*

No.

INTERVIEWER: *You got, like, a leave of absence?*

No, at that time you were working two or three days a week; you wasn't working full time, and there was a lot of people unemployed, on WPA, and there was a lot of people that were not working at the time, laid off, so they were out on the picket lines. There was no problem then getting pickets because there was a lot of idle people, and everybody was pitching in.

INTERVIEWER: *What did your family think?*

My wife was kind of peeved at me being gone every day, but that was part of my job.

INTERVIEWER: *How did the very first officers get in, before the union was really going?*

There wasn't no officers at the time; there were just organizers. You see, maybe there was a half a dozen people passing out these application forms and talking to the people about the union, explaining to them about what the union can do for them.

INTERVIEWER: *Would the AFL send organizers, or were they local people who did the first organizing?*

Usually people in the plant who wanted a union were the organizers. They would talk to different people and ask them to sign applications for the union. You got the union in the plant first, the representation of the union; and then you'd call a meeting for all the members, and then the officers would be elected. And then you'd have election of constitution and by-laws committee and stuff like that. You'd have your own by-laws and constitution that you would go by, your rules and regulations.

INTERVIEWER: *Who would make decisions? Would just anybody be able to make suggestions, or would the leadership decide things?*

Anybody from the floor could make a suggestion; and then the body would vote on it and, if the body would accept it, that would be it. There was no certain group of people or certain person that could make any by-laws or anything like that. The people would present certain rules, regulations; and the body would vote on it, and whatever the body would accept, that was it. The majority would rule.

INTERVIEWER: *On May 23, could any strikebreakers get past the pickets?*

Everything was closed down then tight—the plant was. At times you had a couple thousand pickets. You had a lot of spectators out there just watching what's going on. Every once in a while somebody would get an urge to pick up a rock or something and throw it at the building.

INTERVIEWER: *Did you throw many rocks?*

Well, I did some, not too many, though. The people on the outside thought those inside were foolish for staying in, because they knew that they couldn't stay in for very long and keep on going. And they stopped the food trucks from going in. Then it got so that they were begging to get out. The women were a part of the picket line same as the men.

INTERVIEWER: *They participated in the violence, too?*

Oh, yeah, sure. Yeah, the women weren't any better than the men. They fought just as hard, yeah, oh, you bet.

INTERVIEWER: *The way you're smiling it seems like you have some memories.*

Oh, they did. The women were—they weren't any better than the men. They were out for the same purpose, and they fought just as hard.

I was supposed to have my tonsils taken out on a Friday morning, and Thursday afternoon all this tear gas was going on—and I was right in the midst of it. I went to the doctor Friday morning, and I never told him anything about that tear gas and I was full of it. So, in his office he was taking out my tonsils, and the ether wouldn't mix with the tear gas, and I got sicker than heck. I guess my heart stopped a couple of times. He had a heck of a time with me. He thought I was drinking, see, but it wasn't drinking—it was that tear gas.

INTERVIEWER: *How did it feel, that tear gas?*

It choked you up, made you sick to your stomach, and your eyes water and swell up. But the throat was terrible, you know, burning sensation.

At that time, there were a lot of people who were Communist minded, and we wouldn't allow any of them on the picket lines. If we found out anybody like that, they'd be told to get off and stay off and stay away. They didn't want any Communist-oriented people mixed up in anything like that.

INTERVIEWER: *Was that because they were talking about revolution?*

Right. Right. Communists.

INTERVIEWER: *Were they serious organizers, Communists?*

Oh, yes.

INTERVIEWER: *Were they pro-union?*

They always acted like they were 100 percent for the union, but their main purpose was organization for Communist purposes. That's why the United Auto Workers here, Local 18384, wouldn't have nothing to do with them at all. If they found out any member of the union or any officer belonged or was even close to some Communist organization, why, they would get rid of them in a hurry.

INTERVIEWER: *What did you feel about the National Guard coming?*

I just couldn't do anything about it. That was it. For a couple of days they fought, but it was too much for the pickets. The settlement was pretty good. The employees were pretty well pleased. They got the representation, rights, and wages and they got cafeterias in the plants that they wanted. It was Buddy's at the time. That's Gladieux now. It was Buddy's Box Lunch.

The strike usually, in them days, was not for what you could get now. It was for the future generations. That was the thought of the people at that time, you know. Many people used to say, "Well, you lose so much time, you'll never gain back what you've lost." Their thought behind the strike was that it wasn't what they're gaining but what they are gaining for the future generation. They was going to have better working conditions. You can see for yourself today the wonderful working conditions you have. Look at the pensions you get today. People retire from the factory; they get five, six hundred dollars a month. You know that's a pretty nice pension. And medical benefits, hospitalization, vacations, working conditions, stuff like that, see.

JOHN [J. J.] JANKOWSKI
Punch press operator in Department Two at Auto-Lite; union organizer.

We were walking out of Claude Pound's office April 13, on a Friday afternoon, all of us guys on the committee at that time. Little Rigby, he was a small guy, was ahead, walking with Minch, side by side. We were walking behind him. And the other negotiators were behind us, too, walking down the center aisle to the stairway to go out. And Rigby said, "Minch, you bought yourself a fight," he says. "We're going to fight this to the last man. We're going to hold out to the last man. You guys just bought yourself a big loss." And Minch sort of like laughed about it, see, so that's the last word that was said to him.

When the strike hit on April 13, 1934, well, we had about two, three hundred people out of possibly about a thousand. But your outside sympathizers were walking the picket line. We were recognized by the union, by William Green of the AFL. There was no funds or nothing given to us.

We were walking the picket line, and things got a little rougher. See, scabs was hired in there while we was out. Some workers stayed in, and we'd go to their homes and say, "Look, stay out of the plant because you're just hurting yourself." Some of them would listen to us. Their wives would tell them, "Don't go in there. You might get hurt." Some guys would stay in there, and they'd go to work; and they'd join the Auto-Lite Council while we was out on the picket line. I think the "red apple" boys were the reason there was a council, because they didn't want no union because the foreman favored them.

Chester Dombrowski was at the Auto-Lite. He worked in my department. He was one of the boys that stuck with it. He went out in 1934. Yeah, he was one of the guys. I think his seniority started about 1930 or something like that.

I remember like today. During the strike, we used to sit on his front porch and talk, you know, in the evening and afternoon. We couldn't be there twenty-four hours a day; we had certain times. We'd take turns. And Chester Dombrowski was on the picket line. A lot of these guys that was out there sympathizing with us, they were ex-Auto-Lite workers, because they were canned one way or the other.

In April when we went out, women were more active in some spots than the men were. Oh yeah. I can't take that away from the women, boy. They were really in there with both feet. They were vicious, because a police officer or sheriff couldn't do nothing to them. They'd scratch his eyes out—that's the way they were. They helped a lot with it in their own way. And when it come to signing up membership, hell, I'd go through with the book to get some members. Sneak out there. They'd take the book out of my hands, go over on rest or something, come back, give me ten, fifteen members. Ten, fifteen dollars. They were active. They didn't give a damn about the foreman. In other words, they got awful when they knew they had a backing, see. Prior to that, they were all quiet and just looking over their shoulder and watching.

INTERVIEWER: *They were on the picket lines right away, Friday, April 13?*

Right after dinner. Everybody on the picket lines; we had signs and everything made. The beginners was on there, and they stayed right with it. And the negotiators were going back and forth to the management whenever they got a chance. But they would get bogged down; and they started horsing around because they were getting these guys to come in and scab. So, then they could dock you a little bit, and they'd say, "We quit negotiating," see. So, the union kept it going, going, going.

All of a sudden, they got riled up. Started fights in front of the gates, started shooting tear gas. And when you think about it years back, it wasn't the strikers themselves. A lot of them strikers were home, didn't want to go on the picket line. It was the sympathizers that was doing all the damage and the raising hell. The few leadership was there, too. A lot of the wives of the leadership were there, too. You know what I mean, they were helping talk to the women and all that.

INTERVIEWER: *There wasn't any difference about whether you were German or Irish or Polish as to who would be on strike?*

No, no, no, there was none of that.

INTERVIEWER: *And the guys who went on the council—there were Poles and Germans?*

Oh, sure, there were a lot of Poles. We went to their doors, slapped a couple of them around because they were going to work. In one case, I remember, we went and we slapped a guy in the face in front of his house. And his wife come out there and she says, "What's this all about?" And we told her. She slapped him for us. She says, "I told him he's not supposed to go there." And things like that happened. But later on, the guy was one of the best buddies. Drink beer and everything. You'd go to his party, he'd come to ours, good friends after that. But some of them had to be knocked in the head to have the sense.

A lot of them would go to one another and tell them to go in there and go to work. Yeah, there were a few. In the Polish families, too. They'd say, "Well don't be a damn fool. I'm with Department Two, I'm sticking with them guys." Well, this sister of mine been working in Department Seventeen or Nineteen. She'd be in there scabbing. Before the lock-in, when they were locked in there, she'd say, "Well, I'm not going in there, they're getting too rough around here." And they wouldn't go in until they were cooled off. But after the fight was over, they were the first ones to join, because they didn't want to be left out in the rain.

INTERVIEWER: *Did you feel funny about that?*

You got used to it after a bit. You know what I mean. From the beginning you feel bitter. You'd see one of the guys that worked in there, he's still working. He was under the Auto-Lite Council. He was in shakey business. And 90 percent of them guys that they kept in there to scab on us, they didn't know how to run a press. They were just dummies at it. They were there just to put themselves in there for the reason to break the strike. But as far as experience running the machines and stuff, they didn't have it.

Most of the experienced workers were all on the street, boys that knew how to set them dies. The trick in a pressroom is the diesetter. If he sets the machine right, it's going to make the right parts. He puts them in backwards, turns them around—breaks them, breaks the punches, don't put oil on it or something. There's lots of things to each different job. And if you don't know how to operate, you're just stuck. Some of these guys would come in, maybe run a plow someplace out in the country. They'd work a couple of days in the winter months at the Auto-Lite. So, they'd get canned—so, they'd come back. They called them, "Hey, come back." Weeks on the job, make a few extra bucks. Some scabs come from the South. A lot of them come from the South. And at that time, there was no black ones in the Auto-Lite at all.

There were police around, but some of the policemen—bless their souls that are alive yet today—they themselves was in sympathy with the strikers. Anybody that you talk to, a businessman, we'd go down LaGrange Street, down Adams, down any street to get collections to help the strikers at Auto-Lite. We'd come back with buckets full of money, because everybody was in sympathy in them days, see. They were. Toledo was going wild in union recognition.

You see, the police department didn't give the Auto-Lite too much cooperation. They'd see a picket do something wrong, they'd turn their head. See what I mean? The police towards the end didn't have no part of it. Well, maybe they were ordered, but they didn't act like they should live up to their orders.

So, the company was putting pressure on some place. So, they got ahold of this Krieger. He was the deputy sheriff in Lucas County at that time. They notified him, and he come out there with special deputies, trying to get us off the picket line.

His deputies, they were in plain clothes. You didn't know who they were. A couple of them had badges. But the rest of them were walking around, watching what the pickets were doing. In the meantime, reporting what's going on, what's going to happen. You could spot them guys real easy.

INTERVIEWER: *They were outside of the plant?*

Oh, yeah, outside. There was nobody but scabs in the plants, but they wasn't inside the plant to watch them. They were watching us outside, what we're going to plan to do when they're ready to come out—like a spy system. They were planted in there. But it didn't last any too long; because when the militia come in, Krieger and all them police and all them were told to stay the hell away from there.

Well, in the meantime, quite a few of us during the period were arrested by Sheriff Krieger, put in the county jail for a couple of hours. They didn't want us in jail. Well, we wrecked the county jail. Because we wrecked the toilets and everything. You lock up one hundred fifty, two hundred men in a jail like that with jigsaw puzzles they had over there and all that stuff. They threw it in the toilet, kicked over the bowl, water leaking all over. So, the sheriff says, "Oh, hell, I don't want them in here no more." Well, we were arrested a couple of times.

INTERVIEWER: *There was an injunction at one point, I recall, prohibiting picketing.*

Yeah, well, we ignored that. The sheriff served that injunction, and we run the sheriff off the picket line. We didn't pay no attention to it. We were called into court. Us guys was in court; the others were picketing.

What did we care? We were in and out of court. We walked in there in answer to that injunction. Judge said, "Get out of here." He didn't want no part of us. (Laugh.) In other words, that crowd was uneasy. They would have tore up the courthouse; they were just looking for something. What is he going to tell us not to picket? We didn't pay any attention to anybody.

What started the worst thing of all was one of them scabs from the fourth floor threw a piece of steel—we called it a cold piece—that was inside of a generator in a coil, dropped it, and hit a woman on the head. Right on the side of the head. Cut her head open while she was on the picket line. That's what started it. Blood started streaming down her head. All them people, all them women around there, they were just screaming like mad. Boy, that was—I wouldn't want to be guilty of anything like that, because they were ready to tear them screens down to get into that building and get that person who threw that down. So, that's when that war started.

The sheriff brought tear gas and everything; it was just flying around there. Well then, you can imagine a riot like that; all of Toledo started gathering around from all these other factories. Especially these people from Spicer's and Willys-Overland at that time. They all come to see the picture, to see the scenery. Some of them were unemployed; they were laid off. They come over. Well, that's where you got your help, your sympathy—from these people that didn't even think of a union; they'd come over.

Now, them flower beds in front of these homes across the street from the Auto-Lite have brick in them. They'd sort of make a little fence out of them. Then kids, seventeen, sixteen, fifteen years old, breaking them up and throwing them at the windows. And when we got in there, in Auto-Lite, up come the Communist boys; they come in to help. They rented a private home couple of doors down the street, across the street from the plant. They made signs, picket signs. "Hang Miniger, Hang Minch." You know how they produced that stuff.

Well, they asked us to be members of their club. Well, some of us guys was anxious to stay together. You see, like unity you stay together, divided you fall. So, we figured we'd join.

One day, it was about five or six of us was sort of like the leadership, they asked us to come to their meeting on Jefferson Avenue. They had a private home was converted out of an apartment home to a meeting. And at that time, Spain was fighting that revolutionary war, Loyalists and the Republicans. Republicans they called themselves. The Loyalists was the Communist party.

So, this Selander and Pollack were the two guys that was the head of that outfit asked us to come to their meeting, over on Jefferson Avenue. So, about ten, fifteen of us went over there. Meanwhile, Auto-Lite was on picket, see. We was still picketing, come over there. And we went over there; and we were all members, see, because we joined in that private home when they was getting members. So, we all joined. It cost us fifty cents. And not a dollar, but fifty cents, so we joined. If we had to borrow a quarter from somebody else to join, we did. We had that meeting over on Jefferson Avenue one evening. The strategy was, approximately, they wanted to burn the place down. I said, I want to go back to work over there if I possibly can. What the hell am I going to listen to them two guys on the roster up there preaching.

They give us ideas. They organized a group of men, their own group, I guess. They took electric bulbs, cap off, and filled them up with some kind of an acid or something and put a cork in there. Then they'd go along the building and throw them inside the plant. That's supposed to eat up steel and everything—dangerous to human beings. Well, they were doing that.

But before we adjourned that meeting, he says, "Well, uh, gentlemen and ladies" (there was a few women there on the picket line), he says, "we'd like to have you people—we're going to pass the hat around to help the Loyalists in Spain, their air corps over there fighting the capitalists over there in Spain." So, a Catholic like myself, and there was four or five of them sitting alongside of me, they was worse

Catholics than I was. Well, he said, "That son-of-a-bitch is a goddamn Commie! What the hell are you talking? What, help the Loyalists?" Alex Donachevsky, I remember like today. He got up, he had this little cardboard to get into the meetings. He pulled that card out of his pocket and he shouted, "You can stick this up your. . . ," you know what I mean, and he threw that card out. And everybody around him—Bill Collins, Rigby, me, all of us, standing right behind Alex. When he shoved that card, he bumped my face right there on the side. We threw the card right out, we walked out. We didn't want nothing to do with them at all. We didn't want no part of Communists because they were anti-religion. You know that. Especially the Polish speaking was religious as hell at that time.

So, we got back on the picket line. But they wouldn't give up. They still kept a-coming. Helping here and there. And when that big riot started, they were the ones that pushed the people. And I'm standing against the building, protecting myself against the tear gas. I remember like today. They were pushing people: "Grab that chair, grab that watchman, grab him by the head. Pull his hair, girls. Grab him, grab him." And when that big fight started, I looked over at the big advertising signs. They were sitting on top of the signs there watching—the two agitators, Pollack and Selander, they were sitting up there watching the show. While these people here were all lit up, fighting the guards and everything.

INTERVIEWER: *Were you down there with the tear gas?*

Oh, yeah, all the way through. Had to be there to see what's going on because, in fact, we were responsible to begin with. And in the meantime, you had to see how it's going to come off, what you can do to try to stop it. Because right at that time, when the people was really getting out of line, at that time the company give Charlie Rigby a phone call that they're ready to negotiate. And we couldn't get these people away from there. After the militia hauled the people out, they were still noisy.

People get riled up so bad. What you gonna tell a kid off the street over there? "Don't do it anymore, now. We're all done." He might think you're a company stooge, and he'd throw a brick at you. See what I mean?

They burned the cars that were parked. See, the ones that were parked in them lots that were burned, there were no humans in there at all, not a soul in there. They were inside the plant working.

After it got dark, they burned them and turned them over and everything. They ruined a lot of them in the lot next to it, too. They took a concrete cement block. Stand on the goddamned roof of the car and throw it right on the hood, cave it right in. Bang everything all up. They ruined a lot. That's what I mean. Now each one of them cars and everything, Auto-Lite was responsible for. They had to pay these people after the strike.

They were all beat up in that strike, the company was. Because all of these other manufacturers around here, I think they were saying to Auto-Lite, "Settle, settle." And Auto-Lite figured they were going to take the fight on themselves. And that's the reason why they went through their capital, money they had on hand, to fight it. And they got a pretty bad beating. So, that's why they merged with Moto-Meter after they called us back into work, started settling it. So, now they got money; they were in the hands of receivers, damn near.

When the strike broke out, Virgil Gladieux had a beer joint on the corner there. His dad put him in the business. He was giving us coffee and doughnuts in the morning for nothing. The pickets were getting lunch along then and hot dogs and stuff like that. Meantime, that company called him when the scabs were locked in. "Hey, how about you coming in, giving lunches to these people that's inside?" Gladieux turned them down, him and his brother, Nelson. They turned them down, nothing doing.

Homemade had a concession in there, too, with a wagon in there. They volunteered to give the scabs the food they wanted. Once the strike ended, anybody buy from Homemade, they'd push that sandwich down his throat. They'd crowd right around him, and guys would watch. Them poor vendors was going through that for a long time without selling a thing, because one that would want to buy was scared. Only a few of them that did buy was Auto-Lite Council, but the vendor never came close. They dumped the wagon over for him. Oh, yeah, they were vicious against him, because they knew he was feeding them scabs in there when they were trying to get them out of the plant.

INTERVIEWER: *Did the fire department come out?*

The fire department come out, and we let them in. We wouldn't bother them. But the minute they left, the guys were ordered by our chairman, Rigby, like I said, "Listen, whoever is building these goddamned fires, better cut it out. We want to go back in to work someday." He sort of calmed that down, Rigby did.

They had grates on the window. Them people pulled them off. They hooked on a hook with an automobile bumper and a chain and pulled.

Yeah, we were all over, mixed up here and there. Everywhere there was excitement, we're there. Lots of times you'd stay home, get filled up with that fumes from gas and sleep for a couple of days. But I mean you'd go back and forth. You couldn't be everywhere at the same time. It was pretty tough. But sometimes you'd report there were hours during the night that were quiet. "Oh, last night," he says, "I nailed a guy coming out with a car. I run a brick right through his windshield. I don't know if I hurt him or not, but he skidded awhile. But he skipped anyway." Things like that they'd report to you next morning. We were captains. See, I was on the committee. We had captains.

Then we had some of these guys that were militant. We didn't care whether they were a captain or they wasn't; just so they was there to help in, that's all we cared about. Then later on, that Pollack and Selander got into the act, which we didn't know. Them birds were really fighters. Know what I mean? They were paid, I guess, by that outfit, that Communist outfit. But they went out there, and they really led the people into everything. Them people, like some of them women, them guys that didn't know much about personnel of that type, they'd walk in right behind them and supported them. Once they'd started the thing a-going, they'd sneak out and let you do the battling. That's how they operated. Oh, I seen that act so many times.

JOHN SZYMANSKI

Auto mechanic, self-employed during the strikes; later, Auto-Lite machinist and union supporter.

When that strike started over there, I felt so sorry for those people. That strike was really brutal. The company had these goons running amongst these people, beating them, throwing rocks at them. Those who were in the building when the pickets were in the street would throw items at them—generators—any parts of those, and they had all kinds of stuff in their hand to throw at you. Actually, they antagonized the people. People amongst the strikers were antagonizing them, standing back there, these rabblerousers like you got today. They will sit back and say, "Get in there. Do this, do that." That's working you up to a frenzy, where you could almost tear that building apart brick by brick.

You see, in February it was tough; it was cold and you were, well, say, throwing snowballs. In April, in spring, it was rainy; that's still bad weather. But, boy, when the sun starts shining, they really had to make up their mind one way or another because, brother, them guys would be out there in that sunshine. They'd stay all day and all night, you might say. It was warm. For a company to let a group of people go on strike in the summertime would be a dumb thing to do. If you're going to strike, get them to go move in the wintertime, in the fall, when it's bad weather, winter or spring when it's raining, because a human being can't take it. But he sure can take a lot of sunshine. All he had to do is find a little shade and, gosh, he can stand there all day and talk and, as far as that goes, and carry a banner around.

ALBERT ABERLING_____
Punch press operator hired into Auto-Lite during the strike.
&
MARY ABERLING_____
Production worker at Auto-Lite; supported the union and honored the picket lines.

MARY: The committee there, like Rigby and that, would tell so many to get on the picket line and be peaceful. They'd say we could talk to them and razz them but to be peaceful, don't touch them. We'd go down there in the morning, we'd be down there when they was going in and be down there at night when they was coming out. You see, they said, "Just razz them and ask them maybe in a nice way to stay out, but," they said, "don't touch them in any way."

ALBERT: I was upstairs in Department Sixteen.

MARY: He moved into the department that I had walked out of.

ALBERT: Used to have a driver come after us to take us to work in the mornings, some mornings. See, I lived about three and a half blocks away from the Auto-Lite; and the driver used to come pick us up there, and he'd have the .45 revolver setting aside him on the seat in case something happened. He was a company man. He used to go around and pick up the different people. Some was brave enough to walk down the street. I walked down the street quite a few mornings but, I don't know, it was taking an awful chance. Before you got there, even a block away, the pickets was always after you right there. See, they'd be in back of you, and you don't know when somebody was going to hit you. I was one of the lucky ones and didn't get it.

INTERVIEWER: *There were unlucky ones?*

Well, if you didn't say nothing, why, they wouldn't bother you. But if you start arguing with them, naturally something was going to happen. I wouldn't say anything. Then, I told them I'm not walking in no more; you'd better come and pick me up. And that's what they did then.

MARY: Jobs were hard to get at that time, and they figured they wasn't doing any harm by going in, you know. Never thinking, 'cause unions were unheard of really, and they figured they were going in to get a job and would be working, and that would be the end of it. Sometimes you couldn't blame a man for going and getting a job working. Had they known it was going to cause all the trouble, they probably wouldn't have went in. We tried to talk to them to tell them we were trying to get better working conditions, maybe a little more money, but it went in one ear and out the other.

TED SUSKA
Auto-Lite production worker and early union supporter.

No, there was only about ten of us when we first went out. Then, some guys would come in one day and go out, go back in the next day.

INTERVIEWER: *How many were in the department?*

Oh, I'd say a couple hundred with the automatics. Some of those fellas never did go out. They stayed in all the time, and they never lived that down either after that. It was hard to live with, but I never carried no grudge. I did for a while, but what are you going to do? You can't be mad at everybody for life.

When the strike started in April 1934, just a few of us belonged. We had been going maybe five or six weeks and nothing doing. It looked pretty bad for us, you know. I didn't think we'd win this strike. Things began to get a little tough with the strikebreakers. When they come in, we started to kick them around a little bit—kick them in the shins and stuff like that, you know—because we were getting desperate. It would have been our jobs. I had a family and two children. Had to pay the mortgage and stuff like that.

INTERVIEWER: *You were afraid you were going to lose the strike for a while?*

Well, it didn't look too good because they were hiring new people. They weren't getting no production or anything. When we come back in, they had stuff piled up that we had to go over and redo; but they could get enough to make it miserable, to make you believe that they were doing good. You can't blame the companies. They're out for their interests, and the worker was out for the interest of the worker.

INTERVIEWER: *Were there any planning meetings during the strike?*

Oh, yes, we used to hold meetings pretty nearly every week to see how the strike was going along. It wasn't going too good, don't let anybody kid you, because it didn't start until the National Guard come in. Then they started negotiating and quit hiring.

INTERVIEWER: *Were there long hours on the picket lines?*

Well, you had to be there most of the time. It got so bad at last, well, we run out of money. I didn't even have carfare. So, we had to walk down from here.

CHESTER DOMBROWSKI_____
Punch press operator in Department Two at Auto-Lite; union organizer. [His wife, Elizabeth, joined the interview.]

In the second strike, the big strike, we all stuck together. They tried to break us real bad; boy, I tell you, they tried to break us bad. But friends would help. Right from work at Spicer, Tony Quanter would come out and picket. While they were working up there, we were on strike and they knew it. One would help the other—people stuck together then. I mean when we first got organized. See, if one company walked out and another had trouble, they would stick. Nobody would cross the picket lines. We had unions. If we didn't stick—oh man—if we weren't stickers, you wouldn't have this.

We tried to explain to the people that were taking our jobs, that went in to work. We called them scabs. Many times I was there for twenty-four hours. I had picket duty to do, and others had picket duty to do—and I mean everybody had to take a crack at it. Then they got an injunction against the union. So, when they got an injunction against the union, the leader says, "Walk right across the whole side-walk, three or four across." There was quite a few people there. I think there was twelve hundred of us at the time. We just take the whole walk up, and we just keep walking back and forth, picketing.

And these people that were going to work—they had lead pipes, iron pipes, every which way, I mean some weapon that in case of something. A lot of times we'd take that stuff away from them. I mean, we'd take care of it, let's put it that way.

The sheriff come in there, and he fired tear gas on Chestnut Hill and Champlain. That did it. Everybody was crying but, boy, everybody was fighting. They had their duty, I imagine. I mean, I've got to put it that way because they were told to do that. I was in military service, too; and if you was told to do something and you refuse to do it, you know what would happen. We didn't like a lot of things they did, but they were told to do it. I mean, you've got to be broad-minded there, you know.

I remember going there early in the morning, and I stood across the street; and these guys were all parading down, back and forth, and there was hundreds of pickets. There was plenty there. Some of the guys I knew said, "Come on over, Chet." I made one round, and I was in the pie wagon. I was in the county jail. Of course, they didn't do anything, but everybody went there. The county jail was so full with women and men, with the employees, that they had to let us out anyway. They couldn't feed us, they couldn't hold us, they couldn't do a thing with us. There was so many. The patrol wagon and the police were standing there, and they just said, "Get in the wagon." So, we piled in, and they took you out there to the county jail and that was it.

ELIZABETH: Here I come from work—I was working at the Boss Glove at the time, and we were about to organize—I looked at the headlines, and here was my husband on the front page—smiling, bright as day. I thought, what, I'm working and he's in jail? Then, I happened to think, should I start it? There was a German girl with me from another department, and I said, Elizabeth, how about starting this place and get started and organize?

CARL LECK

Stockroom worker at Auto-Lite and union supporter. [His sister, Marie Rosselit, joined the interview.]

CARL: In fact, I had a cousin who was working in the planning department there. He came out here after [my brother] Barney and I were on strike the second time, and he talked like hell, "Oh, you'll never get your job back. For god's sake, go back to work." He was salary help.

But my landlord right now, he's an old railroader—Earl Welch across the street—and a few more when we were on strike used to tell, "Carl, you're out on strike. If you ever go back, I'll kick your ass."

MARIE: This is a union neighborhood, you better believe.

INTERVIEWER: *Well, so you were quite successful in recruiting people that had been working there for a while?*

CARL: Yes, we were. The new people, no. They knew what they were hired in for, that they were going to stay.

There was no negotiations. You're out on strike, you're on the picket line; forget about it. They got enough people in to keep the plant running, and that's the way it drifted along until summertime, until this violence started.

INTERVIEWER: *There was no attempt to talk with you?*

No, no way.

INTERVIEWER: *Who was handling the organization for the strike?*

Well, that would be more or less our executive committee, that would be Stucker, Ginny Bshara, Rigby. There was something like six hundred fifty of us put down in the county jail, and we almost tore the place apart. So, they decided to try us. There is a tunnel from the county jail over to the courthouse. So, they took the six hundred of us over to the court-house. I think it was Judge Stuart, he has these cops out there, he calls the name—six of them. "I'm going to call these six in and try them." And here's six hundred of us jammed in the courthouse and probably five thousand outside of the courthouse, all around the courthouse. I don't know who passed the word, but the word was passed. So, a cop would come out, read these names; and every cop that come out, the whole gang would fold their arms and just walk him right into the courtroom—push him right into the doorway. When you try us, you try us all. So, that went on for two hours. Finally, they tried all of us at one time; dismissed the charges. What else could they do?

MARY ABERLING_____
Production worker at Auto-Lite; supported the union and honored the picket lines.

INTERVIEWER: *When do you remember them first talking about a union in the plant?*

I didn't pay much attention to it. They just told us that they were getting ready to organize and did I want to join; and I said, well, yeah, because the rest of them did, and I said I might as well, too. So, and then they set this date to walk out and not go into work, and that was it.

INTERVIEWER: *Who talked about unions?*

There was just some of the girls that got involved in it, and they'd come around and ask us if we'd join. They were from within the plant.

INTERVIEWER: *Why did you join the union?*

Well, because they was supposed to get us better working conditions. I figured, well, what else could you do, either join them or—I don't know. I thought that as long as they could get us better working conditions, that would be a lot. Because, you know, they had a lot of these sweatshops around. I done my work all the time, so it didn't make no difference to me; but I thought the rest of them are joining, so I'd join, too.

INTERVIEWER: *You went out on April 13 with the rest of them. Did you start on the picket lines right away?*

Well, they'd tell us when. We'd take turns on picket lines, so I'd take my turn and go back home, 'cause I lived right there. About once a week or twice a week I go over and see what was going on.

INTERVIEWER: *Were there any new ones coming in?*

Yeah, they hired new ones in our replacement.

INTERVIEWER: *How did you feel about that?*

Not too good. I figured we were trying to do the right thing, and then they go in there and take our job. So, how would you feel? It doesn't make you feel too good.

INTERVIEWER: *Did they ask you to go when they were violating the injunction?*

No, I didn't go then. I figured I don't want to be picked up and hauled down to jail, 'cause they picked them up left and right. They had the paddy wagon down there and filled it up and took them down. I don't like strikes myself, anyway, because you're out of work so long, and you don't know whether you gain anything by it or not. Of course, at that time, they was just starting organizing; it was rough.

Jobs wasn't to be had. That's all there is to it. I really hated to go out because I needed the job, but then I figured I'm not going in there and get myself in trouble. You don't know what could happen, but I wouldn't take that chance. I'd rather be on the outside than inside.

Later on, the sheriff was there when they had that riot that night. That was a night of nights, I'm telling you. What started that was, I think they was out there picketing, and somebody threw something out of the window and hit one of the girls—hit one of the pickets on the head—and cut her head open; and that's what started the rioting that night. Then they threw bricks and all that. Oh, that was a night. They killed every canary around that neighborhood.

INTERVIEWER: *Every canary?*

Every canary. Every bird, you know. They had tear gas. They were throwing it.

MARGARET BYRD
Wife of the late Lester Byrd, a union organizer at Auto-Lite.

There was a group that was active, you know, for the union. There were probably twenty-five or so, and then they were bunched off. And one man would have ten men under him, and he'd tell them what to do. It was very well organized, the strike. The Auto-Lite was a big place. My husband was the only captain, but he had these co-captains and he'd tell them. Each co-captain had ten men, and he'd tell them what they wanted done; so, nobody got in or out of the Auto-Lite after it was organized. They got very little help from anybody, very little help. They had to do everything themselves.

INTERVIEWER: *Except people would come to the picket line to help support them?*

Yes, that there is about all the help they got. Of course, everybody was in the same shape I was. They didn't have money to do anything else. We had a grocer we had went to and he said, "Well, if you didn't go out on the strike, why, you wouldn't need food." That's what this grocer told us years ago.

People from the city, the workers, and a lot of people that had to quit their jobs—like retired—they couldn't work anymore. They would come down and walk the picket lines. They had one of the biggest picket lines known. There was probably hundreds of people there all the time. You see it was workers. And it was the people in the city of

Toledo that had worked and didn't get fair play. They should have had more money, and they were all in sympathy with the strikers.

I know we suffered terrible; and I think anyone that was in the Auto-Lite strike suffered terrible, especially those that had a family. I know people that would only eat one meal a day. Sometimes they didn't have enough at that one meal. Clothes was out of the picture, and shoes. Of course, I was awful glad when the summer come on because I didn't have to buy shoes. The children could have went barefoot, you see. But, we were sure short on food. If we didn't have a garden, I don't know what we'd done; and they wouldn't give you no relief, because they said you had no right to be out on strike.

INTERVIEWER: *The city wouldn't provide relief because you were on strike?*

Yes, they didn't want the union here, the city didn't. Naturally, all the business places didn't want the union either because they could do as they wanted to. They could hire you and have you work all day and give you a quarter, as far as that. There was nobody to say to give you more.

And the city wouldn't give you relief, and they wouldn't give you medical attention. It was just lucky at that time when my daughter was born. The doctor knew of our condition. He charged me five dollars. I didn't have a stitch of clothes for my Florence; and the nurse at the school came over one day, and I explained it to her. Her name was Miss Pope, at that time, and she picked up a few things at the Red Cross and brought them down for the new baby.

But people at the Auto-Lite were just like I was. When people that had their children raised had extra food, they brought it out to us, or we never would have been able to make out. It was milk and eggs and, you know, things like that we didn't have. We didn't have the money to buy them. I had a few chickens; I used to sell the chickens to get gasoline for my stove. See, we didn't have gas out here. We didn't have electric out here when I came out, so we had gasoline lanterns and gasoline stove.

INTERVIEWER: *What kind of food was available?*

They went and collected food from different groups and business places. There wasn't enough to go around.

INTERVIEWER: *Who collected this?*

Well, they had a food committee. And they would go to the bread company and get so many loaves of bread, and they would go different places. There was hams and meat shops would give hamburger and different things like that, but there wasn't enough to go around. I remember one time, Mr. Rigby (he was a helper of my husband over there at the Auto-Lite strike) and his father came out. They brought two cans of corn, a little sack of potatoes, and that is what my children had for dinner and for supper. There wasn't anything else. We were right down to the bottom of the bucket at that time. Of course, I can't forget them because that meant so much to me that day. I didn't know what I was going to feed the children. And that didn't only happen in my home, but it happened in a lot of other homes where the men were on the picket lines over there. And there was no work available if you was picketing, you know. If you were a striker from the Auto-Lite, there was no work available for you anywhere because nobody else would hire you.

INTERVIEWER: *You were sort of blacklisted?*

That's right. And you couldn't get no credit anywhere.

INTERVIEWER: *The stores wouldn't?*

Oh, no, they didn't know where the money was coming from if they gave you credit, where they'd get paid, 'cause we didn't know how long that strike was going on. And there was no grocery stores trusted you because they figured you had no right to go on a strike. There was plenty of them we talked to and tried to get credit, but they said, "How do I know I'm going to get my money?"

INTERVIEWER: *Were there evictions in the neighborhood?*

Oh my, yes, one right after the other. One time a family of seven that my husband and I knew. And we heard the sheriff was going to be there at 7:00 that night. There was about, I would say, close to five hundred people over there, and the sheriff left the people in there. He said he wouldn't come back. That wasn't the only time. My husband was a railroader before he came here.

INTERVIEWER: *Was he in the union then?*

My goodness, yes. He was always a great union man. He believed in what was right, and the worker should get paid for what he did. Yes, he was a great union man. He was a union man from the end of his toes to the top of his head. Everything was union. He wouldn't even wear a suit of clothes unless it had a union label on it.

Gladieux's—Buddy's Box Lunch—was very wonderful with the strikers. They donated their coffee and sandwiches to the ones on the picket lines, all for free. And they had a small place. They really couldn't afford it, but they were sacrificing themselves at that time.

INTERVIEWER: *It was very close to the Auto-Lite factory?*

Right across the street. But I really think that the strike was what made Buddy's—the Auto-Lite strike.

INTERVIEWER: *There was a lot of tear gas, I understand.*

I have that one cylinder from the tear gas. And, I'll look and see if I can find the piece of steel that was thrown out.

INTERVIEWER: *You mentioned that your husband and some friends and union people were followed around by the sheriff?*

They naturally were followed all over. You know, the police didn't know what these strikers were going to do next. But when they would be following my husband, he would lead them to a different place; and then, he'd have his men take care of things he wanted done over there. They were following the wrong one. They were very well organized. They put nails down in there all along the front, about the time the sheriff and the deputies were going to come in, and every one of them had flat tires. The nails were all in the police cars, paddy wagons.

INTERVIEWER: *Your husband was arrested then for picketing?*

For picketing. Of course, he was captain of the pickets, and they took them all down. They took—well, I don't know how many times they took him down. And then, he got a warrant served against him that he shouldn't go back down there anymore. But, anyhow, then he took cork and blackened his face, and he went down and served as captain just the same. They got this, well, it could have been called an injunction, I guess. They were trying to keep him away from there. And then, the Auto-Lite was bringing in these people in cars in the train—boxcars. Strikebreakers and, of course, he went to the railroad, being an old railroader, and they didn't know that. So, they took care of that right away. They didn't bring any more in.

INTERVIEWER: *Were there any families who were divided about whether they should support the strike or not?*

Yes, that was the main thing. These women didn't really understand why their husbands had to be out on strike, and there was a lot of trouble over that. Almost down to divorce. And my husband had to go and talk to them people. He was called some names weren't very nice, but he did talk to them and explain to them. And then they became more militant, these women was; and then, they'd come down on the picket lines. Quite a few of them brought sandwiches and things.

Of course, there was a lot of people against the strike; 'cause, at that time, you know, things weren't booming. You'd heard a lot of people talk against it and said they had a right to go back to work. There for a while, I was quite disgusted myself. I didn't think he'd ever, they'd ever, go back.

STEVE ZOLTAN_____
Set-up man at Auto-Lite; stayed out with the strikers but did not picket; later became a plant superintendent.

So, they called a strike. People began to get hungry, needed money; they began to get rough, destroy things. More and more, it got dangerous to walk around on the streets around the Auto-Lite because everyone would say we're the potential strikebreakers. They didn't know, see. You do have people in every crew which may be very mean—killers, and good people—you don't know these things. When they start throwing bricks and turning cars over, you didn't know who were the good people.

Of course, organized labor had to do that because they were just coming up. They had just started to grow, and they didn't want that to be wrecked. But the company dominated so many years. Oh, "We'll never give in," you know. "We'll just let them starve. When they get hungry, well, they'll come back." That was the temper of the matter, which is wrong. I can see it today.

You didn't know who you was talking to—if you was talking to one of the employees of the Auto-Lite or Young Communists, or whether the guy wanted to break the picket lines and go to work. You were afraid. Your speech wasn't free. Everybody was a potential enemy. Then, maybe you thought you were talking to management. They had guys out there, you know, feeling you out.

I do recall one day they were going into Michigan. And we did stop along the way, and the bus pulled up. There was quite a number of men; and one introduced themselves as the Young Communists from Chicago or Detroit, headed for the Auto-Lite strike, and asked us how to get there. So, you see it was more than just the Auto-Lite people of

Toledo organizing. It was something behind that they didn't know.
There was Communists from Detroit, Communists from Chicago, see.
They traveled the country to organize these factories. Of course, at the
time, we didn't know. But the deeper we got into it, then we knew that
the Communists were behind it because they held meetings, communistic meetings. This guy got up and said, "I'm a Communist," introduced himself as a Communist. They passed papers around,
pamphlets—why it's good to become a Communist—oh, yeah.

INTERVIEWER: *What did the things say?*

They say you will never amount to anything until you join the Communist party; then you will share with the riches, see. There were a lot
of people was just hungry enough to get some of the riches. Even if
they didn't have to work for it. That's why organized labor then has got
to stick to one another—because they wasn't part of that big pie. It was
the communistic propaganda—join the Communists and get richer,
see. But they didn't last very long in Toledo. I think we run them out
after a few weeks. No one attended the meetings. We had more non-
believers than we had believers, see.

INTERVIEWER: *What did women do? I understand there were women
working there at the Auto-Lite at the time.*

Who do you think can be the meanest and dirtiest in the human race?
You'll never believe. You never saw a bunch of women get together, did
you? Well, during the strike they were out there cutting wood, bringing
wood, bringing suppers, making suppers, using profanity and, oh,
they'd do anything that a man wouldn't think of. Women were mean. I
think they're the toughest ones to work. I had twelve hundred of them.
I'm telling you. They didn't differ from the men. We had more women
on the picket lines than they had men. I don't know how their homes
looked during the strike, 'cause they were always on the picketing
lines; but women are very militant. They're very outspoken.

INTERVIEWER: *During the strike, were there any planning, decision-
making meetings to direct the strike?*

Well, after this Communist clique took over, the people, the workers,
didn't have any direction. There was no plan. They kept telling the
people, "Stay out, stay with us. They're getting weaker. No plan of
what you're going to do, you're just not going to work. You're just not
going to let the company make a profit, that's all. Just stay out, weaken
the company."

INTERVIEWER: *Did you go down to the picket lines when you were on strike?*

No, I didn't go to picket.

INTERVIEWER: *What were the union meetings like?*

They were orderly. Union meetings were very orderly. You had the right to question. I asked questions by raising my hand. They were very orderly. But you see, the element that did all this trouble, they didn't attend these meetings. They had a clique of their own. The union tried to get enough money together and pay these pickets; but they couldn't pay them because they just started in 1934, you see. Even the unions didn't have any money. Now they have strike funds; those days they didn't have. They had what they called soup kitchens. You see, you'd leave your picket line and you go down to the hall— union hall—and get your meals. Then when these women started up, they fixed the meals at home and bring them out to the pickets. The women, in my book, is the meanest people in the world, you know. Of course, there are some mean men.

A lot of those guys went out of town, looking for jobs, you know. That created a little dissension, too. Who does he think he is? Here we organize, we're holding a picket line for him, and he's working at some other place, see. That created a lot of trouble.

INTERVIEWER: *You mentioned strikebreakers. Where did they come from?*

Oh, southern states. They brought in a truckload of them guys. Some of those, in fact, got a job in the Overland, too. Not only that, but I believe (I can't really prove this), but let's say like one company would get a truckload of these strikebreakers. Some of those were professional strikebreakers. They'd bring them in, like say, to work for the Overland because they're looking for more men. Well, they'd ship them from there to the Auto-Lite. They took care of these guys during that period. Of course, none of them made it in the Auto-Lite. They lost money on that because they had nobody to teach their strikebreakers right. They ruined more equipment than they did any good. I know when I was called back in after the strike, I was busy about two weeks just straightening out the automatic machines. Broken tools, camming—the distance of travel of those machines to make a good piece—that was broken. Oh, it was awful. I don't think that the company would want another strike. Of course, I suppose they claimed it as a tax loss. There was a lot of damage.

The depression really helped the strike grow because so many people were thrown out of these homes. People couldn't pay rent, so the owner would get the cops and throw them out. The cops would come over and take all the furniture out of people's homes; and they'd wait 'til they'd leave, and the union would come and put the furniture back in. It wasn't very far that I could see where a general strike was about ready to take over; and that would be vicious because everything would be ruined in town. I hate to think about it because I just don't know what would happen if we had a general strike. A general strike in Toledo would be a general strike in the state of Ohio, Illinois, and Michigan.

INTERVIEWER: *How were the union leaders?*

Well, they were good. I mean Rigby, he had a cool head at all times. He was always a level head, and he wasn't one of these rowdy guys or a big dictator, either. He was a good kid. He knew what he was talking about. He understood the union then. He was *just*, that's what I liked about Rigby. If you didn't have anything coming, he told you so.

11

Lifting the Siege:
The Ohio National Guard

The siege of the Auto-Lite factory fell early the morning of May 24 when the National Guard, ordered to the scene by Ohio Governor White, marched down Mulberry Street to Champlain Street, moving the strikers and their sympathizers away from the factory gates back to Michigan Avenue, a block away up Chestnut Hill. Machine gun emplacements at Elm and Champlain and near the Buckeye Brewery anchored the National Guard's line.

Around 7:30 in the morning, the people held inside the factory left, much to their relief. The factory itself was then closed to all but the National Guard and some managers and secretaries. Production ceased. An uneasy calm settled over the area, ruffled now and then by the hostile glares of the strikers; but the calm did not last.

For the next three days, the strikers and the National Guard fought, culminating in the famous Battle of Chestnut Hill. Strikers advanced down Chestnut Hill as the guard fell back under a rain of stones. Guardsmen returned the stones and rocks, regrouped, and charged up the hill with fixed bayonets, throwing tear gas ahead of them. In retrospect, the result seems inevitable. On one charge, the young and inexperienced guardsmen opened fire, wounding several. One bullet found Frank Hubay, who had once worked at Auto-Lite, hitting him in the neck and head. He died on the sidewalk on Michigan Avenue.

The fighting did not end with the discharge of National Guard rifles during the Battle of Chestnut Hill. Rocks and tear gas continued to fly that night and the next day. Additional troops were ordered into the area, and again, National Guardsmen fired at the strikers; but no one was killed. By Sunday, however, the fighting had essentially ended, for negotiations between the Auto-Lite executive shop committee of Local 18384 and Auto-Lite management had begun in earnest; but tensions remained high. The pickets identified a strikebreaker, stripped him, and marched him downtown where the police rescued him. Other minor clashes between strikers and the National Guard marred the peace.

A week after the siege of the Auto-Lite factory, labor unions, Auto-Lite strikers, and union sympathizers paraded through downtown Toledo to demonstrate their support for the strikers. Talk of a general strike was in the air, and many unions voted to support one. On June 1, Governor White recalled the National Guard; shortly thereafter, the strike settlement was announced.

One's view of the National Guard depended on one's position in the strike. Those held in the Auto-Lite factory saw them as saviors reminiscent of the U.S. Cavalry coming to the rescue, as in the movies. The strikers saw them as one more threat to their success. Virtually all our narrators saw them as frightened young men.

MARY ABERLING
Production worker at Auto-Lite; supported the union and honored the picket lines.

That night, when they called in the National Guards, they unloaded right in front of where I lived; and they come in about 4:30 in the morning, and they set up their guns around the plant. It was just like a young war. That night, I didn't even go near the place. They was throwing bricks in the plant and breaking the windows. And they were shooting the tear gas out because they had called the sheriff, and he was in the plant; and they were throwing the tear gas, shooting it out. These fellows would catch it and throw the tear gas back into the place, and they were going to set it afire. I don't think there was a window that was left in that place that they hadn't broken that night. And that was going on all night long. I could hear it from where I lived. We had to close our doors because the tear gas come way over to where I lived. That was just like war, I'm telling you. That was going on the next day and the day after that, and that's a night of nights I'll never forget.

INTERVIEWER: *Where did these people come from?*

I couldn't tell you. I wouldn't have wanted to be one of them that was in there 'cause I heard about these men running back and forth. They'd give five hundred dollars if they could get their wife out of there, you know; but what did she want to work in there for?

INTERVIEWER: *Did you go down to look at the National Guard at all?*

Well, yeah, I went down to Michigan Street to see what they were doing—just to be nosey—to see what they looked like. Of course, I was watching them unloading in front of our house there in the morning. They was hauling all of their things out. I said, oh, my God, the army's in town. They had the regular uniforms on; and then, they had their trucks in front there, and they was unloading machine guns and taking them down there. They never used them, I don't think. They had their other guns. They was just young boys. That's all that belonged to the National Guard—young men.

JOHN [J. J.] JANKOWSKI
Punch press operator in Department Two at Auto-Lite; union organizer.

INTERVIEWER: *How'd you feel when the militia came?*

Well, what could you feel like? Harassed them. They were all young kids, about my age at that time. They were young men, twenty-four, twenty-five years old. Some of them were scared. You could see them shaking with that rifle in their hands. They had bayonets, everything fixed up. On Champlain and Elm streets, right on the corner there, they had a machine gun spread out on legs, pointing towards the approach into the Auto-Lite property on Elm and Champlain. There was three guardsmen, see. There was one of them sitting on each side, one in the center sitting like on the lawn, on the ground, you know. And Ralph Holmer—bless his soul, I think he's dead—he was loyal; he was a loyal man in the fight. He went right up there. He says, "Do you know how to shoot this goddamned thing?" He says, "If you do, you might shoot yourself." And he went over and he kicked the machine gun over. He says, "You ain't got no bullets in there." Ralph wouldn't have done that, but he was half-loaded, see. He was a beast, boy, when he was loaded.

So, the militia came in there, and they had a couple of charter buses. They backed inside in the private grounds of the Auto-Lite company in the yard there. All these scabs was loaded in these buses, militia men sitting on top of the roofs, rifles, machine guns on corners of Champlain and Elm, and by the Buckeye Brewery, a couple of more machine guns. They got them out of there. I don't know where they took them. But nobody faulted them; we were tickled they were threw out of the plant.

So, after they were all gone, the militia was there for a couple more days, three or four days longer. But they couldn't let nobody into the work under them conditions. The militia says, "No, we're not going to protect them guys." They got them out. That was the reason they were there mostly. The crowd was so riled up, and they were just ready for blood. So, they got them out. So when the militia hauled them out of there, then there was nobody to throw stones at and nobody's car to tip over. Well, then they quieted down. And when they was quieting down, then they started negotiating again, see. The militia took over completely, the whole thing. Not the local militia, like I told you. Not the local boys, just the outsiders.

Then a couple of days later, the militia was still there and a whole crowd was standing around watching. Then a guy says, in a crowd he says, "Boy," he says, "I can't get in there to get my paycheck." The guy standing alongside of him says, "What do you mean, paycheck?" He said, "I worked in there. I was supposed to get paid today." "You worked in there?" "Yeah," he says, "I worked all during the strike." He says, "They hauled me out of there on a bus." "You did, huh?" They stripped him, right on the street there. Beat him up, stripped him, marched him clean up to the Safety Building. The police rescued him. They painted a tie on in the paper picture, but there was no tie on him at all.

STEVE ZOLTAN

Set-up man at Auto-Lite; stayed out with the strikers but did not picket; later became a plant superintendent.

I wasn't on the picket line. I'd go around and visit the guys that I knew. They had these young kids in the National Guards. They'd have their rifles and stand there in the middle of the street. People way behind— crowds, thousands strong. They'd pick up, like, dead rats, throw them over their heads, and hit these guards. These guards just stood there, you know, get him in the stomach and head—just stand there, they didn't do nothing.

Of course, then they started shooting gas at the people. The pickets got so clever, they'd wear gloves—they'd catch these gas bombs and throw them back at these militia guards. If the wind blew just right, they'd scoop them up like a ball and throw them right back. Oh, we had fun. I got hit by gas. You cry, then it itches. Everybody was walking around with handkerchiefs and throwing bricks at the militia. Then, of course, they arrested the people, and they begin to get tough. They started these riots, shooting at one another. They killed an innocent bystander.

DOROTHY MATHENY
Teacher; organizer and member of Toledo Federation of Teachers; witnessed Auto-Lite strike events.

People were upset about the National Guard arriving, considerably, because I don't know that the National Guard had ever been called into Toledo for anything before. They were very young. Again, partly because there weren't jobs. I mean this National Guard was something they could do, you see, with some income. Just like going into the army might help when you can't get work to do. We did go over to see what was going on, because you'd see headlines in the paper, pictures in the newspaper, and see the marches down to the Lucas County courthouse, the rallies on the lawn down there. So, we went over to see what was going on after school one afternoon.

Well, we got caught in a barrage of tear gas. I don't even know what started it. They were shouting things at each other occasionally. That's all we had noticed. Of course, they had their guns ready. They were standing there with their guns pointed. I don't remember whether they had bayonets or not because we were behind them. We were just so horrified at the sight of the thing. Just sick.

JACK C. LATHROP
Foreman in Department Two at Auto-Lite; crossed picket lines and worked during the strikes.

Of course, Sheriff Krieger did have to call for the governor, which was the law. The chief of police can't do that; it has to come from the sheriff.

A hill goes up to Michigan Avenue, and strikers kept on coming down. I guess they thought these guys were bluffing and maybe that they didn't have only dummy ammunition, but they were loaded. So, they let go. That's where the shooting was when they started up that Chestnut Hill. These guys started down and a couple of them kids let go. In fact, a guy working for me—a diesetter, Joe Wyslick, he's still living—he got shot. It bothered him for a long time, I guess. I remember real well, because his legs bothered him even after he come back to work. Yes sir, she was a rough one. Tough battle.

INTERVIEWER: *Were any of the upper management in the building at the time?*

To my knowledge, the only one that I recall being there all night was Dan Kelly, who was executive vice-president. I happened to be alongside the desk when he called the governor and told him they wanted troops. He told the governor that we would not tolerate this condition any longer without shooting back. Now, you see, we had our own guards up on top of the office building with machine guns, and one of them was in the office entrance right at the top of the steps. There were probably eight or ten steps; one man was placed right there with a machine gun. And, like I say, Mr. Kelly told the governor that we wouldn't tolerate that condition much longer if it were getting to the place where the lives of Auto-Lite employees were being endangered. And if they didn't send troops, they would start firing. So apparently, he must have gotten some word later.

The troops got there. I watched them come in. And as soon as they established security lines, we were allowed to go home. And then, of course, there was a cordon put up around the Auto-Lite several blocks away. Nobody was allowed through without passes. The police and the National Guards had guards right there at those streets, and no one got through unless you had an authorization. Then we were notified that we would have a week's vacation, and we weren't to come back for a week after everything was set up and it was safe to come back. Then, we had our tickets, too, that would let us through the National Guard several blocks away, and we could drive into the territory, into the plant.

INTERVIEWER: *So even a week later, the guard was there.*

Right, 'til the strike was actually settled and the gang disappeared.

LYNN G. WATERS _____
Toledo policeman; on patrol at Auto-Lite during the strikes.

INTERVIEWER: *When the National Guard came, were you glad to see them?*

Oh, my God, yes. Sure, anything that we thought would be of help, because I think at that time we only had about three hundred men on the whole department. We were all assigned to sixteen-hour duty. Oh, I'd come home, all right. Oh, heck yes, and lay down and get something to eat, take a bath and go back.

FRED C. [WHITEY] HUEBNER _____
Management in Auto-Lite's time study department.

It seemed to be, whether it was political or what, that the governor and the politicians were rather reluctant to order the troops in. I do happen to know that Art Minch, the vice-president that we had in charge of the plant at the time, was a fiery individual. And he blew his stack and called them everything he could think of because he wanted the National Guard in there to preserve and save his property and the property of the government.

But the outcome was at 7:00 in the morning. The National Guard came in, and I happened to be up standing on the roof of the office building, which was a corner building. And we saw the National Guard squads coming—one from this street coming down the street, and one from this way coming down the street. And you know—no, you're not old enough—but I had come from an era where you went to a nickelodeon show and the last was the troops coming in, the American flag flying, and all the trumpets going, you know, and so we all cheered. That's the way I felt this morning when I saw the National Guard coming in.

GLEN LANGENDORF _____
Toledo resident; truck driver for the Toledo Blade *during the strikes.*

We were on the front porch of neighborhood houses, and the National Guard unit had men walking down the center of the street sort of patrolling to keep the civilians off the street. But down at the corner, near the factory about one block away, there might have been as high as two hundred people there on top of this hill. The National Guard was assembled at the bottom of the hill. And the people would throw rocks as a group, and the sky was actually cloudy with them. And then they'd retrench; they'd run back quickly, and then the guard would sort of charge throwing some of the same rocks back. And that went on for some time.

All of a sudden, they ignited some type of a bomb that had a yellow smoke to it, and that dispersed some of the people. But they still kept throwing the rocks; and then, all of a sudden, on some order, the guard put their guns up to their shoulders and fired some shots. And after that, things calmed down quite a bit. No more rocks were thrown. And I stayed there a very few minutes. And I got out of there. That was the time when the people, some of them, were injured and killed, I believe. But the guard really had to use some force, because they were being hit with hundreds of rocks; and they had no protection, none at all.

One evening, why, we were milling around there again about two blocks from the Champlain Street side. I remember a fellow, he had no business being there, but he probably wasn't aware of what was going on. And someone from the top of a building threw a tear gas bomb, and it exploded pretty close to his face and tore some of his face away. And I got out of there again.

I was only a spectator in those days. What it got to be was that when people didn't have anything else to do, they used to go down. "Oh, let's go see how the strike's coming along." That's the attitude that people had. Most of the people on the porches, that day I was there, were all harassing the guardsmen who were doing their job in the streets, calling them names and trying to agitate them. But it seemed like the public opinion around there was all in favor of the strikers, not the guardsmen.

INTERVIEWER: *How did the National Guard, in your opinion, behave?*

Very good. They just took a lot of abuse, harassment, and name calling, and the crowd was trying to agitate them. And they were pretty calm and cool about it. But it seemed the sympathy from my friends was all in favor of the strikers and against the management. In fact, there was one of our acquaintances who was accused of being a strikebreaker at that time. He was on the roof of the Auto-Lite throwing bombs down on the rest of the people, and nobody in the neighborhood really liked him too much after that.

EARL MOORE
Auto-Lite worker and union supporter; went out on strike.

National Guard load up the truck, five or six guys in the back, and then drive; and then they'd throw pepper bombs at 'em.

INTERVIEWER: *What's a pepper bomb?*

Well, it's something like a hand grenade. It was full of some kind of soft metal. Why, it burned in. When they'd see that truck coming, why, the boys would take off between houses. Sometimes, they didn't get going fast enough; they'd get peppered. They called them the "Dutch Pepper Bombs."

Then, there was one fellow that run a grocery store; he was shot in the leg by one of the guardsmen. I can't tell you his name. He run a grocery store two blocks away. And they shot at one of the fellows that was out there. Missed him, went over and through his front door, and hit him in the leg.

INTERVIEWER: *Were you happy to see the National Guard come?*

Didn't make no difference, because I was figuring if it kept up much longer, I was going to find me another job.

KATHRYN SCHIEVER
Stenotype operator for Auto-Lite management; crossed picket lines and worked during the strikes.
&
MARGARET JACOBS
Payroll department worker at Auto-Lite; crossed picket lines and worked during the strikes.

KATHRYN: The National Guard got there in the morning, and we went home. Then we were called back to work on the settlement of the strike. They had to have figures on the payroll. So, we had to go down and work in that gas-filled building—an enormous building. We were the only ones in there, except the National Guard. And to go to the ladies' room, we had to go through where they were sleeping; and they would be running around in their underwear and everything else.

The National Guard picked us up every day and escorted us home every night. You know, the strikers knew we worked in the office. They wanted their checks, obviously. We went back to work right away, but the rest of the office didn't, well, until it was settled. I don't know; how long was that?

MARGARET: Quite a while.

KATHRYN: The plant was closed down. It was just us and the National Guard in there. They had to camp there. So they set up their cots, which was an ideal solution to them, and they just camped.

INTERVIEWER: *How many were there?*

KATHRYN: Oh, gosh. There must have been more than twenty in there, wasn't there?

MARGARET: Oh, yeah, I would say so. There were a lot of them.

KATHRYN: So when they'd throw this tear gas in, it just hung in there. It sort of penetrated everything. Our clothes—you know, usually you wear a different dress every day. Believe me, we did. The odor got into your clothes, your eyes, your hair. But we worked very hard. Our boss would phone and tell us what they wanted, and we'd get it out. They sure wanted figures. I think one of the stipulations as far as Minch was that he leave Toledo. Why they were so mad at him I never could figure out, could you?

MARGARET: He always seemed to me like a pretty good guy. They all went all out for him, remember?

KATHRYN: They didn't pay us overtime for that, but they gave us time off to compensate for the hours.

MARGARET: They didn't pay overtime, but they bought your dinner.

KATHRYN: Yeah, bought dinner, but you had to keep working. It was an eerie feeling, too. Here was this enormous plant and just us in there, except for the National Guard, of course; that great big plant, windows out, tear gas hanging on. It felt like you're the only ones in there, and that's kind of a funny feeling. Nights especially.

VIRGIL BARNHART
Owned small candy business near the Auto-Lite factory; wiped out by the depression and hired into Auto-Lite in 1935.

I did go down to the Auto-Lite once after the guard was there. Here was this plant with all the windows broken out. And there was a parking lot just this side of the administration building towards Elm Street, and there was at least half a dozen cars upset in there; and one of them had been set on fire, and there was still smoke. We walked down that street and turned around and came back, and nobody stopped us at all. But I thought, boy, what a terrible mess that must have been when the melee was going on the night before—glass all over the street, bricks. Champlain was paved in bricks. At least half of the bricks were gone in the street; they were all inside the plant. There wasn't a whole window, I think, left in that side of the building.

ROBERT A. CAMPBELL
Auto-Lite machinist and MESA member; continued to work during the strikes.

The sheriff didn't have enough men to handle things, and he hated to admit it. He didn't want to call the National Guard in. They would only be called in on his orders. So at midnight, he made the call.

The National Guard got in there, oh, I would say about 4:00 in the morning; and they barricaded all the streets within a two-block radius of the plant, and they started to go through and get everyone out. They went into every home within that two-block radius to be sure there was no one in there causing trouble. I went home that morning, and then my foreman called me about 9:00 a.m.—wanted to know whether I'd come back to work. So, I went in that day in the afternoon, and we had to spend about two to three hours cleaning the brick and glass so that we would even start to work.

They had their guns. They were all armed, and they had clubs. Oh, yes. And they set up barricades. They set up a truck at the entrance of each street. There was no possible way for any cars to come down through. They had men at all times at all street entrances.

CLAUDE W. POUND
Production manager at Auto-Lite. [Mrs. Pound joined the interview.]

When the troops came, they put a circle around the plant and around . . .

MRS. POUND: . . . our homes for a while. It was like an arsenal. They had guards with guns at our home. They sent me west, to California, to get out of the way.

INTERVIEWER: *What was that like for you?*

MRS. POUND: Well, I was just gone ten minutes and called my home and had a strange man's voice answer me and tell me quickly, though, that my husband was all right. But they had threatened to kill both my son, Billy, and I. So, they got me out of town and left Billy there to fight with his dad. So, it was an upheaval for the families, too. They just had to keep watch of our house all the time.

INTERVIEWER: *How long did that last?*

CLAUDE: We had guards at the house for weeks after the strike was over with.

MRS. POUND: They just wanted to see that nothing did happen to our family.

INTERVIEWER: *Did Auto-Lite do that for a lot of people?*

CLAUDE: No. Not very many. Every time I left the plant, I had two troopers right with me—two state troopers. One of them would stay at the house, the other would sleep; every night, we had our house guarded.

INTERVIEWER: *Did the company provide you with the troopers?*

CLAUDE: No, that was the state.

INTERVIEWER: *The state, you say, because you were management?*

CLAUDE: Yeah, that was part of the reason.

ALBERT ABERLING_____
Punch press operator hired into Auto-Lite during strike.
&
MARY ABERLING_____
Production worker at Auto-Lite; supported the union and honored the picket lines.

ALBERT: We all had some iron bars and different things with us in case we had an outside fight, but then they told us to leave everything in the plant. We had a lot of armature shafts, nice handy things to have.

When I saw the National Guard, they were around the corner. They had set up a machine gun on one corner. A buddy of mine, we chummed around together when we were kids, got shot in the hip on Chestnut Hill. He was working there. He was outside, and he was over on Chestnut Hill there standing on some porch; and he got a bullet in the side of his hip. That was Ed Flynn.

MARY: It was the National Guard against the radicals doing all the fighting. There was just everybody down there. You always find a bunch of radicals that's all for starting trouble, and them's the ones that was fighting the National Guards.

INTERVIEWER: *But he was up on the porch when he got shot.*

ALBERT: Yeah, he wasn't doing nothing. He was a picket there at the early part of the strike. He never got in amongst the radicals though.

CARL LECK

Stockroom worker at Auto-Lite and union supporter. [His sister, Marie Rosselit, joined the interview.]

CARL: When the National Guard got there, then they let them out.

INTERVIEWER: *Was that the end of the demonstrations?*

Oh, no. There were several killed after that. We threw bricks at the National Guard. I found out after I went to the army that was the wrong thing to do. You don't throw bricks at a man with a rifle, 'cause a couple of them got killed that way. They shot tear gas, long tear gas; and Orville, one of the guys from the south end, he lost an eye down there.

But I still remember, and I'll never forget, the gal directly across the street. Whether her husband ever worked there before, I don't know; but she says, "I got a brick foundation on my porch, take the bricks." And they did. That wasn't the only porch that was ravaged there.

When they started throwing the tear gas, there was a little store the next block up, and there was about ten of them went in there and told this guy, "We need your work gloves." They just took his whole stock of work gloves. Now, these ones that they shoot out of a pistol, these tear gas, you couldn't throw them back too fast or too far. The tin cans they would lob right back at them, put the gloves on, and throw them right back at them. My clothes stunk for weeks after from that tear gas.

MARIE: They had strung barb wire and everything down there. Oh, yes, machine gun nests, everything set up. And the houses were all barricaded up. People barricaded their windows up within four or five blocks all around. It looked like no-man's-land to me.

INTERVIEWER: *What did the National Guard look like?*

CARL: A lot of them were kids that didn't know what the hell they were getting into. I saw one of them give his rifle to a striker; the striker walked away with it.

MARIE: There was even talk of a general strike in Toledo to back up these boys.

CARL: And many of these days, after this thing started, I would guess that (not the picket line but around the plant) anywhere from five thousand up people jammed in there to see what was going on.

MARIE: There had to be a lot of people helping.

CARL: Everybody helped or tried to help.

INTERVIEWER: *Were there concrete expressions of support from labor unions? They'd come down and help you picket; for example, say the carpenters' union?*

CARL: They all came down, but the group was so big that you couldn't pick them out; let's put it that way.

JOHN GRIGSBY

Newspaperman for the Toledo Blade; *worked as a reporter around the Auto-Lite factory during the strike.*

That was one thing that impressed me. Here would be the soldiers lined up with their guns, and there would be this huge crowd of people standing in the streets facing them. I mean, they were just more or less facing each other.

There was a lot of shouting, a lot of cursing, and I'll never forget a couple of times when women would come up and these guardsmen—of course, they were a lot of seventeen- and eighteen-year-old boys—would be standing in the middle of the street. I'll never forget some woman; I just never heard such language in my life. She stood right up and shouted at this fella and spit in his face and called him all kinds of names; and, of course, the kid probably didn't know what half of them were. I don't remember how old or anything about her except that she was awfully noisy and screaming.

I think it was that next day or so that they had this Battle of Chestnut Hill. I saw, I would say, dozens of the soldiers fall. They would get hit with these rocks, I mean in the arm. Some of them were bleeding. They would get hit in the head, and they would gradually fall back down the hill. They would have stretchers, and they would carry them off. They'd help them off, and they'd be limping, and they would carry them down and take them into the factory. They had some army ambulances. In a period of some of the fighting that was going on, I'm sure I must have seen fifty or sixty of them fall or be helped away. Now, some of them would come limping down, or they'd be holding a head or their arms or something like that. That was quite a dramatic part of it, to see that. It was noisy, a lot of shouting. And they would get more or less down, and they would more or less regroup; and they'd fix bayonets, and they would march right back up the hill, and it would seem awfully slow. Gradually, the crowd would melt back.

They would have these night battles going on; and then, they'd send scouting parties out of these National Guards. They'd come back in and bring in ten or twenty or thirty people that they had round up in a scouting party, and they'd haul them into the plant. They would bring them in to the provost marshall. I don't know whether the military took them or Toledo police took them or where they took them; but they would send them to jail or supposedly off for detention.

All of a sudden, they came in with this big fellow. He had long hair, and he was very slovenly dressed—very uncouth looking and everything—sloppy, big, and, of course, this was in the days of redbaiting and here he was. He had a key to the Commodore Perry Hotel with him. Well, he was one of these Reds that they had imported, one of these fellas staying at Commodore and all this sort of thing; and they brought him in, and they were poking him—right behind him with these bayonets. Of course, this was Heywood Broun. I guess he finally let them know who he was, but he had a bad time; and, of course, he wrote about that for years later. But we happened to be in this room set aside as our pressroom in the plant. He wasn't the fastest moving, and they was right behind him with the bayonets. They said who they had, and then, we looked out and saw him; and they brought him past. He was a big man. Big in many ways. Of course, they had talked about the Red Menace at times. And you know they were always at the Commies or Communists, which was going on even then. And Heywood Broun sort of fitted the picture of a Bolshevik, I guess.

These National Guards were high school kids that were getting a little money, twenty-one dollars a month probably. Now, whether they were in for the thrill or for the money, I don't know; but I can't recall looking to them as anything knowledgeable of philosophy or anything.

I can remember one point, I don't know whether it was the Friday night or when. We'd go around and talk to these National Guard; and this one time, it was kind of a quiet period, and we got to talking. And here were these kids, a couple of them I think were crying. It turned out that his high school graduation was that night and he was on duty; and he said, "I'm supposed to graduate from high school tonight," so I mean he would be a seventeen-, eighteen-year-old kid.

INTERVIEWER: *You don't recall any other force like the sheriff and the police being around?*

No, I don't. No, that's strange, because I remember reading about the sheriff hiring the guards. There was some questions why he did it; but, of course, I think the sheriff was a Republican at the time. Sheriff Krieger was a Republican; and, of course, the Miniger outfit that ran the Auto-Lite were very strong Republicans. And I think they wielded a lot of power with the sheriff's office. Now, whether the sheriff had a certain jurisdiction over labor at that time, I just don't know.

INTERVIEWER: *When you came back inside the plant in the day when it would be lighter, what was it like inside?*

Kind of ghostly. I can remember just faintly the machinery. It was all standing idle in there.

12

The Aftermath

On June 5, 1934, the doors of the Auto-Lite factory reopened, and workers returned to their jobs. The settlement, negotiated over the previous weekend, assured reinstatement of all workers who had struck fifty-four days before, on Friday, April 13. Workers employed by Auto-Lite before the strike were treated as old employees and immediately returned to work. Workers hired during the strike held lower priority for reinstatement. Many returned only months later, and some did not return at all.

In the essential clause of the very brief contract, Auto-Lite recognized Local 18384 as the legitimate bargaining agent for its members. That recognition laid the foundation for all future negotiations. The contract also recognized the Auto-Lite Council as the legitimate bargaining agent for its own members. Negotiations quickly demonstrated that Local 18384 represented its members more energetically and more successfully. Thus, the Auto-Lite Council waned as Local 18384 grew; and by 1936, the Auto-Lite Council ceased to exist. Its existence immediately after the strike exacerbated tensions created by the strike, for council member and local member viewed each other with suspicion and often hostility.

The persistence of these hostilities for months, sometimes years, after the strike testifies to the intensity of the experience. Even forty years after the event, partisans still defend management and council members. Few defend the scabs. Workers who did not strike or who hired in during the strike still feel compelled to explain or justify their actions.

187

The aftermath of the strike might be calculated quantitatively, using the mathematics of cost and benefit. We might calculate the cost of repairs to the factory and of repairs to damaged property. Auto-Lite certainly did that, as surely it calculated the loss of production and profit. Workers who struck those eight weeks surely calculated, in their own private ways, their loss of wages and the disruption of their lives. We might also tally the gains Auto-Lite experienced through an organized and stable work force, gains which resulted in increased profits. And like the workers themselves, we might weigh the value of increases in wages and benefits that came with collective bargaining. But how shall we calculate the other aftermath: the human aftermath?

In fundamental ways, the Auto-Lite strike altered the relationships between worker and management and between worker and worker. Auto-Lite managers still ran the plant after the strike, often paternalistically; but the concentration of power they had enjoyed before the strike diminished. The strikers wrenched it from their hands in their struggle to establish greater equality of bargaining power. Solidarity eventually displaced suspicion and distrust between workers. Neither came without sacrifice, even of life itself.

We must not exaggerate these alterations, however, for no revolution occurred in Toledo. The same people returned to the same jobs in roughly the same relative positions. Managers remained managers, and workers continued to work for them for wages. The strike did not alter relationships to the means of production.

Nevertheless, important alterations did occur materially and in spirit. Fear and uncertainty no longer haunted the workers' lives, because they now received something closer to a living wage at more secure work. The right to grieve without reprisal restored dignity and self confidence. The union embodied the workers' strength.

Auto-Lite reluctantly accepted negotiations forced by the strike, but it did not cease to resist the union. The contract recognized Local 18384, but the company continued attempts to manipulate the union and its leaders, even to break the union. Labor spies hired into the plant attempted to bribe or hook union members and leaders. The LaFollette Congressional hearings on "Violations of Free Speech and the Rights of Labor" conducted in 1936–1937 revealed not only that Auto-Lite prepared for the strike by accumulating munitions in the plant, but that it hired private "investigators" to infiltrate Local 18384. And Auto-Lite was successful. It hired Corporations Auxiliary, whose agent, Bart Furey, found his way into the union members' favor and to the presidency of Local 18384. Eventually uncovered, he escaped retribution from union members; but these spies within the union's ranks could sow seeds of suspicion and disrupt its activities. Local 18384, which evolved into Local 12 of the UAW, CIO, was able to withstand these efforts. However, it was less successful in meeting the challenges of Auto-Lite's reorganization.

In 1962, Auto-Lite closed its operations on Champlain Street. The factory building stood, a decade later, virtually empty—without machinery, without work, and without workers. The industrial union the Auto-Lite workers created, like most unions in the United States, rested upon an important assumption: the union assumed that the company wished to remain in production. However, as it was for Auto-Lite, that has become a shaky assumption for other companies. Decisions to close are often simply economic matters, made in board rooms far from the point of production and on the basis of profitability; large corporations may find it more profitable to close rather than salvage a particular operation.

From the very outset, Auto-Lite faced competitive pressures from the automobile assembly companies. The instant an assembly company could manufacture Auto-Lite's products cheaper, Auto-Lite lost a customer. That happened in the early thirties when Ford cancelled its contract with Auto-Lite. Chrysler's account saved them; but inevitably, it was merely a reprieve. Eventually, Chrysler built its own electrical equipment factory, taking many Auto-Lite engineers into its management. Constantly striving to reduce costs and increase worker productivity, Auto-Lite fought a losing battle.

The decision to discontinue production on Champlain Street resulted partly from economic considerations based upon Auto-Lite's market difficulties, but also influencing that decision was Auto-Lite's contractual obligation to provide pensions for its workers. Meeting that obligation would apparently be possible only through allocations from current profits, thus affecting net profit calculations. The resulting decision to close transferred some operations to other plants and permitted workers to transfer to those plants hundreds of miles away. Some did so to protect small pensions. Others, only a few years from retirement, refused to leave Toledo, their home for most of their lives. Auto-Lite workers over fifty years old received a small amount of money from the pension fund. Those under fifty, even though they had worked for Auto-Lite for thirty years, received no pension at all. Those who qualified for pensions received twenty to fifty dollars a month, after thirty or more years of service to Auto-Lite. Clearly, the struggle for full protection for working men and women continues.

ELIZABETH NYITRAI_____
Production worker at Auto-Lite; crossed picket lines and worked during the strikes.

[Reads from Diary] "June 6, 1934—We're making it pretty tough for the strikers. Razzed Marge so much she cried. She can't take it."

You know, after we got back it was kind of tough on us, too, you know, because they played jokes on us. They'd call us rats, and it was nothing for us to go to work in the morning and get our table ready for work and find big hunks of cheese all over it. There were those who had been out on strike scattered around, and that was how they made fun of us. And some of them wouldn't speak to us for months; but towards the end, before I quit, we got back on good terms. But a few of them, they never did forgive us, you know, for sticking with the company.

"June 8, 1934—We sure booed the strikers all day. They don't say a word."

But I'll tell you, when the unions got in, they did away with the fancy forelady. She had to sit down on a bench and work hard and get dirty like the rest of us did. No more fancy clothes. She had to sit down on the bench there and work hard for her money and not parade around with her fancy clothes and her fancy hairdo. We had to laugh because she sure gave us a bad time.

INTERVIEWER: *After the strike, were you forced to join a specific union or anything like that?*

Well, I don't think we were forced, but we decided that it was the thing to do on account of—the girls they razzed us, yeah, pretty darned good: "We fought for this. We fought for a raise, and you are enjoying it." So naturally, well, you know, you're going to go along with them after you got a raise and conditions were much better. And, well, I think after going through all that horror, you see the light, don't you, because it was really scary.

EARL MOORE_____
Auto-Lite worker and union supporter; went out on strike.

I could understand it a little better *after* it became consolidated, not before. Because I figured like this, what was the use in just a few of them taking off and marching around and hollering and screaming and, you know, going through their antics? If everybody did go out, they should have stayed out for another week instead of taggling back, even if Auto-Lite hired the new help. Because the new help was costing them more money than that two pennies that they was paying extry per hour. They were green, get what I mean? They were green people. Just the same, if you were to go out to be a dentist, you'd have to learn that. It cost them more an hour than they would have had to put out if they'd went ahead and paid the two-and-a-half cents and not had the strike.

INTERVIEWER: *Well, the guys in receiving with you, did they eventually join the union?*

Yeah, eventually, they came around.

ROBERT A. CAMPBELL
Auto-Lite machinist and MESA member; continued to work during the strikes.

I feel sure they could never have gone on the way they were. It was either recognize the union and try to get things settled or just go out of business. It was that serious. Finally, they had a vote and the AFL won out. The Auto-Lite Council didn't have enough votes, so they decided to go with the union because they were outvoted. The vote was right after this strike.

There was some hard feelings after the strike. All I know is what I heard. There would be people arguing, and they didn't like to cooperate with each other. I imagine it was years before people would get over these things and start to cooperate together and work together again. It took quite a time to get things back to normal.

CLAUDE W. POUND
Production manager at Auto-Lite.

INTERVIEWER: *How did you feel about them striking when there wasn't very many jobs going on?*

Well, a lot of them lost their homes and everything else due to the strike. At that time it didn't take long because nobody had any surpluses. That's right, oh, yes. A lot of our employees afterwards: "God, what a mistake we made."

INTERVIEWER: *You said after the National Guard came in they started organizing again?*

No, after they had left. After they had left, things started quieting down, and we started up again; and that's when they started to organizing. Awful. Groups of girls would surround a girl and tell her, "You better do it. You know what you went through before, you're going to go through it again." Everything. It was just vicious.

INTERVIEWER: *What type of relationship did you have with the workers?*

Oh, at the time of this strike, they'd have murdered me any time. Most any of them. But after that, we got to be pretty good friends.

INTERVIEWER: *How was the strike settled?*

I can't tell you the details of it. There was money involved principally. When the strike was over with, we put them to work. Of course, we had a lot of work. They weren't satisfied with this, that, and the other thing. You can't satisfy all the people.

INTERVIEWER: *Did they put a lot of pressure on you?*

Oh, yes, never let up. I retired in 1956—January 1—and up until the last three or four years that I was there, I spent more than half of my time on labor relations. It was just constant, constant, constant, nagging, nagging, nagging.

CHESTER DOMBROWSKI
Punch press operator in Department Two at Auto-Lite; union organizer. [His wife, Elizabeth, joined the interview.]

After that big strike, they closed the whole plant down. They wouldn't hire anybody. They wouldn't open it up. During the depression, before we got organized, those worked that was brown nosing the foreman. Those like me that had seniority, we didn't have no union. But after we got a foothold with the union in there, we got recognition. They had to go according to seniority. Recognition was first, then seniority rights, and so on down the line. Everything was in the contract.

That union money that I paid in there, I never felt sorry for. My seniority rights were worth every dime of that money, because I'll never forget how it hurt me during the depression when some of the guys that I knew were hired in after me, worked at least two or three days a week, and I was out on the street going hungry. I'll never forget that. Now, you got the rights of seniority.

But you got to have it in a contract. Like I told Duane when I worked at Spicer after Auto-Lite closed down. I said, Duane, what's the protection the employees in here at Spicer have? Like they're moving some of these departments out of town—to Spicer, of course—but they claim they're going to arrange things different. "Well," he says, "we got the company's word for it, Chet." I laughed in his face. I said, boy, ain't you guys got something. We had that over to the Auto-Lite. Look where I'm at, I says, they put me out on the street after thirty years. I said, they had it pictured in the Toledo *Blade* on a heap. Do you remember that? He said, "Yeah. Well," he said, "this company is pretty good." I said, they're all pretty good, when you've got it in black and white. They've got to be pretty good. When you don't, that's another story.

They made a mess at the Auto-Lite. There was twelve hundred of us people that was left there, and there wasn't anyone that had less than twenty-five years, at least. But the company wanted to see how many would go here and there, which they knew that there was a certain percentage that won't go. They figured they're saving that much money, too. They got that figured in one way or another, you know. So, I guess they wanted to make a mess of the people's pension plan; that's what they're trying to do. Now, in the Spicer, they got it so if you've got ten years, your pension's okay. You don't lose it like I did at Auto-Lite. There for a while the both of us felt we'd keel over because our nerves were on edge. We'd wanted to start building this house, and they come out with this: that Auto-Lite's going to move the place and there I was, at my age. They say at thirty-five they won't hire you anywhere, but I was fortunate. I was one of the fortunate ones that I got a job.

ELIZABETH: We kept praying, and that's the best medicine. We prayed to Saint Jude. He's a great fellow to watch TV, and I said, Chet, instead of watching that idiot box, you can always watch that another night—the novena is tonight. I said, let's have an early supper, get dressed, and go to church and say a prayer for work. He said, "Oh, that's not going to help." I said, you're not supposed to talk like that. You're here—put by God—and what He wants to give you He'll give you, providing you have faith in Him. So, he went. We went two or three times; and one night we come back, and I said, well, how do you feel now? He said, "Oh, I think I feel better since we're going to church like this," he says. So, the next morning he got three telegrams for work. I said, see there. He said, "My God, look, one in the morning, one right after dinner, and one late in the afternoon." So, from then on Saint Jude is his buddy.

LYNN G. WATERS

Toledo policeman; on patrol at Auto-Lite during the strikes.

I tell you one thing, some of those fellas you spoke about that was working inside—strikebreakers as the strikers called them—had a hard time getting a job after the strike was over. They knew who they all were.

INTERVIEWER: *The strikers and the rest of the union men in town?*

For instance, now we had one of the policemen that was fired for drunkenness, and he went to work at the Auto-Lite during the strike. They were just about ready to reinstate him on the police force, but they found out that he was one of the guys that was a strikebreaker inside so, oh, man!

INTERVIEWER: *What happened to the sheriff?*

I know how thin he was when he left office.

ELIZABETH SZIROTNYAK

Production worker at Auto-Lite; crossed picket lines and worked during the strikes.

Now, they pay these pensions, too. That's another big deal. You know what they did to me? For thirty-four years and nine months I worked there. And I get twenty-six dollars and seventy-five cents a month. These smart, you know, college guys, they sat down there (laughs), they set down and they worked this out. If I would have waited 'til I was sixty-five, I would have got forty-one dollars; but I took mine as soon as I got it at sixty, so I only got twenty-six dollars. They figured it out by the hour, somehow or other, I don't know. We had a sheet of paper that showed how it worked. That's not even a dollar a day. I take the twenty-six and I'm thankful for that. It takes care of my utilities. But the point is, by themselves, they will not give you a nickel! Nothing; if you don't go out and get it. I worked both sides, see. After the union came in, then I was with them. But before that, well, I was with the company because, well, like I told you. I needed it badly.

BERNICE KELLER

Production worker hired at Auto-Lite just before the strikes; crossed picket lines and worked during the strikes.

I was so tickled to have gotten this factory job. I thought, oh boy, I'm all set. And then along came the strike and, of course, I didn't know which side to be on. You know, I'm a young kid. I know from nothing. Well, everybody was against the union in those days. Like I said, it was just getting started in Toledo. But people of my own age at that time, we wanted it. We wanted it because it meant security for us. Like now, I'm retired and everything because of the union. Otherwise, I wouldn't have a pension.

ALBERT ABERLING

Punch press operator hired into Auto-Lite during the strike.

&

MARY ABERLING

Production worker at Auto-Lite; supported the union and honored the picket lines.

ALBERT: I signed up with the union right away.

INTERVIEWER: *Did your first wife sign up, too?*

Yeah, she signed up right away. As long as you didn't join the council, if you joined the union, then you were okay. They'd see that you meant right.

INTERVIEWER: *There must have been some tension with your family after the strike.*

MARY: Oh, they didn't speak to us for twenty-five years. That's because they had us arrested during the strike, see.

ALBERT: My wife had you arrested.

MARY: Yeah, your wife had us arrested for assault and battery. We never laid a hand on them. We had to go to trial, and the judge said, "Well, it's more of a family squabble than the strike." So, he said he'd put us under a peace bond for one hundred dollars for one year, all six of us: my husband; his sister and her husband; Tim and his wife, both. Well, that was for a year. It went on for twenty-five years, until his brother-in-law died; and my daughter said, "Well, we're going to call them up and tell them that your Uncle Joe died." This had been going on long enough—twenty-five years.

SEYMOUR ROTHMAN

Newspaperman just entering the trade in 1934; reported some events during the Auto-Lite strikes.

I think that Toledo has been a strange city—I'm sure of this. I'm sure the strike sort of took care of our taste for violence. I know that nobody was either proud or happy with what had happened here. And yet, I think here in Toledo it taught management, at least in the auto-related industries, that they are going to have to do business with labor and better work out contracts both sides can live with. We had a reputation here—partly undeserved, partly deserved—of being a horrible labor town. We had a lot of strikes in here. This was completely turned around by the [Toledo] Labor-Management Commission. The record was just completely turned around from where we were a city of strikes to where we were a city of no strikes, or where we were a city of short strikes or little quick walkouts.

JOHN SZYMANSKI

Auto-mechanic, self-employed during the strikes; later, Auto-Lite machinist and union supporter.

There was one thing I wanted to insert. At this labor and industrial institute we had some time later, there was a representative of the company. Oh, I think he was their public relations man, and he was quite a guy. And I'm setting there listening to him talk, you know, and he's talking about manufacturers and investments and machinery and so forth. They don't seem to talk about the guy that runs the machine, and he don't talk about the guy that punches the clock.

I'm listening to that, and the guy next to me says, "I wonder what you do with a guy when he gets to be about forty, and he can't produce. What do you do, take him out in the back there and shoot him? At least a horse you can turn him out to pasture and let him graze after he's worked faithfully for you all these years. What do you do with the guy when he gets to be forty years old? You know, you can't get a job when you're forty." At that time, if he was forty years old, he couldn't even get a job. It was amazing what a man as intelligent as that representative had to say. He says, "Our first interest to us is our company; and the most important thing to us is that machine, because it must produce, and our stockholders must have profit, but," he says, "we can always get somebody to run that machine." Now, what was more important, see? And I always thought that he was a fairly intelligent man.

ELIZABETH FRITSCHE_____
Stenotype operator and secretary to the manager of the service parts division at Auto-Lite; worked during the strikes.

Later, we went down to the Hillcrest Hotel downtown. At that time, our president was one of the owners of it, so they rigged up a big suite of rooms for our particular department—just a skeleton force—because we were the parts and service division, and we had to keep things going. So, he hauled my typewriter and all my paper and everything down there, and we just worked there for quite a few weeks until this thing was all over and we could get back and we cleaned up the mess.

I took depositions for people who had damaged property. You see, I'm a stenotype operator. I use a little machine like you see in court. And so, I had to sit down for days and take stories from employees, even factory people who stayed home peaceably but still had their homes damaged: black paint smeared on white houses and rubbish thrown on them; glass was broken.

INTERVIEWER: *Did they live near the factory?*

Not in every case—in the general area—I'd say maybe quite a ways out, Elm or LaGrange streets, but not immediately surrounding it, no. I know at that time Pict and Cavanaugh handled all our insurance for the company, and one of their agents came in that day visiting, just on business; he didn't get out, either. He wasn't related with the company, but he didn't get away; he had to stay in all night with us. They covered it, I do think, because at that time most of the companies had strike insurance because strikes were prevalent then. I know we were glad it was settled, but we hated the union. There was an awful feeling, an anti-union feeling in our office.

INTERVIEWER: *Was that pretty consistent, running through the different offices and secretaries?*

Well, I couldn't speak for them any more at this time. But I know in our particular group we—well, the damage that was done—we all were pretty much anti-union. But it just scored me agin' the union until this day. Like I say, we need them, but not to that extent. I'll tell you, it fed me up with unionism. I just never have gone to it yet. We need it—

there's no doubt about it; but I thought if that's the way they fight to get what they want, it's a hard way to get what you want. Now, they unionized our time office and I think our accounting section. Whenever they legislated for the union, I talked it down just as hard as I could. And we always defeated it. So, they finally didn't let me vote because of my capacity working as the secretary to the manager. They finally just took my vote away, but I still talked against it.

CARL LECK
Stockroom worker at Auto-Lite and union supporter.

So, I would go back through the lines where these girls were, the gals that stayed in there. All right, now I'd check your stock. All right, what are you short of? They wouldn't even look at me, wouldn't tell me nothing. Just shrug your shoulders. Well, sister, a couple of days from now when you run out of stock, you'll holler. Just skip them, no report on them at all. It only took one week, and they started telling me what they were short of.

INTERVIEWER: *Why wouldn't they talk to you?*

Because we were strikers, they were scabs—that's why. That deep feeling between the union here and the Auto-Lite has never changed. It's still there. The upper echelon of the Auto-Lite got beaten. They didn't have to move out of here; Bay City is not as big as here. They had more plants than in Bay City by far. Right now, every time they get an increase in production, they got to add on to their plant up there. They could have kept it right here.

INTERVIEWER: *Figure it was to escape the union here?*

Certainly.

INTERVIEWER: *The hard feelings never died?*

And they never will.

RAY GARBERSON
Supervisor in Auto-Lite's cost and budget department.

INTERVIEWER: *What was it like after the strike?*

Oh, it was good. People forget things. That was my impression, at least;

and even the union committee didn't seem to be antagonistic after it was over. They wanted to get together and get going. That's their job, to make jobs for people they represent, so it would only be natural that they would be reasonable and continue for their own good and the good of the employees because that's their bread and butter, too. They keep the people out on strike all the time, why, they won't be voted in on the committee again; it isn't likely. People want to work, at least they did at that time.

MARGARET BYRD_____
Wife of the late Lester Byrd, a union organizer at Auto-Lite.

Right after the Auto-Lite, the Chevrolet struck. Now, I made sandwiches and coffee for the Chevrolet workers. I had a very good friend by the name of Clarence Nagle over there, and he was on the executive committee. And I walked the picket line over there. Then Toledo Furniture was on strike. I walked a picket line over there. I walked the picket line at the Fisher Body in Flint, and we used to go out and walk the picket lines at the Conklin Pin; we walked the picket lines there.

After the Auto-Lite strike was over, we all stuck together like glue—the union people. And then they would—each one would put so much money together—and then they had a picnic, and they gave prizes and baskets of food to the largest family.

But, I think the Auto-Lite strike made Toledo.

KATHRYN SCHIEVER_____
Stenotype operator for Auto-Lite management; crossed picket lines and worked during the strikes.

I remember Art Minch was the vice-president, and they seemed to take a personal vengeance against him. As a matter of fact, he was sent to the Port Huron plant after that. They had to send him out of Toledo. He and his wife lived out on the River Road, and they always had a guard out at their home. Now, that's pretty bad when you live in the United States that you have to have a guard around your home.

Obviously, I have some feelings against unions. No, not against unions, against the abuse that unions often take and the advantage they often take.

HILDAGARDE & WILLIAM LOCKWOOD_____

Office workers at Auto-Lite; crossed picket lines and worked during the strikes.

WILLIAM: I had an incident that happened to me, personally. In fact, I was asked by two of the officers of the Auto-Lite Council to join the council and I made the remark that, I said, if I joined anything it's going to be that outside union, and that's just the way I put it. Well, I had been on this particular checking job for, oh, probably seven, eight months. The next morning they took me off of my job and moved me down to the heat-treat department—the dirtiest and the hardest job they had.

I went over to one of the committeemen that I knew, and I talked to him. I asked him about joining the union. He said, "Sure, come on and we'll go right down after work." So, I went down and joined the union. About two days later, he got ahold of the chairman then, and I told him what had happened; and, of course, right away they went right to my boss and wanted to know why I was moved. In other words, to me it was a case of discrimination, because I felt that because I refused to join the Auto-Lite Council that I was taken down there and give this other job. Of course, they denied that. They don't agree that that was the reason. But anyway, after two or three days of haggling, I was put back on the other job. This was in, I'd say, oh, somewhere around November to January of late 1934 or very early 1935. This was after the strike.

There would be a continuous hassling between the Auto-Lite Council and the automobile workers within the plant. They ostracized each other, and one tried to be persuasive on the other. There was nothing that was major as far as hostility was concerned, but there was that ill feeling among the employees because at the outset there were more people belonging to the council than there was the outside union, actually.

The company still fought the union after the strike. The Auto-Lite hired the Corporations Auxiliary. They spent ninety thousand dollars, according to the LaFollette Senate investigation records, to break the union after they had recognized the union. The LaFollette hearings uncovered Bart Furey. He was the third chairman of the Auto-Lite union. Moore was first; Rigby was the next, then Bart Furey. He was a Corporation Auxiliary agent. He was a Canadian that was brought in there. A very brilliant man. I knew him personally.

HILDAGARDE: He was pretty smooth.

WILLIAM: I'll say this in defense of Furey. He did the union more good than he did it harm because he was found out before he got a chance to actually get to a point of destruction.

STEVE ZOLTAN

Set-up man at Auto-Lite; stayed out with the strikers but did not picket; later became a plant superintendent.

After the strike ended, I felt like a stranger to the management because some pride you've lost. Being away from them or out on strike for so many weeks, you don't feel like one of the employees for a long time; and then to top it all off, when the Auto-Lite Council organized, you was a total stranger.

The Auto-Lite Council was an organization of employees who did not believe in the union. But that caused more trouble than the first organization did because they worked so contrary to the union rules. Everything was 100 percent management. At that time, I recall the management favored the council because it was their union, see. Of course, the union members outnumbered the council. They were so much stronger, and they accomplished more than the council. In fact, when it come to some rough words or rough actions, the union was much stronger than the council. So eventually, since the production went bad, they couldn't accomplish anything with the council intact. They then dissolved the council, and things begin to go again. I don't think that you would have had that many organizations in the plant. They were just troublemakers, because everybody just hated the Auto-Lite Council because they figured they were part of the management. They didn't recognize them as employees, just part of the management.

Most of them guys were sweepers; they call them sanitary engineers. After dissolving the council and they joined the union, you know, and peace begin to reign and everything was just normal. But it took at least six or seven years before all the people got back to the common sense, you know, and liked one another.

I never ate so many potatoes in my life as I did during the depression. Used to eat them fried, boiled, through the mill, fried again with a little cabbage mixed with the potatoes. Today, if you want to go to the show you say, Ma, give me five bucks. Those days, you got ten cents every two weeks. That is the difference between unorganized country and an organized country. It's because of the organized labor and the companies who recognized the labor that causes the good times. We're going to have some bad times, too; the union and the manufacturers are both going to suffer. Where before there is only one type that suffered—the guy in the shop. Not only that, if you work six months and you thought you had a little savings, you got laid off. That's why you never kept any money in the bank in those days. Didn't have time, didn't have enough to put in the bank. When you spend everything that you've saved and that you have under the pillow or somewhere in the corner, then you had to go back to work or look for a job. If the boss liked you and gave you your job back, you got a job. If not, you had to go without for another month before you found a job.

Of course, when they recognized the union, practically every man in the department become a job setter or a master at his trade because we teached; you had a better chance. Seniority was recognized. It wasn't because I hate you, I'm going to lay you off. If you had the seniority, you worked; if you didn't know, you were shown. That way, I think the union did very good. Those that had the ability, I can't see where the union helped. In fact, if I had the ability and I wanted a dollar more an hour the company was willing to give, they wouldn't, because the next guy would say, "I work as much as he is. I belong to the same union. I want the same money." That's the way it happens. You couldn't raise one and forget the other in the argument.

People who had pulled the strike remained with the company. I was there forty-two years; and I know that the people that began to retire, they were the same ones that started this union organization. So, it must have been a good place to work in. Auto-Lite—I can see today, after being retired for twelve years—they did more good for us than other companies. They did cooperate with the employees and, of course, I was one of the lucky ones, too. I got top jobs with them.

FRED C. [WHITEY] HUEBNER

Management in Auto-Lite's time study department.

After that, it was a matter of just negotiating and bargaining back and forth until we reached a conclusion; but they had already gained their objective, and I say that advisedly. I say that because the main thing, if they got nothing else, they would have settled for recognition.

INTERVIEWER: *You said you used to exchange words back and forth with the pickets. Was that the only hostility that you experienced from them?*

I never had any serious trouble with any of them. They were always decent to me. To give you an idea—after the strike was over, we had to set a way of dealing with the union, so I was the one that had to deal with the union. We had fifteen committeemen, I think, and they used pretty rough language. And we had three or four women among those. When we started the meeting, I said, now I want something understood. We're here to do a job of business; and we're not here to swear at each other, to curse at each other, and I won't stand for it. I'll tell you this, that I will deal with you just as long as you want to deal; but if you can't use decent language, I'll walk out and that's that.

Well, I walked out twice, and they called me back. And we had meetings thereafter which were very orderly, very nice, and very decent; and probably the worst one we had to fight was a woman. I think this was one of the major things that helped get things on the right foot. Because, after all, it's pretty hard to quarrel with a moral standing; and if you maintain a moral standing, you're on pretty safe ground.

The strike resulted in R. G. Martin taking active charge of the plant. As a result of the strike, the vice-president that we had was under the gun. In other words, the people all blamed him for the situation that developed.

INTERVIEWER: *Was that Art Minch?*

Minch, yes. So, as a result of the strike and Minch's militancy, R. G. Martin came in to change management.

MARY ABERLING
Production worker at Auto-Lite; supported the union and honored the picket lines.

INTERVIEWER: *What about the people that hadn't gone on strike?*

Well, they give us a pretty rough time when we went back to work. They kind of razzed us. Like you'd walk away from your place, maybe they'd go grease up your screwdriver, grease up your chair. When you come back, you'd have to watch where you sit; you know, play tricks on you. But I didn't pay attention to that. It didn't bother me. I done my day's work and went home. I minded my own business.

JOHN [J. J.] JANKOWSKI
Punch press operator in Department Two at Auto-Lite; union organizer.

We done all negotiating ourselves. We didn't have no representatives.

INTERVIEWER: *Were you in on the first negotiations, at the settlement of 1934?*

Oh, yeah. Yeah, I was on the first one. That's when they just said they recognized the union and so forth. We signed papers on the desk right across from one another. They took our copy, we took their copy. And that was the first one. Art Minch was there. The first one I'm talking about now. Remember, the first one is in February. When we went back in June, them guys were all pretty scared. So, Claude Pound and all them—Minch and all them—they agreed. Minch agreed from another room.

INTERVIEWER: *He wouldn't be in the same room with you?*

No, he was scared, because everybody in there had signs of him. They were going to hang him and all that stuff. You know what I mean, the guys would act up. Claude Pound, Whitey Huebner, and Bob Thornton—them are the guys that negotiated with us. The committee, well, we was only four or five of us guys.

INTERVIEWER: *Who was doing the negotiating for the union?*

Negotiating? Charlie Rigby was the first chairman, Bill Collins, Walter Moore, John Jankowski, Leo Kapurski, and that's the first ones on the committee that represent the people. All the members that were coming in, we'd represent.

And Miniger throughout the negotiations—whether in the hotel or in the office there—never once was in the negotiation. Not once.

INTERVIEWER: *What about Minch?*

Minch? He used to come in there now and then. But not too much, you know. But Minch was more of the type to: "Give them this, give them that." But he sent it through Claude Pound or Hossmeier or Thornton or Whitey Huebner. They were the boys that would do the talking for him. Then they'd report to him on the side office every few minutes, you know. Or call him by phone in another office.

Later on, some of the guys that was in that council joined the union. And they were good members, too, you know what I mean. After, after. Because once we got in there, the company always give them what they give us first—what we asked for, fought for, got through negotiations. So, we said, what the hell, you belong to the company? They wanted something extra; they were promised something extra. They didn't get it. So, they jumped the fence, come over on our side. They were members.

Toward the end, their council was losing their members to us. He's alongside of me, he belongs to the council. I'd give him a hard way to go. And he knew I was in the majority around him. So, what did he do? Can't beat them, you join 'em. That's what they were doing.

The things we were getting was great; guys that was there before knew what they were treated like. We got better holiday pay and stuff like that with good negotiation. Then we got the real leadership, after the 1934 strike, when they started hiring. Then they got Bill Caswell, Earl Stucker, Floyd Copeley—they come in after the strike, see. They were the new help hired. They were active as hell. So, guys like me, we took it easy. Let them guys do the fighting. We pave the street; let them walk on it.

When the strike was over, boy, did you see that Buddy's climb. Everybody and his brother was patronizing. They were buying booze and whiskey and lunches, everything from him. Union negotiated. We're going to have Buddy's in here as a canteen. So, we had them; the company put canteens in from Buddy's. Because he supported us, we supported him. So, Homemade had only one canteen, and Buddy's had the rest of the whole plant, all over. But you see, it was no use the company fighting the people. What the hell, they enjoyed their union, so they're going to eat union food.

Every time you'd mention Minch in the factory, they'd start throwing things. They had his picture in the factory. Throwing weights and coils and stuff at this picture, like that. So, they figure it was best to get him out so nobody would notice that he was around anymore. He was still in the corporation. In June, he was sent to Bay City, Port Huron, by Mr. Martin.

It improved extry good when we went back to work in June. About a month or so later, Auto-Lite was near dead—damn near broke. Royce Martin picked them up off their knees. Martin was a wonderful man. He was one of the best men you could want. A top management corporation man like he was, he was so strong for union it was surprising. That's why we got such a baby contract, such a superior contract. He agreed that you got it coming, you got your troubles. And whenever we had any confusion in our departments—now this was when Martin was in charge of the Auto-Lite corporation—he'd come out and he'd get on a stack of generators. He'd get up on top of there with one of his assistants, a young lawyer or something. He'd tell his people in each department (he'd go around the buildings and departments), "You got trouble with your wages," he says, "I'll give you more wages. But I want some more work from you guys. I don't want no dogging around. You do right for me, and I'll do right for you, because I want you guys to be well fed and well paid."

Under the agreement we had in 1962, the Auto-Lite corporation would have to have fifty-two million dollars by 1972 in the pension fund. They had to have that kind of money, according to the agreement. Early in 1962, we had a meeting of the Auto-Lite union. Ralph Brown was the chairman then. He called us to Scott High School for a meeting. We went across the board, completely voted 100 percent woman and man that worked for Auto-Lite, that we take a fifty cents cut in wages per hour. "They refused it," Ralph Brown says. The company refused it, because they had to raise fifty-two million dollars by 1972 if they kept Auto-Lite in Toledo. So, what'd they do? Spent five million and moved it out of Toledo. That's what happened. And that's where it died from then on in. Auto-Lite was washed up then.

Understand, everybody I talked to has said Auto-Lite was paying too damned much wages. Auto-Lite went out of this world with their wages. That wasn't it at all. These other plants was getting close to our wages and everything, but Auto-Lite closed the door and told everybody they're done. A labor relation man by the name of Elgin Brooks come around to the departments and picked up twenty-five of us and told us to come in the following Monday and help pack machinery, tools, sweep up, clean up at the rate of two dollars and fifty cents an hour at that time. It was 1962 when they closed on June 22. So, we stayed there, cleaned up. We worked about six and a half, seven months.

Then, the top management run into us in the cafeteria eating our dinner. The ones from the old school of the management that was bitter against union, they walked into that cafeteria to have dinner or breakfast, whatever they were up to, and we were eating our dinner. We went under the promise from Brooks that they was going to open a short-order department in the old Auto-Lite, in the Champlain plant. Us guys that he picked out was experienced set-up men, experienced operators of generators and electrical parts for the automobile industry. He kept us because he said he was going to set up a mail order department to take care of that. In the meantime, he wants us to stick around so he wouldn't have to look for us. The top management, when they seen us in that cafeteria, they come up, asked us what are we doing here. I says, we're cleaning up, fixing things around here. He just shook his head, laughed a little bit, off he went. Right after that dinner, about twenty minutes to three, our boss, Stevens, which was in charge of us clean-up men there, he come in there and he says, "From now on, you guys are all done. All done completely."

That same day when we was done at 3:30, a couple of us fellows walked over to the personnel office, which was moved in another building next to the plant, and we asked, "Well, now that they let us go for good, how about our transfer to Bay City?"—which we had the right when they closed the plant. And they told us—Mr. Day, I think he was the personnel man at the plant there—according to the agreement with the union, the deadline was January 1, no more transfers allowed.

INTERVIEWER: *When Auto-Lite left, did you receive any retirement from them?*

Yeah, later on. Later, the company sent me a letter: "John Jankowski, if you take your pension now, you will get twenty-five dollars and ninety cents. But if you wait 'til 1972, you will get forty dollars and some cents." So, I says to the wife: If I wait that many years, I might be dead by that time. So, I took the twenty-five dollars and ninety cents pension.

INTERVIEWER: *After working there thirty-eight years?*

Thirty-eight years. That's all I got. No. Nothing else from Auto-Lite whatsoever. No insurance, nothing at all. See, pension was taken out of our checks, so much per hour, towards a pension fund. So, when Auto-Lite closed up, some of them wasn't fifty years of age—they didn't get a penny. What they put in or nothing. Nothing at all. Not even a kind word they didn't get out of the deal. These fellows are the ones that suffered.

13

Charles Rigby: Organizer

C harles Rigby was about five feet six inches, had a rotund build, and peered through thick glasses as he spoke. In his own terms, he was a "little fat man." He did not dominate through physical presence or a powerful voice. His leadership rested on enthusiasm, judgment, and commitment. Rigby chaired the first shop committee of Federal Labor Union 18384, organized in the plant, and developed strategies for the strike. His fresh ideas, resiliency, and determination inspired others to follow his lead. He gained respect by giving it.

Rigby spoke to us in his modest home. We were joined by his wife, whose support, he reminded us, had been essential to his leadership, for she had shared his hopes and aspirations for a better life for workers. She had stuck with him, even though he had risked their livelihood and perhaps his life—for Charles Rigby had been a marked man. He recounted an attempt in 1936 by a Corporations Auxiliary agent to hook him—to manipulate him into working as an agent. That attempt backfired when Rigby wrote to the LaFollette committee, which was looking into "Violations of Free Speech and the Rights of Labor," and offered to testify. He was spirited secretly from his Toledo home by committee investigators, escorted to Washington in a closed train compartment, and smuggled into a guarded hotel room. At a most dramatic moment, he was brought before the committee, related his experiences at Auto-Lite, and pointed out in the hearing room the agent from Corporations Auxiliary who had attempted to hook him.

Such courage and enthusiasm sparkled throughout Rigby's interview. He spoke carefully and precisely about his early life and about the evolution of his involvement with the union at Auto-Lite. He recounted events for us chronologically, in detail, and in an orderly— although excited—way. His excitement was infectious; we readily saw he was a man who refused to sit idly by and allow himself or others to be victimized, which reflected his activist philosophy. He believed that life demanded involvement; conditions could be changed if only one tried.

Rigby not only tried, he succeeded. No individual can be credited with organizing the Auto-Lite workers, but Charles Rigby deserves special acknowledgment for the courage and imagination of his leadership. He continued his leadership beyond Local 18384 and became an international representative for the UAW, a position from which he had retired when we interviewed him in 1973. In the following narrative, Rigby recounts his personal development and his organizing efforts at Auto-Lite.

CHARLES RIGBY
Organizer

There was a natural gas well hit in Arcadia, and so a glass factory was built which used lots of heat. My father went from Fostoria to Arcadia, Indiana, to work in this glass factory. And he was active in the Flint Glass Workers Union. And, fortunately, he met my mother, and they lived in Arcadia for, I'd say, approximately four or five years. And then they moved to another town called Alexandria, Indiana, where there was a glass factory. He always was a glass worker. Then he decided he would move back to Fostoria, Ohio, where they opened up another glass factory. His folks lived in Fostoria. So, he moved the family—my sister and I—back to Fostoria, and then he went back to work in the glass house there. He was active in the labor movement. That was about 1905 or 1906.

So, he worked there and I went to school in that town. And during my summer vacations, I would work in these glass factories. I received seventy-five cents a day. And the union hours in that plant was eight hours; but the men worked six hours, and they rested one hour in the morning and one hour in the afternoon at that time, see, on account of the terrific heat.

INTERVIEWER: *It was a union shop?*

Oh, yes, yes, it was a union shop.

INTERVIEWER: *Was everybody organized? When you were working there in the summers, did you join the union?*

Just the skilled trades. The skilled trades, the glass blowers, were organized, but the punty boys [who took care of the rods used to blow the glass] and the carrying boys and the common laborer wasn't organized. They didn't know what a union was. Just the skilled trades, and they were organized. They could sit down and negotiate their contract, which they did every year. They said when the fire is out, they would negotiate a contract. So, every July—I think it was July and August—the plants closed down, on account of the intense heat they had. It was out of this world, the heat in those plants. So, during that time that they were out, they would have picnics and they would have ball games and they'd have all kinds of gatherings; and they lived it up for those two months. And they knew they wouldn't go back to work until that contract was agreed to. So, they always got a contract; they didn't have to worry about anybody taking a job. Because it was such highly skilled and technical work that you had to be trained to do it.

INTERVIEWER: *Your father was a glass blower?*

Yes, he was a glass blower.

INTERVIEWER: *How did he learn that?*

He started out when he was a boy, like an apprentice, and he'd work all around there. And you had to be of a certain age, I guess, the way they worked it then; and you had to be capable of learning all of these jobs before they would give you an opportunity to step in and learn this skill. So, that's the way he learned it.

INTERVIEWER: *Was there any pressure on you to learn the trade, too?*

No, my dad didn't want me to learn the trade. He didn't want me to because you have to travel around the country. If one glass plant folded up and another one opened up, you'd be on the road a lot. So, he advised me not to, so I took up another trade. I took up an apprenticeship training as a sheet metal worker. I served four years as an apprentice to a sheet metal trade.

INTERVIEWER: *Your father was active politically and an active union man?*

He wasn't as active in politics, because the average person didn't agree with his philosophy of politics. Because those days, you're either a Republican or you're a Democrat; and my dad—it so happened, he seen how the working class was treated that he was a Eugene V. Debs Socialist. Let me put it that way—Eugene V. Debs Socialist. And he followed him. Most people are not hero worshippers, but my dad thought that he was tops, let me put it that way. And he followed the theories and the philosophy that Eugene V. Debs had.

INTERVIEWER: *Your dad talked to you about politics, too—about the Socialist party and Debs?*

Yes, when I reached twenty-one, I was indoctrinated to take part in political activities. And his theory was be active, no matter where you are, be active in politics. And I have followed that theory, not in the early days as much as I did until I got in the labor movement in 1933. From that time on, I became very active in politics.

INTERVIEWER: *Weren't you in labor unions before 1933?*

No, I never was in a labor union. They didn't have any to speak of. When you mentioned labor unions in a plant, they fired you. So, there was no such animal as a labor movement to join. You had to become a highly skilled person. And most of these towns didn't have any trade union councils, and you had to go to a city in order to put up an application to get a job as a skilled tradesman. But your small communities didn't have them. So, there was no unions to go to. You just took whatever the employers offered you.

INTERVIEWER: *You went into an apprenticeship in sheet metal working. Did you go on with that?*

No. No, I served my apprenticeship training and learned to be a sheet metal worker. I followed with that for a while, after I learned the trade. And then, I decided I wanted to do some traveling. So, I done some traveling. I just traveled around the United States. And I became, not a boxcar vagrant (laugh), but a knight of the road where I'd go in like a town like Chicago, and I'd go down on Canal Street and deposit two dollars to any one of these agencies they called "shipping out" in those days; they called that a "shipping out" place. I would pay a dollar or two dollars—usually I could get him down to a dollar—and they'd give me a ticket and I'd get on some train that they would designate to go out in some area—it could be Wyoming, Nebraska—it can be any place that you want to go. So, I'd go out there for a dollar or two dollars. But there was strings attached that you had to work on the railroad. Gandy dancing, you know, that's where you use the old spike-mall and do hard work. I didn't mind it; I was a young fella and I wanted to see a little of the country, and I'd go out there and I'd maybe work for a week, two weeks, if I felt like it. If I didn't, I'd quit and keep right on going.

INTERVIEWER: *Were there any unions there?*

The IWW [Industrial Workers of the World] was out on some of the railroads, and I had a card for the IWW. And I had a lot of respect for the organization. People run that organization down, but it done a lot of good. It helped those people that worked on the railroad. See, they used to bring them in from Mexico, and they'd go in these Chinatowns and bring out Chinese. And the foremen, well, they'd have to speak Spanish or Chinese or something to tell these men what they wanted done. So, I was fortunate, I didn't get in any of those gangs; the gangs I would get into was some of these Americans—young fellas like myself that was out to make a buck or two and see the country. And a lot of the fellas that would ship out, they didn't even take a job; they'd just keep on going, just the same.

INTERVIEWER: *Were there many Wobblies [members of the IWW] on the railroad routes?*

There was quite a few in the Northwest, in the railroads in the Northwest, and in your lumber camps.

INTERVIEWER: *Where did you run into the IWW first?*

On the Northwestern Railroad; there was a few of them. That Northwestern was running up through Nebraska at that time. And I went into Nebraska and worked. I lived in a camp car. And they had bunks and everything else that went with it (laugh).

INTERVIEWER: *Bedbugs and all of that?*

That's what I had reference to. I just traveled like that for a couple of summers. And then I'd come back, and then, I got established one time with this Electric Auto-Lite. That was 1921, when I got established with Auto-Lite. So, I went in there and run punch presses, and I was a diesetter.

INTERVIEWER: *What did that involve?*

There's not a skill about it, to speak of. You just take a die and set it in a punch press; and you put it down and set the die in, tighten up the bolts, tighten up the bolster plates. Of course, you have to set it exactly so; it has to be set in perfect in order to shear the metal. And after you get the bolster plate, you get the die set and you switch on the belt—those days they had belts, today they have gears.

INTERVIEWER: *Where was the belt fastened? Did it have its own little motor?*

There was a line shaft that would run across the plant; and there would be pulleys on each one, and the belts would run down to the machine.

INTERVIEWER: *So, the power shaft went across the top of the plant?*

That's right. And each place had a pulley. They eliminated that eventually; and later on, they got the little individual motors to run a punch press.

INTERVIEWER: *Were the belts exposed?*

Oh, yes. Everything was open. And it was nothing to see men get their fingers chopped off. It was a common occurrence. And this was right here in Toledo. And I started out in an Auto-Lite plant in Fostoria, transferred to Toledo. And the conditions during 1928, 1929—the money wasn't very good, no, a maximum of sixty cents an hour you could make. That was your piecework. If you went over sixty, sixty-five cents, then you were cut. That was a common occurrence, all the time, even in good times.

INTERVIEWER: *What do you mean, you were cut?*

They'd come 'round and restudy the job, so you couldn't make as much, or else they'd stand behind a post in the plant at your back. Some time study man would time you while you was working, and you didn't know it. And then the next day they'd come out with a new time study, and the job would be cut. And you'd look at the card and you'd see you'd took another cut. Well, along about 1928, an engineering department came in; it initiated the Bedeaux system. This Frenchman, Bedeaux, developed this system that you would work. Sixty minutes in the hour was the equivalent to sixty B's. B's was equivalent to a money value. Now, that was your base rate. Now, if you was making forty cents an hour, then you had to produce sixty B's an hour to make the forty cents. Then if you went over that, say you made a hundred B's an hour, then you got forty extra B's; but, in that forty B's, the company got a share of that—the worker didn't get it. Now, the rest of that was split up between all the officials of the company, the foreman, from the president of the corporation down, received a share of that.

When the depression came along, the first ones they rapped on the wages was the girls. You talk about the girls that have a right to fight in your women's lib: they sure have, in all these plants. They made those girls—instead of producing the sixty B's per hour, which was equivalent to sixty minutes, they raised that up to seventy-two B's. If they could run up ninety to one hundred B hour, they would eventually wind up with about—well, their base rate was around twenty-five cents an hour, I think. And they could probably make themselves thirty-five, some of them could go up as high, maybe, as high as forty cents.

The men, when they set this new rate in, they restudied all these standards of these jobs, and you really had to work in order to make seventy-five or eighty B hour. And your take-home pay sometimes would run, oh, anywheres from eighteen, twenty, twenty-two, twenty-one dollars a week. If you were lucky to work that and make that, that was really luck on your part. Because I'll explain to you why that was luck. When these men would come in to go to work, the foreman would place these men on the machines—the men that he wanted to be placed. They would set over on the benches, and he would place them on the jobs. Some of these men would be able to work, some of them would be sitting there, and some of them would sit there for hours; and they didn't get paid, not one penny—they didn't get paid a dime. Then, some men might come in four or five days in that week and wouldn't get a day's work, but they'd still come in, in the hopes that they would be placed someplace. Then, sometimes the boss would let them work for a day or two. Now, these men all lined up here, trying to support families, trying to live, and not receiving one penny. Some of them would walk three, four, and five miles to work, and sit there for days, day in and day out, and maybe get in a couple of hours work now and then, two or three hours. And they'd walk back home. Some of them would have a sandwich in their pocket, if they was lucky to have enough at home to eat. And this condition existed in the Electric Auto-Lite plant. I seen it with my own eyes, and I can verify it by the people that I worked with and the committees that I represented.

INTERVIEWER: *How would the foreman pick people to work?*

Pick them at random. Anyone he wanted.

INTERVIEWER: *Didn't he try to spread the work around amongst the guys?*

No, in a lot of cases, he didn't. But he would pick out the ones, in his opinion, that could produce more and could get the B hour up so the schedule, his schedule, would show a higher productive rate for his department. That was his bonus. So, the more production they produced, the bigger the bonus for the foreman and the officials of Electric Auto-Lite.

INTERVIEWER: *Was there any personal favoritism?*

Not too much. You take a person like myself. I was what you call a highly-skilled operator. And at one time they made electric clocks, besides their automobile ignition system. They got a order to make so many electric clocks. And the gears were so fine, some of them, that you had to have good eyes and have a fast hand to operate them. And I was always fortunate; I could set my own dies. I worked, you might say, all the way through the depression—maybe three or four days a week, at least—and I managed to get by. But we had some tough sledding just the same. I lost my home. I lost everything. But I came out a millionaire: my wife and son survived.

The first time that we had a discussion about unions was with a group of my friends, my favorite friends that I could trust. They worked around me in Auto-Lite in the same department. It was in only one department, Department Two, that we started this union. I started talking to these fellas, and I told them what we could accomplish if we had a union. And I told them about the NIRA, at that time. I said the National Industrial Recovery Act was approved. It's law. I said we do have the right now to organize and bargain collectively. And I had the law there, and I read it to them, and I tried to explain it to them, what we could do. So, I said, I'm not going to say too much here, fellas, but I'd like to have—and there was five or six of them there—I'd like to have you meet at my house and park your cars away from the house and walk over to the house and in the back. And we'll go down in the basement.

INTERVIEWER: *Why those precautions?*

Well, at that time, the Electric Auto-Lite threatened anybody that, if they organized, they would be fired. They also tried to threaten people, if they organized, that they'd never work in Auto-Lite again, or any place else.

We had a meeting in my basement, and we agreed to organize the plant—or organize the department, not the plant—just the department. Because the department, Department Two, made all the parts that went into every piece of ignition system that the company made. If that was tied up, they couldn't make them. So, that was a little reasoning on our part that we figured out. So, we went back in—we all agreed to secrecy—that we would go back in and talk with some of them; and then this five or six fellas—I forget how many, five or six—we decided that we would look around to see where we could get a charter and where we could get into the union. We went down to the Central Labor Union, and they wouldn't take us.

INTERVIEWER: *Who did you talk to there, do you remember?*

I think his name was Otto Brock. Otto Brock. And there was another old fella there that used to publish the paper, and he was a nice old fella, too. Gunthro. But he wasn't in a position to give any recommendations. "Boy," he said, "we're with you." And they wouldn't give us a charter, but they sent and they got a Federal Labor Union charter; William Green granted the Federal Labor Union charter that would take in all workers. Now, that meant millwrights, electricians—it meant all skilled trades. Plus all of the production workers that worked in a factory. And that particular factory would go into the industrial organization, into a union.

INTERVIEWER: *They got this for the Auto-Lite factory?*

No, they didn't get it here, first. They got it at Overland, City Auto-Stamp, and the Spicer, and the Bingham Stamping. This was in 1933. They got it before we were organized. And I was looking around for a place to go, and this amalgamated charter, 18384, was set up to bring us all into the same union. And then William Green, the executive board of the American Federation of Labor, was going to decide what to do after that. They decided that we'd go into this Federal Labor Union, if we so desired. So, we went back and told the boys, and we got our cards to sign. We went back, and we got them all signed in our department. Boy, we really got them signed. Especially the girls, the girls was just so mad that they'd have done anything.

INTERVIEWER: *How many were there in that department?*

There must have been in the neighborhood of a hundred or so in there at that time. And we organized, and we set up our committee. We called ourselves the executive shop committee, to go in and talk to the company. I sent word to the management that we wanted to meet with them. Oh, boy!

And the management invited us in, and they said, "Our door is always open to you to sit down and discuss problems." And I said, all right, we're going to discuss some of them. And I said, we'd like to work out a contract—wages, hours, and so forth—according to law. I think it was Section 7(a). They said, "Well, we have no objections to Section 7(a), but we're not going to recognize any union." He said, "We have at least a million dollars to break your union." Now, this was J. Arthur Minch that said that, the vice-president of the Electric Auto-Lite Corporation. He said, "We've got over a million dollars to break you, Charlie." He said, "You might as well forget it." And then he tried to make some suggestions, how we could develop ourselves; and we could eventually become foremen, and we could become inspectors— oh, we could get some plum jobs. He said, "If you fellas would go in there and help us out," he said, "we'll take care of you."

I got the boys out, and I said, boys, he's trying to get us in a bind now; don't you fall for it. They said, "We don't fall for that stuff, Charlie." I said, if you guys is with me, we'll go down and see the business agent, and we'll call a meeting of our department. And we called a meeting, and I believe every person in that department was there.

INTERVIEWER: *When was this meeting?*

I think it was the latter part of 1933.

First, they elected me as their chairman. That was their number one business, to elect me the chairman and the spokesman. So, I got up and I told them what we had to do, and the business agent was there. And he made a recommendation. First of all, Local 18384 was going to strike Spicer, they was going to strike City Auto Stamp, and they was going to strike Bingham.

He said, "You've only got one department organized." I said, I know it. But the rest of the factory cannot produce, because we are making the parts, the stampings. He said, "Then you've got it sewed up, have you, Charlie?" I said, yeah, we got it sewed up pretty well. He said, "Well, we'll make an agreement that there won't be anybody go back to work at Spicer or at City Auto Stamp or Bingham until Auto-Lite is settled. That way, they'll bring the pressure of these other companies on Auto-Lite." So, we agree to that.

We was only out, I don't know, about four days, I think, in February. About four days, after we had went through so many meetings, trying to work things out. We done a picket job. Yeah, we had pickets.

Everybody showed up for picket duty. We didn't have any problem. And there was a lot of other departments stayed out, too. People, different ones, would stay out—they wouldn't go in. And we didn't hold it against those who stayed in at that time because we were just getting organized. We didn't hold anything against anybody.

We settled that strike, and we went back in there, and, you better believe it, we organized that plant. We signed them up and got prepared for whatever might happen after that. Well, we had a great many meetings—oh, we had one meeting after the other to try to get that company to just bargain with us. They wouldn't. They said, "We'll never recognize a union." So, I said, well, I guess, Mr. Minch, you'll have to spend that million bucks you got there. I said, you could give that million bucks to us in wages, if you wanted to. "No," he said, "we're not going to recognize a union." So, we struck that plant. And that company, you better believe it, was well prepared to break that strike. In the LaFollette Civil Liberties Committee, if you'll note, in the Congressional books that was published at that time, what the Auto-Lite had in tear gas. They had over twelve thousand dollars worth of tear gas stored, which will show in that directory.

The company refused definitely to negotiate for even a penny an hour. They'd meet with us. See, they didn't want to be in violation of the law. They can always say, "Well, we had a meeting, but we didn't agree."

INTERVIEWER: *What did you talk about when you got there?*

Well, I tried to talk about everything we could in regards to a contract. We drafted up a contract with the conditions we wanted. It only covered one page; we didn't know too much about labor contracts. And we had the business agent, Tom Ramsey, from City Auto Stamping, help us; but he didn't know too much himself.

INTERVIEWER: *What did the company say? Did they have any offers or suggestions?*

No counterproposals, nothing. None whatsoever. Just refused to negotiate. They'd negotiate with us but not with the union. They'd say, "You, as individuals. . . ." Now, see under Section 7(a) of the act, as long as they was meeting with their employees, they claimed they was within the law. But they didn't have to recognize the union. There was nothing in the act said they had to. But in the act it gave us the right to organize and bargain collectively. But there's nothing demanding about it. You have to take the law in your own hands and have to put up a fight to get what you want. So, we decided we'd fight.

Then, they got an injunction and limited us to so many pickets. Then, they sent out and got scabs from different parts of the country and brought them in and went through the picket line.

INTERVIEWER: *When the injunction was issued, what condition was the strike in?*

We were on the threshold of losing the strike when the injunction was issued. We was down so low that I thought the injunction was going to ruin us. And some of our people was starting to filter back into the plant. And I seen it slipping.

Here, I would go over there every day and every day, hour by hour. And I'd see just a handful of pickets—according to law, according to the injunction—standing there and the scabs going in. I got the boys together, and I said, let's call a meeting, advertise it, and get them all together; and I told them at that meeting—I don't know whether it was the afternoon or night—I said, I'm a law-abiding citizen but, I said, we're going to break this injunction. Now, I said, in breaking an injunction, you people haven't anything to lose; you got it all to gain now. And I said, you're going to jail. Now, make up your mind tomorrow morning. You're going to jail, some of you. But, I said, be there and make them put us all in jail. They haven't got enough paddy wagons and they haven't got enough room in jail to hold us all.

Everybody agreed. They had that fight in them then, and I put it in there so they would follow me in that fight. Naturally, I was the first one they arrested (laugh). That was all set (laugh). They'd arrest some, they'd take a load of them down, put them in jail, and then they'd leave them go, you know. They didn't have any room to take care of all them people, so they'd leave them go.

We had a hearing before the judge, though. And we kept that up 'til we said that we was not going to abide by that injunction; come hell or high water, we was going to break it. If they put us in jail, if they put us in prison, we'll go. But we're going to break that damnable injunction.

And we took all of our crowd that day, all of the people that was on strike, and went in the judge's end of the courthouse. We were packed in the courthouse. And we had one trick that I had; I had a good lawyer. He advised me what to do. And I, in turn, advised, mouth to mouth, what the people in the courtroom should do. When I went before that judge, I would plead guilty. And he got me on the witness stand, and he asked me about breaking an injunction. And I said, yes, your honor, I am guilty. I am guilty of breaking that injunction. Just then I took my handkerchief out of my pocket to wipe my nose, like this, put it back. Everybody in the courtroom stood up and said, "Your honor, if he is guilty, we're all guilty, because we was all there." But the judge said—old Judge Stuart—he said, "Well," he said, "I can't put you all in jail, and I'm not going to find Mr. Rigby guilty because he isn't any more guilty than the rest of you. So," he said, "case dismissed."

We all went back out on the picket line, and that's when the company started shooting the tear gas at us. And going to bust up our picket line. The company still said, "Our door is always open to our employees, but we're not going to recognize a union." That was the way it was.

When we went on strike, then negotiations of any type stopped, from that time on until this riot. Then, we had all these people, we had officials, we had everybody penned up in that plant. They were eating tear gas, plenty of it. They were inside there, praying, and some of them was on their knees, too, praying, 'cause I got word what was going on. Afterwards, they told me what happened.

See, they threw that tear gas—kept shooting this tear gas out—and we threw it back, just as fast as we could. The air, the wind was going toward the plant, in our favor, see? Oh, the Lord was with us. And to top it off, the wind was there; and that night, just before the guard came, we had a light rain—just a mist—and that wind blew that tear gas in the plant. And we had clear sailing on the outside here.

What really got it started was they threw pole pieces down on us. That's the underpart of a generator. The generator was attached to this pole piece that held it in the automobile. It's like a bracket, but it's a heavy iron piece. And they started to throwing those off of the roof and hit a couple of our women and, from then on, we moved across the street.

And then, they started to shooting the tear gas at us. There was two kinds of tear gas. There was a tear gas and another kind of a gas that I don't know what it was. It made me about half sick, that you felt like getting a little nauseated. Not too bad, but it was a little nauseating. But the other one was a real tear gas. And that's what they were shooting at us.

We had some of our boys that was in World War I that was very active, and most of our guys that was in Department Two was World War I veterans. And we had heavy gloves; we was rather prepared for something like that. We knew what was going on and what might happen. We knew the minute the company started violence, we had to protect ourselves. We didn't want to become violent. But it's just like— you talk about violence—say, take a baby that's running over and going to put its hand on the fire. You're going to grab that baby away. Well, that is not violence. So, we grabbed our people and pulled them on the other side; and when they shot this tear gas at us, we grabbed that up with these heavy gloves and held our nose with handkerchiefs. They had square window lights, you know, square window lights over there on Champlain Street. We'd take them and throw them right through the window light back into the plant. And they didn't know how to operate to get rid of them, you know. We was a jump ahead of them (laugh). So, all this tear gas—we'd watch them, and when one would come down, we was waiting on it; and we'd pick it up and throw it right through a window. We wouldn't try to hit the same window. It was a different one each time until we had those window lights pretty well knocked out and all that tear gas was in the plant.

They was working full blast, these scabs were. We had them all penned in. This was just before quitting time. And the scabs were penned in, and they couldn't get out. They stayed in there. And they barricaded themselves. They didn't know what was going to transpire during the next few hours. And, in the meantime, they kept shooting this gas out. I might say a little something here, that, in that area, some of these people had birds—parakeets and so forth; that tear gas killed all those birds. Well, anyway, this ain't for the birds, this is for us. We went ahead and we threw those back in the plant, and then the plant sent word to the sheriff to call out the militia—make a request to the governor to call out the militia. And we covered the plant pretty well. And, I might say, there was an accident right out in the middle of the street. Some old guy, he had an old truck that had a lot of rocks on it, and I haven't any way of knowing where it came from. But those rocks—the truck just stopped—and it seemed like those rocks were there. And those boys just took those rocks and they polished out the rest of the window lights in the building. Well, I don't know anything about this old fella had that truck.

INTERVIEWER: *Yeah, he just appeared, huh? (Laughter)*

The old fella disappeared (chuckle).

They sent for the militia. I think it was the next morning they came in. But we kept them penned up all night. And we had our boys stationed over on Michigan Avenue, doing picket duty. They was over in Michigan Avenue and somebody must have had a gun someplace. And they was shooting into the windows over there.

That next morning the militia came in. And there was writers that came in, newsmen that came in from all over the country. Heywood

Hale Broun was one. Not this Heywood Hale Broun but his dad. Now, his dad was a real heavy man, oh, he was a big man. And he came in there for a story; he thought he'd cover that strike, 'cause he was a syndicated writer, and he was quite a popular man in those days. He was very good. Well, anyway, he was one of the first men to come down there. Some young—when all these soldiers came in, well, not soldiers, they were National Guard, that's different from a soldier, you know.

INTERVIEWER: *How?*

They're above a boy scout and below a soldier. Well, anyway, they came in; and this one young kid, he seen Heywood Broun down there, and he wanted to get him out of there. He thought maybe he was some guy that's causing trouble or something. Put on his bayonet and he got back of Heywood Broun and started jabbing him. Heywood Broun took off, a lot of meat there going. But you should read the articles that he wrote after that. He done us ten million dollars worth of good.

INTERVIEWER: *How did you feel about the guard showing up?*

Well, we had a strategy meeting, and we figured we'd take them on, too. The only way you can fight an object is at night. And we decided we'd try some night operations. Some of them were very effective. And some of the guard, they just give up, they wouldn't do much about it.

INTERVIEWER: *How did they behave? These were young kids, I take it?*

Well, they learned a lesson. A couple of nights of that, they learned a lesson. Because, you take a ball bearing and you have a sling shot, you don't know where that ball bearing's coming from. And that ball bearing—if you take a sling shot and pull it back, and that hits you, it can break a jawbone, it can put your eye out; or if it hits you in the chest, it can really do some damage. You could hear them on their helmets popping all night (laugh).

The guard put us up far in the street, up on Champlain, and the guard, they didn't take too active a part. I can't say they were vicious or anything like that. They probably started out that they was going to be, until they learned they was dealing with old veterans in World War I. So, the boy scouts come out kind of mild.

INTERVIEWER: *I have a question about the MESA. Was that in the plant in 1934?*

Mechanics Educational Society had the tool room. They were tool and die makers. Their department was right next to the big department for the pressroom. They made the tools and dies and repair work for this pressroom. I tried to get them to take us in the union before I contacted the others. And they wouldn't take us.

INTERVIEWER: *Why?*

Because we was production workers, and the tool and die makers, they were the elite of labor, the prima donnas, you know. They didn't want us scrubs (laugh).

INTERVIEWER: *They didn't go out in sympathy?*

Yeah, one time they went out on sympathy with us. But they went back in. They went out with us and then went back and wouldn't stay out. The business agent for the MESA ordered them back.

INTERVIEWER: *They had a contract, did they? Were they recognized?*

Not at that time. As far as I know, I don't think the company had recognized them either. If my memory serves me right, they didn't receive recognition until after we got it.

INTERVIEWER: *Where did you draw your jurisdictional line?*

All production and maintenance employees but no office help. But we centralized all of our efforts on, like maintenance men, such as millwrights and so forth, and we had electricians. And in some other plants the Local 18384 had the entire group, such as the skilled trades and the production workers. But we didn't. The MESA had some of the machine shop, but not much, and the tool and die makers.

INTERVIEWER: *Where did assistance come from?*

In those days, we didn't have anything. We lost our home, that's true. But our furniture, we was fortunate in having that paid for. But far as financial help for our union, we didn't get any—very little, if it amounted to anything. We was on our own.

INTERVIEWER: *What about local businesses extending credit or that sort of thing? Were they helpful at all?*

Well, people didn't hardly have credit those days. We didn't make enough money to go in debt for anything. We just lived from paycheck to paycheck.

INTERVIEWER: *When the guard appeared, did the company then want to meet with you?*

Yes. It was shortly after that that we entered into the first agreement. It was a one-page affair. The company recognized us, recognized Local 18384 of the American Federation of Labor.

INTERVIEWER: *At that time, right at the end of the strike, you sat down across the table from. . . .*

Minch, and there was Claude Pound, and Fred Huebner. Those were the bargaining committee for the management. And I've got a list someplace of the ragged individuals who bargained on the other side. We were ragged individuals (laugh).

INTERVIEWER: *You mentioned earlier the Auto-Lite Council.*

Yes.

INTERVIEWER: *Where were they at the time of negotiations? They weren't inside the plant anymore?*

No. The company recognized the union like this: for those who are or may become members of Local 18384 of the American Federation of Labor. Then they turned around and after we went on strike, they started this Auto-Lite Council. Then, the company said the Auto-Lite Council was a bargaining unit. So, when we entered into an agreement, they turned around and entered into an agreement with the Auto-Lite Council, because they said they was a collective bargaining group, too. That's what we had to contend with when we went back into the plant. We had these two factions. I mean it was trouble.

That was the company union. They made their own agreement, but they wound up with the same one that we had with respect to wages and hours and conditions of employment, which was only natural. The company was going to give them the same because they were trying to break the union, after we already won the strike, by trying to appease the company union.

INTERVIEWER: *When you went back to work, then, there was a lot of tension between the 18384 members and the Auto-Lite Council?*

Yes, yes.

INTERVIEWER: *There'd be a third group, those that weren't members of the Auto-Lite Council nor were members of 18384.*

There was no trouble with any group like that. Part of the people in the plant, most of them, were in the 18384, our union. The balance of the people, not all of the balance but part of them, was with the Auto-Lite Council. Now, how many members they had, I don't know. I threw that book away. I finally got at their membership book. I had a good soul hand it to me one day. They laid it down accidentally on purpose, you know.

INTERVIEWER: *How long did tension last? You were recounting a minute ago about your efforts to heal the wounds.*

Oh, within a year we had things pretty well under control. I started to work on the council and get them into the union. And every meeting we had, I would explain it to our members—what to do, how to handle it. That they were workers in the plant the same as we were. We all knew their heart wasn't with that Auto-Lite Council, so we started to do a job. And when we went back, we had some girls—well, we had a couple men, too—that got pretty nasty. You get them out there in the hall, you know, and maybe slap some of them around. But we had to stop that. And we put on our educational program and finally got them quieted down to take over the council like we wanted; and we finally succeeded. And finally, it wiped itself out of the picture; there was no more council.

We went to the National Labor Relations Board after we got strong enough; it was quite a while later 'til we got the bitterness out of our system. And when we got that out and signed all those people up, the company still insisted that the council should be recognized. So, by that time, we was in a good position to petition the National Labor Relations Board for an election, which we had. And we won out and that threw the company union out the window.

The strikers were people fighting for their bread and butter, that's what they are—American men, good, honest men, fighting for their liberty, fighting for justice, fighting for just recognition. We was all ready to die, if necessary. We didn't care; we was ready to give everything we had to win that strike. And we won it. And to think what the American workers have to go through. I don't care whether it's in college, whether it's in a factory, a department store, where it's at—the main word, if you can get that one word, you have got it. If you can get recognition.

That's it—recognition. And when you are recognized as a human being, no matter where you're at, and they say, "We recognize you," with respect to conditions of employment, with respect to teaching rights, with respect to this or that, you are a human being again. You have something to say about your own welfare, about negotiating for your own money, for your wages, or your salary, or working conditions. It's that one word. It's one of the greatest words to me, it's "recognition." Not money, not seniority, nothing in that contract. First, is recognition. So, we gave everything we had for recognition.

14

Epilogue

The strike at Auto-Lite in Toledo in 1934, when viewed through the memories of ordinary people who experienced it, emerges as a complex and moving human drama. One set of values clashed with another, and people confronted themselves even as they confronted the wishes and the demands of others. And after the picket lines cleared, after the National Guard left, after the special deputies and scabs tried to fade into obscurity, people returned to work at Auto-Lite and sought accommodations, understandings, and peace with themselves and others.

We look back on this event from the perspective of decades, from a time which accepts unions both legally and socially. The union movement has altered relations between employer and employee materially and permanently. Most would agree that union development, on the whole, has benefited the worker, the manager, and the country. The organized American worker today is materially better off, lives in greater comfort, and has greater protection on the job than he or she had fifty years ago. Wages, working conditions, and the ability to stand up in dignity have been enhanced even in unorganized work, because modern managers have learned from history. They have heard the dictum of millionaire entrepreneur Marc Hanna: "A man who refuses to meet his workers half way is a damned fool."

Of course, detractors remain; and so, workers' rights, though recognized in a broad sense, still require assertion and defense in many concrete circumstances. Some still argue that certain workers have no right to strike, perhaps even to organize. Police, teachers, hospital workers, air traffic controllers—those invested with a public trust—may still be attacked for organizing and defending their interests. Some owners continue to insist that their businesses have no public quality to them, that they are private, exempt from public scrutiny, and beyond the reach of workers' organizations. And even in organized industries, employers threaten and cajole to weaken workers' resolve in order to erode worker confidence and power. Some employers have successfully manipulated their workers into decertifying their unions. Occasionally, unions fail to meet their members' needs and so lose the support on which they depend. More troubling, many younger workers fail to see the link between the wages, conditions, and dignity they enjoy and the struggles of even a few decades ago. They do not know their history, and thus, they may be doomed to repeat its struggles and risk the tragedies so regrettably common in the history of workers' movements in this country.

This combination of managerial insight and worker apathy surely accounts for today's dramatic decrease in union organization among American workers. Managers have come to recognize that good employee relations diminish workers' desire to organize unions. An officer of the United Brotherhood of Carpenters posed the problem in this way: "You can't organize someone who doesn't want to be organized." In a different context, twenty years ago I applied to a union for support for historical research and was informed that they were "a history making organization, not a history keeping organization." The pride is understandable, but who will keep the history if those who make it do not? I was once interrupted during an adult labor history class by a worker who asked: "Why didn't we learn this in school?"

The history exists, of course, as this volume demonstrates; but it is in danger of being lost. We are predisposed to focus our attention on leaders, so we can hope that we will learn about labor leaders who assumed a public figure, a larger character, and played on larger stages than the localities that launched their careers. It is imperative to know about them and to recognize their leadership and their heroic struggles. However, we must not obscure the central reality of union formation; because, as this book shows, workers unite along friendship lines more than they follow leaders. Whether the impetus comes from inside or outside, workers make issues and concerns their own and that generates solidarity, the essential ingredient in union formation.

A union emerges when ideas and feelings are shared and when working people decide to try their hands at shaping their own destiny.

The process may not be neat; it may not be linear but recursive. Though planned, it may demand spontaneity. Though it may choose leaders, it may also insist that all become leaders. Whatever general principles it may publish, organizing remains a powerful emotional issue, fueled by basic human values: trust, loyalty, friendship, justice, commitment.

Such values fueled the formation of Local 18384. But these values alone do not account for its formation. Although their expression was the *sine qua non* for success, in another time or place and under different circumstances, their expression would surely have had a different result.

The depression, which so dominated life in the thirties, molded and shaped but did not create the conditions that clutched at workers and managers of Auto-Lite in 1934. However, it did heighten awareness. Many Americans internalized the depression, interpreting it as a personal failure, a reflection of some inherent flaw in themselves. They would not have suffered so, they believed, had they only planned better, worked harder, saved more wisely. Their plight gnawed at their sense of self-worth, undermined their confidence, and offered them no power beyond a flawed self to remedy their situation. How they must have felt the sting in Henry Ford's characterization of a mild upswing in business: "I think the American people have finally decided it's time to go back to work."

Others discovered in the depression a new synthesis, a different way to explain their world. The system had failed, not the individual. Circumstances and not their own private decisions had caused the collapse of economic life. Those who suffered from that collapse were common victims of forces over which they had no control and for whose consequences they were not responsible. The remedy lay not in individual decisions, not simply in a will to "go back to work," for there was no work. To these people, an appeal to class and to cooperative action to remedy a situation they could not remedy as individuals carried great force. Cooperative action empowered workers in ways that internalizing the depression never could.

Conditions for workers at Auto-Lite were far from unique in American industrial life. Wages at a subsistence level, compounded by uncertain hours of work, challenged workers in many industries and posed a reality that taxed workers' skills at coping. Commonly, oppressive rules against smoking, eating, going to the toilet, getting a drink—rules designed to tie the worker to the machine—rested all authority in the hands of foremen. Auto-Lite's rules and methods of enforcement, in common with rules in other factories, demeaned the worker. In many plants, a rapid pace of work, often driven by piecework systems, kept workers bouncing like a rubber ball. The Bedeaux system, whose injustice is so obvious to us now, governed work in other factories. At Auto-Lite, it rankled deeply and provided a focus for worker discontent. Like other rules and conditions, the Bedeaux system was arbitrary. The worker accepted the rules or quit.

The way Auto-Lite managers handled the Bedeaux system accentuated workers' powerlessness. Managers set standards of production for the class of hourly workers unilaterally. If a worker did not produce the quota managers set, he or she risked disciplinary measures, even dismissal. The worker who exceeded standards and qualified for a bonus discovered, much to his or her dismay, that anyone who regularly exceeded the standard proved that the standard had been set too low; so standards were raised. The result placed a premium on speed and production but failed to reward the worker fully. Even the paternalistic touch of C. O. Miniger could not soften the system. Those near him saw him as a warm and caring man, and perhaps he was; but isolated from the shop and caught up in the business end of the company, he apparently saved his concern for a few and left production under the management of others more hardened.

From the threads of system and circumstance, workers tried to weave the fabric of their existence. Auto-Lite was part of a circuit of companies in Toledo, and occasionally Detroit, where workers attempted to earn their bread by the sweat of their brows. They might work at Auto-Lite months or even years and then move, because they had violated a rule and had been fired, or because of lay-off, or simply because a new job paid more. They might stay in Toledo and move to Spicer, Libby Glass, or Willys-Overland; or they might go to Detroit to work at Hudson Motor or elsewhere, only to return to Toledo to Devilbiss, City Auto Stamping, or Timken. From this mix, they wove something else: friendships and "worknets," personal loyalties, and a class feeling that proved crucial in the Auto-Lite strike of 1934. They were, therefore, able to overcome a narrow, provincial inertia and to welcome, even solicit, the help and support from others. They could also identify and support leaders from their own ranks, leaders they knew they could trust.

These leaders knew something about history, about current affairs, and about unions. Lester Byrd had belonged to a railway union, and Charlie Rigby's father belonged to the glass blowers. They knew about Section 7(a) of the National Industrial Recovery Act and recognized a legal climate and political sentiment that worked in their favor. The legal principle implied that the federal government encouraged formation of unions. They recognized that they could readily use that principle.

They also knew and trusted each other, and that foundation sustained them. From person to person, they talked and shared and advised. They built networks of communication and bridges of trust. They began in their own homes and moved to fraternal halls, such as the Moose Hall, as their ranks grew. Their dedication, their willingness to take risks, and their self-sacrifice paid off on the picket lines on Friday, April 13, 1934. On that day, all knew that the "unholy thirteen," who had stood so exposed in the cold in February, had gained the support and trust of hundreds of Auto-Lite workers. On that day, Auto-Lite workers demonstrated that a union truly existed. The only issues in dispute were Auto-Lite management's formal recognition of that fact and its willingness to bargain in good faith with the union.

There were two issues the leaders always kept to the fore—their objective never changed: they intended to secure recognition from Auto-Lite's management and to enter into normal collective bargaining to settle disputes between them. They did not hesitate to seek support and advice from other unions, from political activists, or from lawyers. They never wavered, though they may have doubted, and they never sought to lead a revolution. The only disruption they sought was to stop work at the Auto-Lite factory on Champlain Street, and the only violence that occurred happened because the company attempted to continue production with scab labor protected by special deputies.

Management at Auto-Lite behaved understandably, if reprehensibly. Union representation and collective bargaining were not new to the industrial world, but unions had barely penetrated the mass production industries that employed modestly skilled workers to operate machines. No company wanted to be first, to set the precedent, to launch into this new, uncharted world. Even conventional union theory suggested that organizing such workers on a large scale was impossible, because they lacked the bargaining power skilled workers had. Workers in mass production industries could too easily be replaced.

Despite the clear intention of Section 7(a), Auto-Lite refused to recognize Local 18384 as the bargaining agent for its workers. They were reluctant, of course, because they did not know whether Local 18384 actually represented the majority of their workers; but the more powerful motive was clearly their hostility to any union, whether representative or not. After they reinstated the "unholy thirteen" who had walked out in February, Auto-Lite held meetings with those who had struck. This satisfied the letter of the law but went nowhere and fooled no one. Nevertheless, without being conscious of it, they began to create a system as they identified individuals who would negotiate with the union. Arthur Minch came to represent the intransigence, the arrogant disdain that so rankled workers. The company also prepared by purchasing and storing tear gas and armaments in the plant, gathering the props and setting a scene that would have such tragic consequences. They also hired new people, replacements they hoped would soften the impact should their workers strike. Thus, another piece of scenery moved into place—a piece that challenged a worker's fundamental right to his or her job. Many workers had seen a foreman replace experienced workers with his friends or relatives, and they saw the new replacements as green hands with no legitimate claim to their jobs. Resentment against these scabs sparked anger and outrage that at times nearly obscured resentment against the company. Here were traitors to one's class.

The company's tactics failed to prevent a strike. Despite "negotiations," and perhaps because of these preparations that certainly generated resentment, the strike came; and Champlain and Chestnut streets filled with Auto-Lite workers risking their economic status and perhaps even their lives to assert their rights and their dignity. They had much to gain; but they also had much to lose. The company risked less because, from its point of view, it had much to lose. A union would alter the way managers related to workers, and managers would lose power. A union meant negotiations rather than orders. A union likely meant higher wages and thus a reduction in profits. And a union at Auto-Lite set a precedent for companies in all of Toledo—perhaps even further. Should they defeat the union, they could rid themselves of "troublemakers" and restore absolute control over their workers—control that had been weakening since February and that virtually collapsed on April 13, 1934, when workers walked out.

Both managers and workers knew quite clearly what was at stake in their confrontation. However, they may not have appreciated the larger significance of their actions at the time, because the strike at Auto-Lite in Toledo, Ohio, had a significance much greater than those who struggled there realized.

The significance of the strike of 1934 can be calculated at four levels. First, at the level of tactics it demonstrated that a few workers who were organized to shut down the most essential operation in the production cycle could disrupt the entire process. In addition, the tactical advantage of organizing community support on and behind mass picket lines—primarily by organizing unemployed workers who were potential scabs—became clear. However, the most important tactical lesson was the effectiveness of striking as a means of organizing a union. One can trace the influence of these tactical lessons through the Chevrolet transmission factory strike in Toledo in 1935 and through the occupation of factory buildings in the great Flint sit-down strike of 1937.

Secondly, at the level of organizing theory, the strike addressed anew the old debate between advocates of craft organization and advocates of industrial organization. The craft union proponent asserted it was impossible to organize workers who possessed no developed skill, because only a common skill generated solidarity. Moreover, the absence of a skill meant that these workers enjoyed no inherent power in their relationship with their employer, for they could easily be replaced with other semi-skilled or unskilled workers. Industrial union advocates asserted a solidarity that transcended skill and that appealed, instead, to class. They contended that power came through mass organizing, which would tie up the employer's entire production and thereby jeopardize his profits.

At the third level, the significance of the Auto-Lite strike appeared in the evolving institutional history of American labor. This strike, taken in the context of the other major strikes in 1934—Minneapolis Teamsters, San Francisco longshoremen, textile workers—illuminated the pressures which split the AFL and created the CIO. Largely as a response to workers' attempts to organize in the mass production industries, industrial unionists within the AFL felt emboldened to press their demands for industrial organization at the 1934 AFL San Francisco convention. In 1935, when the Atlantic City AFL convention affirmed its craft union policy, industrial unionists formed the Committee for Industrial Organization, designed to work within the AFL but also to encourage new organization of industrial unions such as Local 18384 in Toledo. The AFL denounced the committee and ordered it to disband. The committee responded with an organizing drive in the steel industry and with the formation of the Congress of Industrial Organizations in 1936. Therefore, the example of Auto-Lite, among others, justified the efforts of industrial unionists and encouraged them to form the CIO.

At the fourth level, we witnessed the lives of human beings confronted with the problems of survival: of caring—for themselves and their families—in an industrial, capitalist system; and of dignity, of asserting their identities in a working world that demands conformity. Their need for security and significance was challenged by an economic system that offered them little security and by a work system that demeaned them. They found in friendship, trust, and unity a complex and even perplexing source of hope; for from the cooperation of many comes the dignity of one. Amid circumstances that required decisions and actions evoking deeply human values, our respondents confronted their feet of clay and discovered their courage.

Appendix A

The Narrators

ALBERT ABERLING

Born in Toledo in 1901, Mr. Aberling worked in auto-related industries most of his life. In the twenties, he worked at both Willys-Overland and Auto-Lite. In 1934, his wife worked at Auto-Lite, and he was unemployed. Largely at her insistence, he began to work at Auto-Lite in April, only days after Local 18384 went on strike. His brother's wife, Mary, had joined the strike. The resulting bitterness within the family ruptured relationships between them for twenty-five years. The silence between them was broken by the death of his sister's husband. After the death of their spouses some years later, Albert and Mary wed.

MARY ABERLING

Born in Hungary in 1903, Mrs. Aberling immigrated with her parents to the United States in 1907. In 1912, she moved with her parents to Toledo and has lived there since. In 1918, at the age of fifteen, she began work at Libby Glass. She first worked at Auto-Lite in 1925 but quit after a brief time. She returned to work at Auto-Lite in 1930 and remained until her retirement in 1962. In 1934, she worked in production and joined Local 18384. On April 13, she struck with the others, joining them periodically on the picket lines.

VIRGIL BARNHART

Born in Indiana in 1904, Mr. Barnhart moved to Toledo around 1923. He found himself unemployed and on relief in 1934 when the candy business he and his brother had built was forced into bankruptcy by the depression. His business and his residence were near the Auto-Lite factory. He was a witness rather than a participant in the events at Auto-Lite. In 1935, he hired into Auto-Lite, eventually assuming a leadership position in Local 12, UAW, CIO, as the Automobile Workers Federal Union, Local 18384 became after it joined the CIO.

MARGARET BYRD

Margaret Byrd is the widow of Ernest Lester Byrd, one of the organizers of Local 18384 at Auto-Lite. He worked in Department Two, where organizing began, and he helped lead the strikes in February and April. After the strikes, he was repeatedly elected to the executive committee of Local 18384. Mrs. Byrd retired in Toledo.

ROBERT A. CAMPBELL

Born and raised in Toledo, Mr. Campbell began working at Auto-Lite as a young apprentice toolmaker in the model shop in 1928. He joined MESA, a machinists' union unaffiliated with the AFL. During both strikes he continued to work.

AUGUST DANNER

A lifelong resident of the Toledo area, as a young man Mr. Danner was involved in the 1919 strike at Willys-Overland. A metal polisher by trade, he served as his union's representative to the Toledo Central Labor Union in 1934, helping them support the strikers at Auto-Lite.

CHESTER DOMBROWSKI

Mr. Dombrowski began work at Auto-Lite as a young man. In 1934, he worked in Department Two and became one of the original organizers of Local 18384. He struck in February and in April and played a leading role in the strikes. When Auto-Lite closed down in Toledo in 1962, Mr. Dombrowski was not yet fifty years old. Consequently, he lost all his pension rights even though he had worked for Auto-Lite over thirty years. His wife, Elizabeth, joined him for the interview.

CLARENCE FOSTER

Born in Toledo, Mr. Foster entered the employ of Auto-Lite shortly after his graduation from business college in 1915. He worked in the managerial group of the service parts division in 1934. He eventually became assistant manager of the service parts division, a position from which he retired.

ELIZABETH FRITSCHE

A stenotype operator, Mrs. Fritsche worked as secretary to the manager of the service parts division in 1934. Considered an office worker by Local 18384, she was not recruited for membership and continued to work during the strike. After the strike, she took depositions from people with property damage claims against Auto-Lite. She left Auto-Lite in 1950 after eighteen years of work. She received no pension.

RAY GARBERSON

Born in Michigan, Mr. Garberson moved to Toledo in 1915 as a young man. He entered employment at Auto-Lite in 1928 in the cost and budget department. As a member of the managerial group at Auto-Lite, he worked throughout the strike. He retired in 1960 after thirty-two years with Auto-Lite.

JOHN GRIGSBY

Born in Detroit in 1914, Mr. Grigsby moved as a child to Toledo where he grew up. While a student in journalism at the University of Toledo, he worked occasionally for the Toledo *Blade*. During the strike, he worked as a reporter around the Auto-Lite factory. He has worked for the Toledo *Blade* since.

FRANK GRZELAK

Mr. Grzelak was born in Toledo and began working at Willys-Overland as a young man. In 1934, he had become active in the union there and served on the executive committee of Local 18384. In that capacity, he frequently joined the picket lines at Auto-Lite, supporting the efforts at organization there.

NORVAL HISEY

Born and raised in Toledo, Mr. Hisey first worked at Auto-Lite immediately after World War I. He worked at a variety of jobs for different companies between then and 1934, when he worked again at Auto-Lite. During the strike, he crossed the picket lines to work in the factory. Once Local 18384 gained recognition, he joined the union and later engaged in some organizing for it.

FRED C. [WHITEY] HUEBNER

Mr. Huebner worked in management for Auto-Lite for forty-nine years. He began working in the time study department as a young man and soon came to head it. Therefore, he had the responsibility for setting rates and values for production work, such as piecework rates. During the strikes, he crossed the picket lines to work. Once Local 18384 gained recognition, Mr. Huebner played a central role in negotiations. He retired from Auto-Lite.

MARGARET JACOBS

Margaret Jacobs worked in the payroll department at Auto-Lite in 1934. Considered part of the office staff by the union, she was not actively recruited to join. During the strikes, she crossed the picket lines to work.

JOHN [J.J.] JANKOWSKI

Born in Detroit in 1906, Mr. Jankowski married a girl from Toledo in 1926. In 1929, he entered the employ of Auto-Lite, running a punch press in Department Two. He became part of the organizing nucleus of Local 18384 at Auto-Lite. He remained active in the union after it won recognition and worked continuously at Auto-Lite until it closed its doors in 1962.

BERNICE KELLER

Mrs. Keller worked at Auto-Lite for just a few months in 1934. She had recently moved to Toledo from Marion, Ohio, and was hired at Auto-Lite shortly before the strikes. She crossed the picket lines to work during the strike. When the Ohio National Guard closed the factory, she left and never returned to work at Auto-Lite.

GEORGE KESSEL

Born in Brooklyn, New York, Mr. Kessel served as an accountant for Moto-Meter, headed by Royce Martin. In 1934, Mr. Kessel examined the records of Auto-Lite for Mr. Martin, who was considering a merger between Moto-Meter and Auto-Lite. During the strike, Mr. Kessel crossed the picket lines on a number of occasions to do his work.

EDWARD LAMB

A native of Toledo, Mr. Lamb is one of its most successful and well-known attorneys. He was a key legal counsel for strikers and their supporters.

GLEN LANGENDORF

Mr. Langendorf was born in Toledo and was a young man in 1934. At the time of the strikes, he worked as a truck driver for the Toledo *Blade*.

JACK C. LATHROP

Mr. Lathrop began work as timekeeper at Auto-Lite immediately after his discharge from the army in 1919. By 1934, he had risen to the position of foreman in Department Two, the punch press room. During the strikes, he crossed the picket lines and remained at work. In 1973, he worked as business agent for American Federation of State, County, and Municipal Employees Local 24 in Toledo.

CARL LECK

Born in Toledo in 1912, Mr. Leck left high school at age sixteen to work at Auto-Lite. He began in the short order department and the stockroom and was an early supporter of efforts to organize Local 18384, walking out on strike in February. Mr. Leck worked continuously at Auto-Lite until World War II, when he served in the army. When Auto-Lite closed the Champlain Street factory, Mr. Leck transferred to Bay City. He retired from Auto-Lite after forty years of work for them. He was joined by his sister, Marie Rosselit, for the interview.

HILDAGARDE & WILLIAM LOCKWOOD

Hildagarde Lockwood began work at Auto-Lite in 1927 in the time office of the payroll department. She married William Lockwood in 1929. In 1930, Mr. Lockwood began to work for Auto-Lite as a piece-work checker in the payroll department. In 1934, both were considered office workers, and during the strikes they crossed the picket lines to work. A few years after the union won recognition, they were active in organizing the payroll department and participated in other organizing drives by the UAW.

DOROTHY MATHENY

Dorothy Matheny moved to Toledo when a young girl. She attended Toledo public schools and Ohio State University, from which she graduated as a teacher in 1927. She became active in attempts to organize the teachers' union in Toledo. In 1934, she witnessed some of the events around the Auto-Lite factory. She retired from teaching in 1965 after thirty-eight years of service.

EARL MOORE

Mr. Moore moved to Toledo from a small town in Ohio when in his early twenties. After working around Toledo in a variety of jobs, he was hired at Auto-Lite. He joined the strikers in 1934.

ELIZABETH NYITRAI

Mrs. Nyitrai, of Hungarian descent, moved to Toledo from a farm as a young girl. She began work at Auto-Lite as a teenager. In February 1934, she joined the Auto-Lite Council and remained at work during the strikes. After Local 18384 won recognition, she joined the union. In her interview, she reads from a diary she kept at the time.

CLAUDE W. POUND

Born in the 1880s, Mr. Pound moved to Toledo in 1912. In 1934, he was the production manager at the main plant on Champlain Street. After the strike, he continued in that position and was part of the management's negotiating team. He retired from Auto-Lite in 1956.

THOMAS PROSSER

Mr. Prosser was born in 1903. He began work at age fourteen as a teamster delivering for an express company. In 1925, he joined the Toledo Police Department as a patrolman. He patrolled at the Auto-Lite factory during the 1934 strike. He retired from the police department in 1970.

CHARLES RIGBY

Mr. Rigby was born in 1901 in Arcadia, Indiana. In 1921, he entered employment at the Auto-Lite factory as a punch press operator and diesetter in Department Two. He played a leading role in the organization of Local 18384 and was a major strategist for the strikes. After Local 18384 won recognition, he became an international representative for the UAW.

SEYMOUR ROTHMAN

Mr. Rothman was a student at the University of Toledo in 1934 and worked as copyboy on the Toledo *Times*. He reported some of the events during the Auto-Lite strike. Later, he joined the Toledo *Blade*, for which he wrote a local column. We can attest to the wide readership of the column, since a brief mention of our project in it brought many contacts with people who had been involved in the strike.

KATHRYN SCHIEVER

Kathryn Schiever worked for many years in the payroll department of Auto-Lite. In 1934, she was considered office staff and not in the union's jurisdiction. She crossed the picket lines to work during the strikes.

WILLIAM H. STONER

Born in Bowling Green, Ohio, in 1893, Mr. Stoner joined the Toledo Police Department as a patrolman in 1921. In 1934, he worked in the bureau of identification. He retired a lieutenant in the police department in 1963 after forty-two years of service.

TED SUSKA

Mr. Suska was born in 1896 and began to work at Auto-Lite about 1920 as a grinder. In 1934, he joined Local 18384's organizing drive and struck with them in April. After the strike, he was elected steward for his department, a position to which he was reelected continuously until his retirement in 1961 after forty-one years working for Auto-Lite.

ELIZABETH SZIROTNYAK

Born in Toledo, Mrs. Szirotnyak began working at Auto-Lite as a young woman. During the April to June strike, she crossed the picket lines and worked, despite her sympathy for the strikers. After Local 18384 won recognition, she joined the union. She retired from Auto-Lite after working there for over thirty years.

JOHN SZYMANSKI

Mr. Szymanski was born in 1910 and worked at a variety of jobs around Toledo. In 1929, he first worked at Auto-Lite but left that to start his own new car sales and service business. In 1933, he returned to Auto-Lite as a machinist.

JOHN TOCZYNSKI

Mr. Toczynski worked at a variety of jobs around Toledo but never at Auto-Lite. In 1934, he worked for the DuPont Company shoveling sulphur. He went down to the picket lines to observe the strike.

RUTH LYONS UNFERDROS

Ruth Lyons Unferdros is the daughter of Nelson D. Lyons, who served as president of the Auto-Lite Council in 1934. Mr. Lyons was employed by Auto-Lite as a guard and as a maintenance man. In 1934, he apparently worked in maintenance. Mr. Lyons retired from Auto-Lite in 1956 and died in 1961. Mrs. Unferdros was twenty-three in 1934 and went to observe events at Auto-Lite.

LYNN G. WATERS

Mr. Waters was born in Clarksburg, West Virginia, and moved to Toledo in 1923 to work at Willys-Overland. When he was laid off at Willys-Overland, he took a job as a streetcar conductor on the Toledo Railway Line. In 1928, he joined the Toledo Police Department as a patrolman. He worked on patrol at the Auto-Lite factory during the

1934 strike. He retired from the police department in 1966 after thirty-eight years of service.

STEVE ZOLTAN

Steve Zoltan was born in Toledo in 1897 and began working for Auto-Lite as an assembly operator in 1920. By 1934, he had become a set-up man for automatic machines. In April, Mr. Zoltan stayed out with the strikers, but he did not join the picket lines. After the strike, Mr. Zoltan rose to foreman and eventually plant superintendent. He retired from Auto-Lite in 1962 after working there forty-two years.

Appendix B

Note on
Oral History Methods

The oral histories in this volume were collected by a team of three: Professor Philip A. Korth, Michigan State University, and Margaret Beegle and Claude Kazanski, students at the time in James Madison College, Michigan State University. We began identifying participants by examining all printed sources. We made an index card containing all identifying information for each name we found. We compared our file of cards with the current Toledo telephone directory, setting aside all cards that created a lead. These leads were sometimes tenuous, but a few people lived where they had lived in 1934. We sorted these cards into three categories: the actual person, possibly the person, and probably a relative of the person. That reduced our list of names from about two thousand to seven hundred fifty. We then sent individualized letters requesting assistance to each of the seven hundred fifty names. We received thirty-five responses to our letters, about half of which proved useful in generating the oral histories. We also moved to a hotel in Toledo, so we could more easily develop leads, and contacted the union, the police department, and the newspapers.

We also prepared ourselves for the project by reading Arthur Preis's *The Rise of the CIO*, and A. J. Muste's *War in Toledo*, among other pieces. So, before we went to Toledo, we understood the broad outlines of the strike as well as some important details. We knew when the strike began, when the National Guard entered, when the Battle of Chestnut Hill occurred, and what the outcome was. None of this general information gleaned from our readings proved wrong. Indeed, it provided reliable "maps" into which we could fit the experience of individual interviewees.

We were fortunate to have many leads, but two leads proved instrumental. Charles Rigby was identified for us by Local 12, UAW, and Seymour Rothman, a writer for the Toledo *Blade*, published information about our project in his column. Mr. Rigby led us to many union activists, and Mr. Rothman's article brought offers to help from a wide range of Toledoans, most importantly from individuals who had been besieged in the Auto-Lite factory. In almost every instance, one interview led to another. We interviewed a variety of participants in the strike, including managers, police, newspaper reporters, strikers, nonstrikers, and bystanders.

A great deal of preparation goes into a successful oral history interview. Locating people to interview is only the first, tiny step. Placing a microphone in front of a person is definitely not the second. We integrated the process of identifying candidates for an interview with gathering background information on the individual and on the strike. We tried to read about the strike much as someone living at the time would, since newspapers, particularly the Toledo *News Bee* and the *Blade,* proved to be excellent sources. Thus, we watched the strike move from back pages to headlines. Measured against historical research on the strike, both newspapers did a credible job of informing their readers on the events, if not on the issues. That they both carefully published names aided our research. Our index cards carried information that explained how we discovered the name and why the name appeared in public. Before an interview, we pulled the card and discussed information it provided and speculated about the kind of information we might gain in the interview.

We also created an outline of the major events and discussed the issues as we reviewed the cast of participants. New information emerged as we interviewed, of course, as did additional names. We did not formally debrief each other after an interview—though that is surely a good idea—but we did discuss interviews and shared the new, the unusual, the contradictory, and the paradoxical, as well as the humorous. In an ongoing fashion, then, we tried to keep current with each other and with the evolving shape of the project.

We employed standard principles for conducting oral history interviews. First, we tried to interview in the individual's home or some other place in which the interviewee felt comfortable. John [J. J.] Jankowski met us at union headquarters, George Kessel came to the hotel rooms, and, Seymour Rothman talked to us at the *Blade*; but most interviews occurred in homes.

Second, we made appointments a week in advance and let the interviewees know that we wanted to talk about their experiences in the strike. That gave interviewees an opportunity to think back about the events, to gather memorabilia—for example, Mary Aberling had kept a newspaper scrapbook, and Margaret Byrd had a tear gas shell casing—and perhaps even to call friends to refresh their memories. We did not conduct pre-interview sessions, except in the case of Charles Rigby. We found him early in the project and went to his home first to seek names of other union members. During this brief session, we grew aware of his central role in organizing the union, so we decided to return after we had conducted some interviews. That gave us an opportunity to hone our skills and to fill in our understanding with additional background information.

Third, we decided to use simple and unobtrusive equipment—small cassette recorders with integrated microphones—because we feared that larger reel-to-reel machines with clip-on microphones or microphones on stands would distract the interviewee. Because of this decision, we sacrificed quality in some tapes. Integrated microphones picked up machine noise, and voices sometimes sounded distant, because the recorder sat far from the interviewee. On the whole, however, these small machines proved to be an advantage. We could turn one on, set it on the floor or on a table, and quite literally forget about it. When it ran out of tape, it made a noise loud enough to attract our attention so we could change tapes. We lost very little in so doing. More importantly, the interviewee could also forget about being taped.

Fourth, we adopted our interview technique from non-directional psychology. We began with rather open-ended questions about personal history. An interviewee could respond easily and confidently in a relaxed situation and could develop rapport with the interviewer, the single most important development in an interview. We then worked through personal experiences into the depression and finally into experiences in the Auto-Lite strike.

Fifth, we tried not to offer information ourselves. Rather, we questioned. We did not debate. We tried only to clarify. If an interviewee used a term that might not be clear to an average reader today, we repeated the term as a question. For example, an interviewee might use the word scab. We would respond: "Scab?" Invariably, the interviewee would explain or clarify the term. In the case of such an emotionally charged term as scab, the interviewee might offer much more than a definition. Interviewees did not want to waste their time or ours with information we already knew; but we did not know how the interviewee felt and thought, so this technique allowed us to express our authentic interest without steering the interviewee.

Sixth, we listened closely.

We asked each interviewee to grant us the rights to the interview by signing a release form of our own design and by signing the cassette or cassettes on each side that had been recorded. We then transcribed each interview verbatim, producing over five thousand pages of text. This became the raw material from which this book was written. The tapes themselves proved of high enough quality to be used for narration in a slide/tape show, which was shown at a number of scholarly and community functions.

One principle governed both the collection and the editing of these interviews: the words must belong to the interviewee. In editing, as in interviewing, we took care to assure the integrity of the respondent's language. The only words added were clear from context and necessary to an understanding of the respondent's meaning. We punctuated to preserve the natural oral expression, diverging from it only to clarify meaning and sustain flow. We made no attempt to "clean up" the language or "correct" grammar. We reordered interviews to preserve narrative flow, and we deleted extraneous and unnecessarily repetitive material. Throughout, we attempted to preserve the priorities and the emphasis of the respondent. This consideration, we believe, best protects the authentic expression of those we interviewed who speak in these pages.

Oral history adds color to historical reconstruction, of course, but it also enhances understanding; it personalizes history through concrete experience and thus adds a dimension difficult to capture through conventional historical methods. To the thoughtful scholar, history is never dead; but it may sometimes need reviving, and oral history can breathe new life into it. Oral traditions are not merely an anachronistic residue from pre-historical cultures but are important molders of modern cultures. The struggle for dignity and freedom, two abstract terms so central to the meaning of American history, was not abstract. It occurred in real and concrete circumstances where ordinary people asserted themselves. The struggle presented here helped create American culture. Knowing about that struggle can help us understand where we came from and who we are. It may even teach us something about the human condition.

Bibliography

BOOKS

Bernstein, Irving. *The Turbulent Years*. Boston: Houghton Mifflin, 1969.

Boryczka, Raymond, and Lorin Lee Cary. *No Strength Without Union.* Columbus: Ohio Historical Society, 1982.

Davis, Forrest. *300,000 Guinea Pigs*. Toledo: Toledo Associates, Publishers, 1939.

Fine, Sidney. *The Automobile Under the Blue Eagle*. Ann Arbor: University of Michigan Press, 1963.

Galenson, Walter. *The CIO Challenge to the AFL*. Cambridge: Harvard University Press, 1960.

Kramer, Dale. *Heywood Broun: A Biographical Portrait*. New York: A. A. Wynn, Publisher, 1949.

Lamb, Edward. *No Lamb for Slaughter*. New York: Harcourt, Brace and World, 1963.

Muste, Abraham J. *The Automobile Industry and Organized Labor*. Baltimore: Christian Social Justice Fund, 1936.

Preis, Arthur. *Labor's Giant Step: Twenty Years of the CIO*. New York: Pioneer Publishers, 1964.

Rayback, Joseph. *A History of American Labor*. New York: The Macmillan Company, 1961.

United States Senate Education and Labor Committee. *Violations of Free Speech and the Rights of Labor*. Hearings before the Subcommittee, 74th Congress, pursuant to S.Res. 266. Washington, D.C.: U.S. Government Printing Office, 1939.

MANUSCRIPT COLLECTIONS_____

National Archives. Records of the Federal Mediation and Conciliation Service. Record Group 280.

National Archives. Records of Regional and National Labor Boards. Record Group 25.

National Archives. Records of Special Labor Boards. Automobile Labor Board. Record Group 9. Records of the National Recovery Administration.

Walter Reuther Library, Wayne State University, Detroit, Michigan. Henry Krause Papers.

Walter Reuther Library, Wayne State University, Detroit, Michigan. Joe Brown Collection.

Walter Reuther Library, Wayne State University, Detroit, Michigan. "Oral Histories of the Automobile Industry." Collected by Jack Skeels.

PERIODICALS_____

"A.F. of L. Inches Left." *The New Republic*, 31 October 1934.

"Electric Auto-Lite." *Fortune*, October 1936.

"General Strike." *Business Week*, 21 July 1934.

"General Strike." *Commonweal*, 27 July 1934.

"General Strike." *The New Republic*, 25 July 1934.

"General Strike." *Survey*, August 1934.

"Government by Strike." *Business Week*, 21 July 1934.

"How to Make Conservatives." *Colliers*, 25 August 1934.

"Labor Draws Its Sword." *Review of Reviews*, July 1934.

"Labor War Breaks Out in Strikes." *Newsweek*, 2 June 1934.

"Labor Wars." *New Outlook*, November 1934.

Mangold, W. P. "On Labor Front." *The New Republic*, 30 May, 19 September, 3 October, 17 October 1934.

Muste, Abraham J. "The Battle of Toledo." *The New Republic*, 6 June 1934.

"Relief Changes in Toledo." *Survey*, May 1934.

Selander, T. "Death March in Toledo." *Christian Century*, 21 November 1934.

"Street Fighting Marks Toledo Strike." *Literary Digest*, 2 June 1934.

"The Strike Tide Rises." *Nation*, 6 June 1934.

"Toledo and its Creditors." *Literary Digest*, 7 July 1934.

"Toledo Thriller." *Nation*, 29 May 1935.

"What is Behind Toledo?" *The New Republic*, 6 June 1934.

Index of Narrators

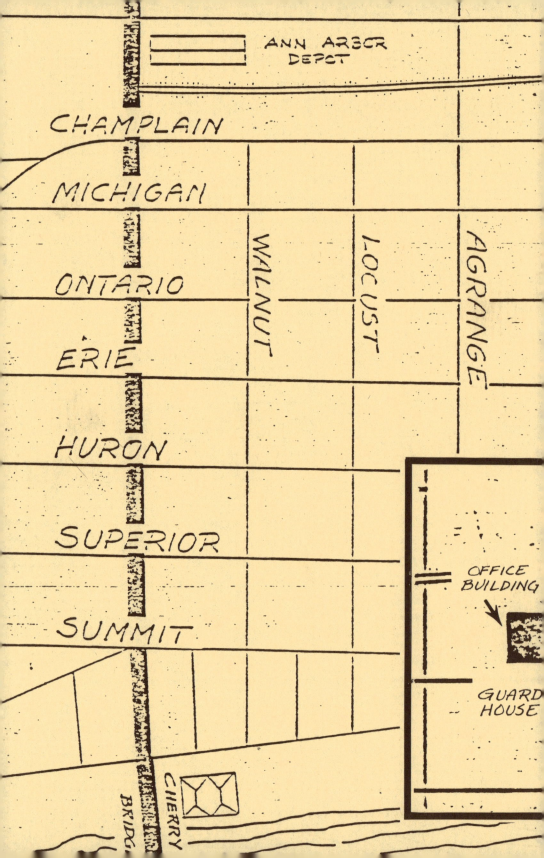

ANN ARBOR DEPOT

CHAMPLAIN

MICHIGAN

ONTARIO

ERIE

HURON

SUPERIOR

SUMMIT

WALNUT

LOCUST

AGRANGE

OFFICE BUILDING

GUARD HOUSE

BRIDGE

CHERRY